An Unchaste Life

Anne Cato

An Unchaste Life
Memoir of a Tudor Queen

Lyon Rampant Publishing
http://www.lyon-rampant.com

AN UNCHASTE LIFE:
MEMOIR OF A TUDOR QUEEN
Copyright © 2005 by Anne Cato
All rights reserved.

Published by Lyon-Rampant Publishing
First Edition

While most of the characters and incidents portrayed herein are based on historical events,
this novel is entirely the work of the author's imagination.

Library and Archives Canada
Cataloguing in Publication

Library of Congress Catalog Number: 2006904526

Cato, Anne
        An Unchaste Life: Memoir of a Tudor Queen
- 1st Edition

ISBN: 0-9781146-0-4

For my family and especially for MDG,
who always knew I could -
and would.

Acknowledgements

The seed for this book was sown when I was first introduced to Tudor England as a child. Of course, when such an introduction occurs, one inevitably becomes acquainted with King Henry VIII—and his six wives. For reasons that I have never been able to fathom, of all those wives, it was his fifth who most interested me. Perhaps it was her youth, her nature, her tarnished reputation, her brief and tragic life—perhaps it was all that or something much more subtle. Whatever the cause, given the chance to write an account of the life of any historical character, I would always have chosen Catherine Howard in a heartbeat. That opportunity did present itself, thanks to my source of inspiration and I am indebted to him for getting me writing again. I was encouraged to continue by my loyal and stalwart husband, and the book could never have been completed without the patience and love of my three children and the wholehearted support of my parents. Heartfelt thanks also to my editors Regina Clarke and Christopher Butler for their tireless help, encouragement and enthusiasm.

Anne Cato.

Table of Contents

Prologue

"Nothing fixes a thing so intensely in the memory as the wish to forget it."

Michel de Montaigne
French essayist
(1533-1592)

Tower of London
12 February 1542

"IT BEGAN AS JUST A PULSE," she whispered. Her eyes fluttered closed as her hand began to move in time to some beat that only she heard, while she uttered a soft sound in accompaniment: *pom, pom, pom, pom.* Mesmerised, I watched the movement and listened to the sound, until she spoke again: "It was low and regular, beating from the direction of the river. I looked up from my needlework so suddenly that my neck cricked."

Her hand now fell to the pale column of her throat and grasped it. She shuddered, and dropped her hand to her side. When her eyes finally opened, I saw that the pupils had shrunk to black specks. I knew then that she was not seeing me or her surroundings, but only the scene playing out on her memory's stage. For memory—even such a one as this—is a refuge for a terrified and tormented mind. She whispered again: "When the beating became intense, I recognised it as a legion of marching footsteps on stone and earth. I was to be summoned to the Tower at last."

Silence throbbed around us. I did not attempt to break it, loath to drag her back to her present ordeal.

"My ladies-in-waiting—I had only four at Syon House—also looked up from their sewing at the sound," she murmured. "I did not meet their eyes, knowing what I would see there: anticipation, curiosity, eagerness—and no compassion. I made busy with my sewing but I could not ignore the marching feet. Now I could hear crunching strides, the jingle of spurs and the clink of swords and the murmur of voices."

I knew why she concentrated so on these minor details—by dwelling on every minuscule aspect of her recollection, her mind became immersed in the past. It was an unconscious endeavour at hypnosis, an instinctive self-protection from the horrors of the impending present. Not for the first time in my long life, I acknowledged the remarkable contrivance that is the human mind.

She had closed her eyes again and her form on the narrow bed was at rest; she either slept or was lost in memory. Anyway, I knew she was free from fear and guilt—for the moment. Her mind had done more for her than I could. I lowered my head to pray for her continued deliverance this night.

Instead, I found myself thinking of the circumstances that had brought her here. A Bill of Attainder had been passed some weeks before: it was now high treason for a woman who married King Henry VIII to not reveal to him beforehand details of "her unchaste life." It had sounded this woman's death knell.

Now she spoke again. The words came without pause, spoken with the sweetest eloquence, holding me enthralled.

"It was the Duke of Suffolk who came for me, the King's greatest friend . . . he and the Lord Privy Seal and other members of the Council and a legion of knights—theirs were the marching steps. All these great and powerful men, to escort me to the Tower! If they were expecting trouble from me, they were to be sorely disappointed. When the Duke stepped into my chamber, all my fear vanished and all my hope. I surrendered to the inevitable. I would go to my death without protest, as protest was useless. More importantly, I would go to my death as a *Howard* who was Queen of England!

"The Duke had hardly uttered his reason for being there, when I lifted my chin and strode forth. He and the members of the Council stepped aside. I walked down the stairs and passed the soldiers, my skirts swishing on the ground. Even when I burst out into the sunshine, the Duke at my shoulder and his entourage filing after us, I did not falter, continuing down the path towards the river.

"When the barges below the steps came into view, I stopped . . . my followers shuffled to a halt behind me. I faced my final journey down the Thames and I well knew what awaited me when I passed through Traitor's Gate. It no longer mattered to me. I was alone, unloved and betrayed. Those I had loved most were dead, through my fault, struck down by the raging jealousy of my despotic husband, my King. I realised I had nothing to live for any longer."

The wretchedness of her words struck a blow to my already aching heart. As I had done many times in the past, I reached out and seized her hands, to let her know that here at least was one who had not betrayed her, and who loved her yet.

My touch was a mistake. It brought her out of the past, and she blinked and gazed about her, as if new to her present surrounds. The full horror of her predicament struck her and she turned pale even to her lips.

I squeezed her hands and managed to utter a desperate prayer. Perhaps it did her good for she relaxed somewhat, and when she spoke again it was directly to me.

"I turned and looked back. My ladies-in-waiting were huddled in the shadows of the house, watching our procession. My servants had also congregated outside, their tasks abandoned.

"Then I saw *you*, standing apart from the rest."

I nodded. I had been in the chapel of Syon House when a page had rushed in to tell me the news. By the time I had arrived outside, my lady, dressed all in black, was walking down the pathway to the river, followed by her escort. On reaching the riverbank she turned to look back, and our eyes met.

"When I saw you," she said to me now, "I knew then that I was not alone, unloved or betrayed. My life had not been in vain. Then panic gripped me. With a cry, I made to run to you but the Duke shouted, 'Seize her!' and the guards grabbed me by the arms."

I nodded again, praying that she would cease tormenting herself thus. Neither did I want to dwell on how she had screamed, thrashed and kicked as the guards dragged her onto the covered barge. I could still hear her screaming my name, over and over, until the boats disappeared down the river; I would hear her screams until my dying day and would live until then with the guilt of not being able to help her when she needed me most.

Weeping now, she grimaced with remembered anguish.

"It was a covered barge, but yet I knew when it passed beneath London Bridge— beneath *them*."

Them . . . the two she had loved . . . two impaled heads on the great bridge, their faces frozen in horror and agony. I had seen them myself. Indeed I had seen the faces before the final blow came, and I saw the lifeblood spurt forth from the fatal wounds. And now, on the morrow, I would witness the final chapter of the tragedy . . .

She stared with desperation into my face.

"Did you speak with them before they were—before they died? Did they still love me?"

"Ah, my dear." My voice was hoarse. I temporised. Those two men had suffered the most grievous torture. They were not heroes, but normal, fallible men who wanted to live. They would have confessed to anything to end the physical agony and, in the throes of torment, they would have forgotten, or even regretted, how much they had once loved this woman. But nothing in their lives became them as did the manner of their going. There were no words of denial at the block. They died with dignity and honour.

"They loved you," I said with truth. "You know they did, my dear. Can you not remember?"

"Aye," she whispered. Her pupils contracted again. Eager to relinquish her to the sanctuary of the past, I released her hands and leaned forward.

"Remember," I urged. "Look back! Look back, Catherine Howard!"

"I remember," she murmured. Her merciful mind took control, and the silence stretched as she travelled back in her memories, to the beginning . . . to the event that started it all. As I let her go and waited for her to speak again, I was struck with purpose. I knew at last what I had been called to do in my twilight years. Catherine Howard had been a shooting star in Tudor skies, lighting them with a fleeting brilliance. Such a spectacle may be soon gone and forgotten, and the stars continue undisturbed in their cycles, but for that briefest of seconds before it falls from the sky, the shooting star captivates us with the radiance that is both its life and its death. It will be my task to be the vessel through which the enchantment of Catherine Howard, above all others, is sustained. Through my inscription, she will talk, and through me she shall receive understanding, compassion and absolution!

She speaks again at last, oblivious of me, and the long, final night has begun . . .

Part 1: Pride

"Pride sullies the noblest character."

Claudianus
Gallo-Roman theologian
(d. ca. 473 AD)

Chapter 1

"One orator in a family, nay even in a city, is enough."

Marcus Tullius Cicero
Roman lawyer, writer, scholar, orator and statesman
(106-43 BC)

I

Norfolk House, Lambeth
4 June 1533

WITH A LOUD GRUNT, our legal guardian, the elderly Dowager Duchess of Norfolk, settled on a stool in our chamber. Like moths to a flame, we fourteen maidens were drawn to her, to sit or kneel at her feet. I made sure I was closest, so near that I could see the tiny silver embroidery stitches in her purple velvet gown, hear the rattle of her breathing in her chest and smell the spicy perfume from her jewelled pomander.

The Dowager sighed, lost in reverie, and I trembled with anticipation. Out of the corner of my eye, I saw my friend Joan Bulmer bounce with impatience. Alice Restwold, kneeling beside Joan, urged her with a sharp elbow and a jerk of her head to rouse the Dowager from her silent reflections. Joan always took the bold initiative and she did not fail us on this instance.

"You have news of the coronation, ma'am?" she asked, breaking the silence.

With a brisk shake of her head, which set her jowls swaying and cast aside her ruminations, the Dowager turned her attention to her rapt audience. Her smile displayed yellow teeth and exuded abundant pride.

"Aye, indeed I do," she said, her gnarled hands clasped in rapture. As one, we leaned forward, eager to hear more. The Dowager continued, with a gleam in her black eyes, and the rose bloomed in her sallow cheeks: "On Thursday last, the Lady Anne, Marchioness of Pembroke, was brought by water from Greenwich to the Tower of London, in a barge richly hung with cloth of gold. At the Tower of London, the King's Grace received her as she landed. Then over a thousand guns fired in salute from the Tower, from Limehouse and from the ships lying in the Thames."

I sighed. This we already knew. Against Her Grace's orders, many of us had braved the rowdy London mob to find a position on the riverbank where we could witness Anne Boleyn's journey to the Tower, the first stage of her coronation. We had exclaimed in awe at the magnificence of the procession, cringed in startled delight at the firing of the guns.

My sigh drew the attention of the Dowager. She nodded.

"Yes, well may you be proud, young Catherine Howard," she said, misunderstanding the cause. "Anne Boleyn is a Howard as we are, your first cousin no less, and my step-granddaughter. This is a great triumph for our family!"

"Tell me more, step-grandmother!" I begged, thinking to hurry the Dowager's musings along. "What happened when Cousin Anne left the Tower?"

"Ah!" The Dowager licked her lips and smiled in grim satisfaction. "That occurred on Saturday, the last of May," she said to her captive audience. "She rode from the Tower of London through the City, accompanied by lords, knights and gentlemen, all handsomely apparelled. She herself rode in a chariot covered with cloth of silver and a canopy of the same was borne over her head by the four Lords of the Ports dressed in gowns of scarlet. Four chariots of ladies followed. Several other ladies and gentlewomen followed on horseback, all in gowns of crimson velvet." The Dowager saw our spellbound expressions and grunted before proceeding. "And there were various tableaux being made on scaffolds in the city," she declared, "and all the guilds were standing in their liveries, every one in order, including the Lord Mayor and aldermen standing in Cheapside. And when Anne Boleyn came before them, the Recorder of London made a presentation to her, and the Lord Mayor gave her a purse of cloth of gold, with a thousand marks of angel nobles in it, as a present from the whole of the city. Then the lords took her to the palace of Westminster and left her there for one night."

The Dowager's thick voice had become strained towards the conclusion of her narrative. She heaved with rasping coughs, and gasped for air. When the commotion had passed, she pressed a hand against her breathless, corseted lungs. With wide eyes and open mouths we waited for her to continue, but the silence endured, broken only by wheezy inhalations.

The other maids signalled to me with surreptitious nods and frantic expressions. I summoned my courage and laid tentative hands on the Dowager's purple skirts.

"My cousin would then have gone to Saint Peter's Abbey, is that not correct, step-grandmother?" I asked.

A liver-spotted hand pressed down on mine.

"Indeed yes, Catherine Howard," panted the Dowager. "And such a procession it was! Monks dressed in cloth of gold and thirteen mitred abbots. And the Archbishops of Canterbury and York! What an acknowledgement! What a triumph! The Duke of Suffolk bore her crown before her and two earls carried her sceptres!"

I wondered if the remembrance was too much for the old woman when again her body became racked with coughing and wheezing. Her page scuttled to her side and waved a pungent handkerchief before the Dowager's face. I decided she was well enough when she snatched the handkerchief from the page's hand and dealt the lad a cuff in the ear that sent him sprawling. She coughed once or twice more into the cloth, drew some deep breaths and, to our relief, geared herself to continue with the tale.

"Anne Boleyn entered Saint Peter's Church at Westminster, beneath a canopy of gold cloth," she said, her voice smooth now. "She wore a kirtle of crimson velvet trimmed with ermine, with a robe of purple velvet over that, likewise trimmed. On her head, she had such a lovely coronet with a cap of pearls and precious stones. Her hair she wore loose, and it flowed almost to the ground. And—," the Dowager straightened her shoulders, "and I, as a Howard and of the highest peerage in the land, carried her train, and wore a robe of scarlet with a coronet of gold on my cap! The Lady Anne was set in her high royal seat, which was made on a high platform before the altar. And there she was anointed and crowned Queen of England by the Archbishop of Canterbury and the Archbishop of York!"

An intense pride coursed through me. What an occasion for my family! Only one aspect of the triumph marred my happiness.

"Step-grandmother, where was my uncle, the Duke? What was his role?" The Duke of Norfolk, or someone of his rank, by rights should have had the duty of bearing the crown in the procession, yet the Dowager had not mentioned him. At my question, the old woman's lips thinned in annoyance and all jubilation vanished from her expression.

"He did not attend," she clipped. "The churl! Not to attend the coronation of his own niece! Bah!"

The Dowager waved her hand, dismissing the subject as unimportant. However, as she launched into a detailed description of the coronation banquet at Westminster Hall, I wondered with unease if my powerful uncle was one of the many who disapproved of the King's divorce and sudden second marriage to my cousin. It wasn't wise to express disapproval of the King's Secret Matter. When King Henry's most valued friend, the Lord Chancellor, Cardinal Wolsey, failed in his petition to the Pope for an annulment of the King's marriage to Queen Katherine, he had been arrested. Fortunately for the Cardinal, he had died at Leicester en route to his execution. His replacement, Sir Thomas More, had resigned over the question of the King's divorce, and it was said that the shadow of the axe hung over him also.

If the heads of such respected men of high rank were not safe, then surely no one could sleep peacefully in their beds—most especially not a Howard. My uncle Thomas, the third Duke of Norfolk, a survivor and an opportunist, was kin to nearly all the peers of the realm. He had led the opposition to Cardinal Wolsey—yet he, and all of the Howards, still lived with the disgrace of having supported Richard III some fifty years since. And surely no Tudor monarch could forget that my uncle had once allied himself to the House of York with a marriage to Ann Plantagenet.

I emerged from my thoughts when Margaret Morton interrupted the Dowager's banquet description.

"What of the King's happiness that day, Your Grace?"

"Ah, the King's Grace never drew his gaze from his Queen. It was rumoured she was with child, and the King cosseted her and doted on her, watching her every bite and her every movement, so as to safeguard his heir."

We sighed in unison, sensing the conclusion of the tale. However, our grandmother had not finished—her gaze was distant, her triumph restored; I guessed she reflected on the child of Howard blood who one day would also sit on England's throne.

"The Howards shall rise and rise," she declared, and issued a barking laugh. "Only the executioner's axe can reduce us now."

Although the other ladies joined her in thrilled laughter, I shivered. I recognised no portent in her declaration but rather was reminded that, beyond the happy small world in which I lived was another—one that was treacherous, ugly and violent, where no one's head was secure.

I suspect it was my uncharacteristic soberness that drew the gaze of the Dowager, and she regarded me with shrewd contemplation. I wondered what she saw in me to captivate her so, for I thought myself of little significance in the family—my father was the impoverished youngest brother to the Duke, one of nine children to my grandfather and his first wife, and I was one of ten children myself. On the death of my mother, when I was nine years of age, I was placed under the charge of this old woman—the Dowager Duchess of Norfolk, Agnes Tylney, my grandfather's second wife. Most of my many brothers and sisters had at some time lived under the guardianship of the Dowager, and it was now my turn to learn from her the art of noble housekeeping and living. However, being one of so many Howards and barely out of childhood, I was obscure and indigent, with only my Howard name to barter in making a future marriage alliance. Still, that morning, the Dowager scrutinised me with an odd and speculative glitter in her eyes. Perhaps now that a Howard was on the throne of England and another was to be its heir, she realised my name had become a more valuable bargaining tool in marriage talks.

I must have made a slovenly figure, kneeling before her that day. It was mid-morning, yet I was still in my shift, for we maids had indulged long into the night in secret feasting and dancing and I had only within the hour emerged from my bed. My shift was old and short, and without its laces at the neckline, so it gaped to reveal a bosom that was mature for my thirteen years. My auburn hair was unbound and flowed in wild, uncombed waves to the ground. All this the Dowager noted, to my shame, yet her interest seemed to heighten as she absorbed the unprepossessing sight I made.

It was a squeal of fright from one of my many cousins, Agnes Ap Rhys, which broke the Dowager's deliberation. Agnes had bounded to her dirty feet, jumping from one to the other and pointing to the far corner of the chamber.

"A mouse! A rat! Oh, horror! Oh, oh!"

More excited squeals mingled with giggles as the page scampered to investigate. I was unperturbed, for rodents were not uncommon in our chamber. The Dowager merely sighed and closed her eyes tight.

"Boy!" she called to the page, who had failed to trap the rodent. "Come hither, I wish to depart from this unruliness!"

The page at once grabbed her outstretched arm. He tugged and pulled, while we watched with stifled giggles. The Dowager wore a heavy, purple velvet kirtle over skirts, as well as a gable headdress with black velvet drapery, and assistance was essential. With a final energetic heave, she rose majestically from her stool. Expelling a great sigh of relief, she turned to depart, but paused mid-stride.

"Oh, yes, I have news," she rumbled. "This morning your new music tutor arrives. Pray dress yourselves and tidy this—this shambles—immediately!"

II

THE DOWAGER DUCHESS OF NORFOLK ruled a large household, numbering in excess of one hundred persons, and divided her time between Norfolk House in Lambeth and her estates in Sussex, usually taking her entire household with her. Wherever she was, her homes attracted visitors and petitioners, and all were made to feel welcome, whilst her stewards struggled to control the disarray. My step-grandmother was a great lover of music and revels, and always welcomed travelling minstrels, jugglers and mountebanks of all sorts.

It was generally understood that if you were young and comely the Dowager would welcome you into her home without hesitation. You were further favoured if, whilst in residence, you provided the old lady with speculation of lascivious activity. It was into this environment that Henry Mannox, the new tutor of the spinet and virginals, was introduced on that hot June morning of 1533.

I usually scorned the wearing of the repressive Spanish farthingale and corset, especially on a hot day. That morning I wore a bodice and trained skirt of pale blue brocade trimmed with gold—with little else. The large sleeves attached to the bodice were dark blue silk and flowed to my fingers. As head wear, I chose a reticulated veil rather than the heavy French hood.

We had gathered in the music antechamber when a steward ushered in Henry Mannox, and made introductions. We examined him with interest, while a flush of discomfiture invaded his gaunt cheeks. The son of an impoverished Sussex gentleman known to my step-grandmother, he was dressed in accordance with his station—his simply cut tunic and skirt were dark green, and he wore a white linen shirt, open at the neck. On his head was flat cap of black velvet, and long top-boots in soft brown leather worn with dark hose completed his garb. Master Mannox was very pale of feature, with wavy, white-blonde hair, almost colourless eyes and luminous skin. A sparse, trimmed beard barely covered an angular jaw. An awkward silence settled on our group.

Taking pity on him, I cleared my throat, drawing his attention to me. I beamed when his eyes met mine.

"We would all love you to play for us, Master Mannox," I said, "and show us the skill to which we must aspire."

"Of course," he murmured. He nodded his head in a brief bow, and moved with fluid grace behind the spinet. We gathered around the instrument as he paused, flexing his fingers.

When he played, his music invaded my soul. Enrapt, I watched his thin fingers and the gentle swaying of his long body, and admired the shadow cast on his cheeks by his fair lashes. Enchanted, I stepped back from the group, to move in languorous time to the familiar pavane, humming softly.

When the music stopped, I stopped dancing and opened my eyes, sighing with contentment. Some of the maids shot me disdainful looks, but Henry Mannox gazed at me with unmistakable ardour. A wave of heat invaded my face—I was always too impulsive, too susceptible to the temptation to dance, too vulnerable to the assault of pleasure on my senses. The disdain hurt and the ardour perplexed.

"Oh!" My cry sounded strangled. Ready tears springing to my eyes, I scooped up my skirts, and spun around to the door.

As I dragged it open, I heard a frantic "Wait!" from Master Mannox and "Catherine!" from Joan. Now embarrassed that I had behaved so childishly and without dignity, I was more intent than ever to flee the scene. Breathing hoarsely, I darted down the hallway, and when I heard pursuing footsteps behind me, I turned quickly, to enter a chamber I knew was empty, shut the door behind me and raced across the bare wooden floors to a door that opened to a flight of backstairs. Norfolk House boasted countless secret passageways and stairways, making it perfect for hiding and chasing games, as we maids knew well, and that morning I seized upon this opportunity with relief.

I half sprinted, half tripped down the dark, narrow staircase until I reached a door at the bottom. There I stopped, holding my ragged breathing to discern if I was being followed. I heard nothing. I opened the door and stepped out into a dim, dusty hallway in the warren of the servants' quarters.

Sniffing and miserable, twirling a strand of my hair with my finger, I wandered down one silent hallway and then another, encountering no one. I imagined rambling forever in this maze, when I heard an odd moaning from a slightly open door. I was about to shove it open when I realised the sounds were of pleasure, not pain. My skin prickled with a strange excitement. Curiosity overcame propriety and I pressed my face to the crack in the door.

I recognised John Hall, the undercook. Standing side-on to me, he grasped something at his hip level, and rhythmically thrust his naked loins at something I could not see. Biting my lip, I gently pushed the door open further to widen my view. Just in time, I clasped my hand over my mouth to cover a gasp. Bent over a chair, receiving Hall's thrusts into her loins was the source of the moaning—a half-naked woman. As I stared she turned her head slightly, and I saw her face. It was Mary Laschelles, our chambermaid.

I tingled with exhilaration and continued to watch, engrossed. I was new to womanhood, and fornication had until now merely puzzled me. My older companions indulged in such activity, and the Dowager turned a blind eye. But with the gentlemen that stole into our chamber to share our secret games I only participated in chaste kisses. This was something utterly different and more enthralling.

"A woman's body is like a complicated, finely tuned musical instrument . . ."

The whispered voice in my ear had me jumping with fright. A firm hand clamped my mouth and suppressed my squeal. I pulled away, turning and shrinking back against the wall, staring in shock at my captor.

Henry Mannox stood before me, wraithlike in the dimness. He put one finger to his lips and nodded to reassure me. I raised my eyebrows in enquiry. He leaned closer so that his lips almost brushed my ear.

"It requires a master to play it well, but when he does, the most beautiful music is made," he whispered.

I drew my head back to examine his features. His cold, colourless aspect did not please me, but his voice was soothing, and the memory of his seductive music was a powerful allure. I shuddered and dwelt on the import of his words until he beckoned me to the door again. I peered through the gap once more.

Hall had reached forward and was now fondling Mary's pendulous breasts. As we watched—I in astonishment, Henry with mild interest—Hall dealt one dark peak a sharp twist. Mary gave a yelp and cursed. I had to shove my fist in my mouth to stop myself from giggling aloud. Henry drew me away and I sank once more against the wall, still stifling my giggles.

He loomed closer, an amused smile on his thin lips.

"I think the knave is not such a master," he whispered.

I nodded in agreement. From inside the chamber we heard a deep grunt of triumph, a female sigh of relief and then silence. Again pressing his finger to his lips, Henry took my hand and led me down the hallway to another door. The chamber beyond was empty, except for some furniture covered in dust cloths. Henry led me inside and half-closed the door. Standing close together, we waited in the musty gloom until we heard the two lovers depart.

Henry's pallor had an eerie glow and his eyes, when they settled on me, were incandescent in his intense face. As his whispered words had indicated, he was not like the simple lads with whom I usually consorted, and I was not sure whether I was afraid, or drawn to him. I still quivered from viewing the intimacy between Mary and the cook.

Emboldened, I spoke out. "I suppose you can make sweet music from a woman's body then, Master Mannox?"

Henry shrugged. "I am a musician, Lady Catherine," he replied, as if that said it all. His face loomed closer and I jumped as his fingers touched my skin, just above my bodice. "For instance—I would not pinch a woman's bosom, but do this—."

I gasped aloud as his hand dropped and I felt his thumb pass across the peak of one barely covered breast and back again. My body responded at once, the tingle sweeping through my breast and sparkling downwards. Shocked, I recoiled from him. He dropped his hand at once and lowered his gaze in contrition. The unspoken apology checked my impulse to flee. My heart thudding, I swallowed and attempted to restore order to my mind and body. When at last I spoke, my voice trembled, yet I feigned merriment.

"And a man's body—is that a finely-tuned instrument as well?"

Henry smiled. "Finely tuned perhaps, but not subtle. It takes little skill to evoke music from a man's body."

I laughed, tilting my head in curious enquiry. Henry shook his head.

"Methinks, Lady Catherine, you are not ready for me to instruct you in that music as yet."

"I am a woman," I exclaimed, surprising myself. "I am quite ready, Master Mannox."

He regarded me but a moment.

"So be it," he said. He grasped my hand and drew it to his groin. I frowned when I felt the hard bulge in his codpiece. When he relinquished my hand, I left it there; I became conscious of his quickened breath. Abruptly, he walked away into the dark shadows of the chamber and for a minute I heard the rustle of clothing and some sharp exhalation. When he returned, he wore a sheen of perspiration on his forehead and a rueful expression.

"You see? A mere touch from a beautiful woman evokes the required response."

I laughed again, this time in amazement. Henry smiled and laid a palm against my cheek.

"I think I shall like being your tutor," he remarked, "of the spinet—and other instruments. I knew when I watched you dance that you were a sensual maid on the brink of an awakening."

How enchanting his smooth voice was! And the thought of exploring new adult pleasures in the hands of an experienced man captivated me. But as a mere music tutor, this man was beneath me in rank—I was a Howard and now cousin to the Queen.

I lifted my chin at a haughty angle.

"Master Mannox, I shall not fornicate with you."

He was taken a little aback, but then shrugged. "I do not need to go in you to instruct you in the arts of sensual pleasure," he said. I flushed at his plain speaking. "But in time," he went on, "you will beg me to take you. Come, let us return now, as I have a spinet lesson to finish."

Not a little affronted, I allowed him to lead me from the chamber. In silence, we retraced our steps to the upper level of the house, where the other maids waited in the music room with impatience and annoyance. As Henry sat himself once more at the keyboard, he dealt me the most fleeting of winks. My affront dissipated with the thrill of shared secrets and conspiracy, and the exciting promise of future clandestine instruction that had little to do with either spinet or virginals.

Chapter 2

"It is easier to exclude harmful passions than to rule them."

Seneca
Roman dramatist, philosopher, & politician
(5 BC—65 AD)

I

Norfolk House
Lambeth
September, 1533

ON THE COVERED COURT Stephen Tyrell, the Dowager's secretary, swung his racquet and dealt the tennis ball a hearty *thwack*. It sailed over the fringed cord and bounced in front of Henry Mannox. Henry flailed, missing the ball by a large margin. Stephen jumped in jubilation. "Game," we cried, and applauded while the players changed sides.

Joan, seated close beside me on my right, put her mouth close to my ear.

"Master Mannox is an expert at making splendid music, but not so at tennis," she whispered. I giggled, knowing well at that stage the 'splendid music' Henry could play; in fact, I also had not been paying a great deal of attention to Henry's skill at the game, but was admiring the way his heated skin glowed through the fine material of his shirt and the long, elegant shape of his bare legs below brief slops.

Following our peeping in the servants' quarters, Henry had played with me a calculated game of wooing and seduction; the wooing almost wore away my resistance to someone so far beneath me, and from there, intimate seduction had been an easy step.

He and I had had another secret tryst in our chambers the previous night, during which we had retreated behind the curtains of my bed. By the time I called a halt to his amorous play, we had both been naked and both delighted with our mutual intimate discoveries.

"Did you lie with him last night?" Joan whispered, observing my rapt attention to Henry's form in its brief clothing.

I shook my head at her wide-eyed question. "No," I murmured. "I shan't fornicate with a mere music tutor, Joan—there is no prospect in such intimacies."

"I suppose you deserve an earl or a duke for a bedfellow, now that you are cousin to the Queen," Joan said, exasperated.

"But of course."

She rolled her eyes and shook her head.

Annoyed, I said, "You could not understand, Joan. You are not a Howard."

"Your uncle, the Duke, does not see the harm in taking to his bed someone of lesser rank," Joan said, her tone acerbic. "He brazenly flaunts his servant-girl mistress."

It was plain to me that a lady could never have such freedom, but before I could respond, Katherine Tylney burst through the doors onto the tennis court. She paused with face flushed and chest heaving with excitement, and then darted across the arena to where we were seated. The players paused and the observers around us became silent in anticipation. All summer we had waited for word of the royal birth—perhaps here was the news that the King had his much longed-for son!

My pulse hammering, I waited for Katherine to come before us. Milking the drama, she bent over to recover her breath.

"I have news," she panted. "The child is born." Still bent over, she grasped her knees and drew several more deep heaves while we hung on her revelation.

I bounded to my feet and grasped her plump shoulder, forcing her to stand.

"Yes? Speak, Katherine!

"The child," she said with a triumphant gleam in her eyes, "is a lass!"

I sank back to the bench, my knees weak. Around me, the ladies exclaimed and murmured, and even Henry and Stephen neglected their game.

"She has been called Elizabeth, after the King's mother," Katherine added. "The Queen is well, by all accounts."

I seized upon the last statement in frail hope.

"Then there shall be more children," I announced with more firmness than I felt. "And a son, next time."

"This is a cause for celebration, indeed," Joan said dryly. "A Howard—a female—in the royal cradle. Gentlemen, please resume your match, we require some enjoyment after this news."

"But of course it is a reason to celebrate!" I said. "There must be feasting and dancing! And in the Great Hall, no less! Stephen," I turned on the Dowager's secretary "you can arrange it? We must have three kinds of roast meats, partridge, eel and pastries!"

"Frumenty, fritters and jellies!" said Katherine Tylney.

Alice Restwold leapt to her feet, entering the spirit. "And minstrels and jugglers!" She clapped her hands with excitement.

"You mustn't forget the Morris dancers," I said. "And a summons must go to all the surrounding households." I added this for Joan's benefit—she had of late developed an infatuation for a clerk in the neighbouring Archbishop's Palace. As I expected, Joan's plain, round face blushed and her interest waxed.

Stephen stared at me, transfixed. A stocky young man with a pleasant countenance and friendly if stolid demeanour, he was a frequent visitor to our revels and, before Henry came on the scene, I had been the object of his romantic attentions. I had been fond enough of him, although I had by now relegated him, and many other lads, to irrelevant childhood fancies. He cast his rival a bitter sidelong glance and pouted in his injured pride before he looked back at me.

"The Dowager is at court," he said. "We ought not arrange such an occasion without her consent."

A chorus of disappointment rose around me. I stepped forward, laid an entreating hand on Stephen's arm and dealt him a sweet smile.

"She would not refuse," I soothed. "You know it! Indeed she would be pleased. Stephen, would you dance the Madam Sosilia with me at the celebration? No one does it as well as you!"

The Madam Sosilia was a new, daring dance, in which couples held hands and embraced. Stephen's placid face flushed. As he hesitated, I batted my lashes (my eyes, large and hazel, were much favoured in the current fashion) and Stephen showed visible signs of weakness as he looked into them. For good measure, I drew back my shoulders so that my bosom jutted forward, drawing his enthralled attention.

The interchange had become something more to me than a way to organise a celebration. Henry had taught me the power I could wield over a man, and I now enjoyed exercising it and exploring its boundaries. When Stephen nodded and patted my hand with his own hot, damp palm, I realised he was another easy conquest. But my triumph was not unreserved. Womanhood brought with it responsibilities that I was only beginning to grapple with. Often, I longed for the simple and harmless amusements of childhood, yet with the advent of Henry Mannox I was putting those aside forever.

Soberly, I watched Stephen bow and back away from me before he ran from the chamber, eager to do my bidding. When I sank to the bench, oblivious of the excited tumult around me, I caught Henry's eye. He nodded and smiled his approbation.

II

SOBER REFLECTION did not occupy me for long, as Norfolk House began to buzz with preparations for the celebrations. Butchers, bakers and other merchants wore a path to our kitchens, and travelling minstrels and players took up residence in the outbuildings in anticipation of the event. Word went out to all noble families in the vicinity. The Dowager returned to Norfolk House to oversee the preparations and a rumour spread that the Duke of Norfolk himself would attend. Despite the disappointing news of the birth of a Princess, the people of the Kingdom were keen to show their support for their monarch.

On the third night after the news of the royal birth, festivities commenced with a riotous supper. Too excited to eat, and imbibing far more wine than was proper, I spent a considerable time staring, rapt, at the high table. There sat a dozen nobles, one of whom was my father's brother, the Duke of Norfolk, in a doublet of gold brocade and surcoat of cloth of gold trimmed in sable. I had met him before of course, although he would likely not know my name or who I was in a chance encounter. Yet he fascinated me. Although not handsome, he possessed a charm that, when combined with his air of strength and authority, was a potent lure for any lady. He also had a reputation for ruthlessness and cunning, and was the second man in the realm, after the King. After the supper, we ladies all retreated to our chambers to change our garments. When I returned to the Great Hall, I was swept up in the boisterous merriment. It was impossible to hear or be heard above the cacophony of every instrument being played simultaneously—the harp, the fife, the trumpet, recorder, fiddle and pipe and tabor. The thuds of many dancing feet and the yells of laughter and song added to the deafening atmosphere. Bellows had been brought in to sweeten the air with the smoke of juniper, and the wine still flowed freely.

Breathless with enchantment, I danced the Madam Sosilia with the sweating, ardent Stephen. After that, barely able to contain my emotion, I partnered the Duke in the Horse's Bransle. I gazed at him in admiration. I smiled at him if he happened to look at me, but when that occurred no change of expression passed across his grey-bearded face—it was as if he did not see me. When the dance ended, I watched him sweep his way through the throng without a backward glance. Yet my fancy, heated by wine, conjured hazy images of the Duke as my protector and admirer.

The clamour and gaiety of the festivities continued unabated. When at last I grew exhausted from dancing and made to retreat to the fringes of the hall, a laughing and shouting group of drunken revellers swept me before them, their combined body heat penetrating my clothing and burning my skin. I staggered away from them, beneath an archway. When I righted myself, a group of mummers caught my attention. Their gay costumes and spirited, abandoned movements made me gasp with delight. As they twirled and thumped, the long, colourful streamers attached to their shoulders created a whirlwind of dazzling lines and curves. The bells at their wrists, ankles and knees were a merry ringing accompaniment to their vigorous movements.

Already seduced by the gay commotion around me, by the sweet, cloying scents from the bellows and pomanders, by the bright colours and sensuality of dance movements, now I was overcome. The thudding of the floor vibrated up through my feet, resonated in my body and tripped my heartbeat. The thrilling dissonance of the gayest sounds in the world consumed my hearing, and the colour, the sparkle and the spectacle of attractive, dancing men in bright, close-fitting garments brought tears of sheer joy to my eyes. As one dancer weaved around me, his brilliant feathered cap tumbled to my feet. With a cry of enchantment I picked it up, placed it on my veiled head in jubilation, and followed his steps. At once, he grinned and clasped my hands.

"Dance with me, sweetheart!" he yelled.

I laughed with breathless elation and grasped his strong, bony hands. The din in my ears faded, and I was aware of only my own breathing and the thudding of my heart. Around we twirled, my skirts billowing, my hair coming loose. Impulsively, drawing hoarse gasps provoked by some new, pent-up desire, I extracted my hands from the dancer's grasp and laid them on his powerful thighs in their close fitting yellow hose. With surprised delight, I absorbed the movement, heat and shape of the silk-covered masculine flesh beneath my palms. The young man laughed, although I could not hear him above the roar of the blood through my head. His teeth flashed, his eyes gleamed, his skin glowed. I pulled him into the archway. Uncaring of observers, my senses conquered, I placed my lips on his sweat-covered chest, revealed by his short jacket of bright orange. I felt hands on the back of my neck, under my hair, pressing me closer, recognised desire as his body seared into mine. My head swimming with the taste of him, I slid my mouth to his neck and sought his kiss, as the last vestiges of control and decorum abandoned me.

A brutal vice clasped my arm and pulled me away, staggering, into the shadows beyond the archway. I fell against another body, this one familiar, and where a second before the dancer's lips had been, there were now another's. I curled my arms around Henry's neck in abandonment. The cocoon of silence that had enveloped me was shattered, and the clamour came surging over me once more.

Somehow above the tumult I heard his husky voice, "You are the ultimate temptress—how well I have taught you! Come with me." I allowed myself to be led from the hall, through the dimly lit corridors, to our ladies' chamber.

As I disrobed, my chest heaving, I examined his face. Gone was the detached, controlled Henry. His breathing was as heavy as mine, his pale eyes wide with reverence when they beheld me.

"You've bewitched me," he whispered. "It seems my tuition has been more successful than I had hoped." He stepped forward to stroke my form and run his hands down my thighs. "Catherine, my Catherine, I love you."

His touch evoked shivers, but as the daughter of a noble family, I knew there could be no prospect in encouraging him to love me. I was not cruel by nature, but neither was I mature enough to know how to rebuff Henry—as I knew I must—without hurting him.

"Are you ready for another lesson in making music?" he whispered in my ear, using the euphemism we had adopted for our intimacies.

I should have demurred. Instead, I replied with unfortunate encouragement: "Aye, but, my love, I cannot. I am not ready for . . . everything. I am a maiden, newly a woman."

Henry raked his hand through his fair hair and grimaced.

"There are other pleasures we can partake of, and I am a patient man," he said at last. "I shall wait until you are ready. Meanwhile, you must know that I love you. You have bewitched me, Catherine!"

I licked my lips in a nervous gesture. Henry leaned forward to follow the path of my tongue with his own, drawing an involuntary shudder from me. Pushing me back onto the bed, he moved down my body, stopping at my parted thighs.

It was not the first time he had caressed me like that and I responded with squirms and gasps, my hidden flesh melting with yearning, eagerly receiving his probing fingers and tongue, yet not attaining the ultimate satisfaction I knew hovered just beyond my reach.

After several delightful minutes, Henry moved up to lie alongside me.

"Time for another lesson," he said. He guided my hands to my own body and encouraged me to seek my own satisfaction.

When I had sampled some sweet delights, I grasped Henry in childlike confusion.

"Was that—that wasn't wicked or wrong, was it, Henry?"

He shook his head, stroking my face and expelling a ragged breath, for he had clearly become agitated by my intimate exploration. "No, my love, it is never wrong to seek and find pleasure, wherever you can find it, however you can find it," he said. The zealousness in his expression startled me. "We are only in this world for a short time, and it is a hard, cruel, frightening world—especially for a woman. Finding pleasure amidst the horridness is giving glory to God for the gift of life!"

The enthrallment of his beautiful, startling words prevailed over their mystery. When Henry kissed me, I kissed him back happily. Notions of giving glory to God by obtaining wondrous pleasures swam seductively through my mind. I wondered if perhaps womanhood was preferable to childhood after all.

Chapter 3

"I am indebted to my father for my life, but to my teacher for living well."

Alexander the Great
Macedonian ruler
(356-23 BC)

I

Norfolk House
Lambeth
Summer, 1533

POPE CLEMENT VII declined to annul the King's marriage to Katherine of Aragon. Undeterred and fuelled with passion, the King declared himself head of the Church in England and thereby legalised his secret marriage to my cousin, Anne Boleyn. In the summer of 1533, King Henry VIII was excommunicated from the Holy Catholic Church of Rome.

With religious tension already rife in the realm, the excommunication heightened the situation. It caught our household in a precarious position—traditionally Catholic, the Howards were also renowned for ingratiating themselves with the monarchy at all costs. Furthermore, we had a vested interest in upholding the current marriage. Fascinated, we maids and other underlings watched the Dowager Duchess of Norfolk, as matriarch of the family, struggle with her conscience in deciding the appropriate course of action. At meal times she could be observed in close, often tense, discussion with the Duke of Norfolk, notorious for his conservatism. At other times the echoes of their arguments could be heard ringing down the hallways.

"What do you think the Dowager will decide to do? I do hope she'll not force us all to retreat to Sussex!" I said to Henry one bright day as we travelled down the Thames towards the City. Worldly-wise Henry was my main source of news about the outside events. I suspect he enjoyed my innocent wonderment when he regaled me with tales of court intrigue and policy. In retrospect, I believe he likely obtained his intelligence in the same way as I otherwise would have done—from servant gossip or lurid tales told by merchants or travelling minstrels.

"I suspect the Dowager's desire for favour at court will be stronger than her religious beliefs," he said, lounging back in the sunshine and crossing his silk-clad legs at the ankles. "She will decide her place is at court where she will be seen in prominent devoted and loyal service to her ruler!"

"I have no wish to leave Lambeth. It is so pleasurable to be here, and to be able to travel to the city on a fancy is something to be valued!"

I'd taken a few trips down river with Henry since his arrival. The journeys slaked my thirst for adventure and danger, and I now regarded myself as quite the mature city-dweller.

Henry laughed. "Properly, a young lady such as yourself shouldn't travel down the river at all, Catherine. It is only because your step-grandmother has appalling standards of supervision that you're able to do so. In any event, I do think her sense of responsibility to her household and charges will come to the fore—at the Duke's urging, if nothing else! Although the Dowager will go to court, we will be bundled off to Sussex, you wait and see!"

"But why? Wherever the Dowager goes, we must go, surely!"

Henry sighed as if exasperated by the questions of a foolish child. "Of course not!" he said crossly. "In any event, the King shall soon remove the court from Whitehall, for fear of the plague. We cannot all traipse after them, Catherine. No, we will be sent to the country . . . speaking of the plague, are you sure you wish to go to town today?"

I felt myself blanch. I had a deep fear of the deadly illnesses—the plague and the sweating sickness—which thrived in London, especially in the summer; but I also longed to be amid the bustling commotion of colourful, twisted streets. I could overlook the evil smells, the noise, rats, beggars and filth. I saw only the pageantry, the fashion, the taverns, hostels and shops with their swaying signs above their doors, inviting eager visitors.

"Yes," I said firmly. "I shall hold a handkerchief over my mouth, and we will wash afterwards."

"Together, perhaps?" Henry asked, hopefully. I smiled without answering, mindful of the shifting of power between us.

We disembarked at London Bridge. On other occasions when we had come here, there were heads of traitors pinioned upon pikes along the bridge, but today there were none, and I regarded this as a good omen. Light of heart, I inspected the cluster of shops on the bridge before heading off with Henry on an exploration of Tower Hill, from where we could see the Gothic spire of Saint Paul's Cathedral to the west. The riotous sounds, vivid colours and overpowering scents thrilled the deepest parts of my soul.

As the shadow of the spire fell over us, I became aware of the increasing numbers of people rushing past us, towards the area from which we had come. Henry, too, had noticed and stopped to look back. The people were in a great state of excitement, calling to each other "It's coming! It's begun. . . . Up ahead, be quick!"

"What's afoot?" I asked Henry. He shrugged. The rush of passing people had abated; now they waited around us. Jeers and cheers eddied towards us in a wave. I heard the shouted word "Traitor!" and the chant "Suffer and die! Suffer and die!" and, barely discernible amidst the noise, the clatter of hooves.

A horse bearing a hooded rider came into view at the turn in the narrow street. The crowd around us staggered back. The horse dragged behind it a hurdle of thin, interwoven branches. Bound to the hurdle was a young man in ragged clothing who cried out in agony as it bounced wildly on the cobblestones.

I knew what this was—the first stage of the penalty for high treason. At the next stage, at Tyburn, the young man would be hanged—but cut down before his neck was broken. Still conscious, he would then be dismembered and disembowelled before his own eyes. Perhaps, if God were merciful, he would die of shock or blood loss. If not, at the third stage his head would be struck off. His executioners would then divide his body into quarters and display the parts on gibbets around the city, a reminder to all who dared commit this most serious of crimes.

I staggered to the gutter and was ill. Only when I felt Henry's cool hand on the back of my neck did I look around me once more. I saw a few sympathetic expressions on dirty faces as the crowd around me dispersed . . . but there were also other expressions that sickened me further, like glee, feverish excitement, delight in another's misfortune. I looked into Henry's face and understood what he had meant on the night of the royal birth celebrations: finding pleasure was a necessity, for it was a refuge, the only passage to God in this terrible world, the only place where God could be found and glorified.

"Let us go home," I whispered to him. I grasped his hand and pressed it to my bosom.

Awareness flickered behind his eyes, and they widened with eagerness. As people filed past us again, he took my arm and we retraced our steps with desperation and impatience. When we travelled back up the Thames, I didn't look back.

At Norfolk House, careless of enquiring eyes or gossiping tongues, I chased the ladies from our chamber and pulled Henry towards my bed, tugging frantically at his hose, hauling my skirts above my waist. We fell to the bed and Henry knelt between my eagerly splayed legs, a dark flush warming his cheeks.

The door to the chamber burst open. As an exclamation of shock erupted from the intruder, we sprang apart, fumbling with our clothing. I stared at the man who had entered. In mingled trepidation and joy I leapt from the bed and took several eager steps towards him before stopping short.

My father, Lord Edmund Howard, had come to Lambeth.

II

MY FATHER HAD BEEN CONSTABLE OF CALAIS since 1531, a position that my cousin, now the Queen, had obtained for him. If his nature had been different, it is likely that he would have held a loftier status throughout his life, for, as well as being the youngest brother to the Duke of Norfolk, he had an impressive and dutiful record of service in the King's army. However, he had declined to adopt the Howard obsequiousness, and was also quite without ambition; thus he had been reduced to poverty and insignificance.

Of course, there were many who said his lot was not the result of pride and dignity, but inability and laziness. However, I remember him talking enviously of the 'honest work' done by our yeomen tenants and others who laboured on the land at my childhood home in Kent. I knew that if his rank had permitted it, he would have been out there with these common folk, toiling in the fields, night and day if necessary to support his large and extended family. Instead he had been forced to make good marriages to wealthy widows and to accept the office of Constable in Calais to keep his creditors at bay.

When I looked at him that afternoon, I saw a man who much resembled me in appearance—thick auburn hair, hazel eyes, short in stature. However, bitterness had impressed a downward curve on his sensual mouth and overindulgence in wine had flushed his cheeks and thickened his body. The colour deepened as he beheld me now, but as the initial shock subsided, apathy crept into his countenance. I took that opportunity to step forward again and throw my arms around him.

Although I embraced my father, he only patted me on the shoulder. When I drew away from him, I saw he was looking at Henry Mannox with a mildly annoyed frown. Poor scarlet-faced Henry was helpless.

"Who are you, lad?"

"Henry Mannox, sir."

"Henry Mannox . . . I do not know the name. What's your station?"

Henry shot a pleading look in my direction, but I dropped my gaze, fixing my interest in a scuff on my shoe.

"I—er—I am a servant of the Dowager Duchess, sir."

"Yes? In what office?"

A short, tense silence ensued before Henry blurted out with desperate pride, "I am the music tutor, sir."

The frown and anger abated and my father sighed. He jerked his head towards the door.

"Leave us, lad."

"Yes, sir . . . of course, sir." Henry bowed. Not looking at me again, he scuttled from the chamber, the door slamming shut behind him.

When the echo of the slam subsided, my father turned perplexed eyes on me.

"Catherine, Catherine," he sighed. "*A music tutor?*"

Naturally, it was not that I had taken a lover, but that I had chosen someone of low rank, which shocked my father.

"Father, we didn't—I haven't—I am a maid!"

My father's eyebrows arched. "It looked very much to me as if you and this *music tutor* are lovers, Mistress Catherine."

"No! We are not! I promise you, father!"

"He was forcing you?"

"No! I was upset . . . not thinking clearly . . . under normal circumstances . . ."

"Then, he was making good use of you?"

"No, no!"

My father crossed his arms and looked at me as if I were a stubborn child. "Then, my dear, if he was not forcing you—and not making good use of you—it does not speak well of your own intentions."

I could say nothing. I pressed my hands to my hot cheeks and returned my gaze to my shoe. My father sighed again.

"Of course this is not your fault. It is mine for sending you here, and my stepmother's for her poor standards of upbringing. It is only through God's mercy that there have not been—repercussions—from this mistake."

It occurred to me that it was my pride in my name and my father's timely interference, not God's mercy, which had prevented disaster, but I said nothing. I glanced up from my shoes. My father was deep in thought. At last, he nodded.

"Aye, that is a good solution," he said to himself. He looked at me. "I shall have to take you away from here for a time . . . you have an impulsive spirit, Catherine, and you require more supervision than your step-grandmother offers. Tomorrow, I will escort you to your aunt's home in Oxenheath. There you will stay for a short time to learn the manners appropriate to your rank. Your sister Mary is there, so be of good cheer!"

I gaped at him in horror. My Aunt Margaret Cotton—my late mother's sister—was a harridan who ruled her small household at Oxenheath in Kent with an iron fist and imposed the strictest and most parsimonious standards. She had disliked me as a child—I was too gay and too spirited—and I saw no reason why she would grow fond of me now. As for the presence of my sister—it had been four years since I had seen Mary, who would now be a mere eight years old. She would likely not remember me nor be worthy company.

"Father, sir, no! Please, do not send me to Oxenheath, I beg of you!"

"That's enough, Catherine. I have made my decision. I will send word to your aunt and we will depart at sunrise. Pray gather your belongings."

The chamber door swung open and the Dowager rolled in, her black velvet skirts billowing. She stopped short, absorbing the scene.

"What has happened?" she asked.

"I found Catherine in bed with the music tutor," my father announced grimly.

The Dowager gasped. Before I could react, she stepped up to me, swung back her arm and, with a *crack* as of a whip, slapped me across the face.

I cried out, staggered and fell to the ground, my ears ringing. The pain in my face brought tears to my eyes. Unrelenting, she hauled me to my feet once more. Again the arm swung back.

"Stop, stepmother!"

As I burst into sobs, my father grasped the Dowager's arm. The old woman glared at me with fury; yet, even in my tumult I detected behind the fury a shame and embarrassment of her own. She drew her gaze from me and stepped back, smoothing her skirts with trembling hands.

My father spoke again, saying, "I am taking Catherine away to her aunt at Oxenheath tomorrow—no, stepmother!" as the Dowager opened her mouth to protest. "I shall hear no argument! And I do not wish to talk of blame any more . . . You must decide for yourself where that lies, although I suspect you already know. Perhaps in a year or so, Catherine may return to this household."

The Dowager, speechless at my father's uncharacteristic firmness, hesitated with clenched fists and wounded pride. Summoning the dregs of her dignity, she lifted her chin.

"So be it," she rumbled. "Catherine still has much to learn of the skill of running a noble household and if she is to make a good marriage, she must return to me in due course. However, if you consider that she should first learn to curb her spirit in the home of her aunt, then that of course is your decision."

Without looking at me again, she turned and swept from the chamber. The door slammed and made me flinch.

My father stepped closer and laid his cool palm on my smarting cheek. I pressed into it, hot tears flowing again. I longed for him to take me into his arms and comfort me but he did not. His soothing touch had to satisfy my need for his affection.

"I am sorry that your step-grandmother smote you," my father murmured, and shuddered in distaste. I realised we shared more than physical similarities. When his hand dropped from my cheek, I grasped it in both of mine and kissed it.

He smiled and did not extract his hand but squeezed my fingers. "This is a good decision, my daughter," he said eagerly, referring to my banishment to Oxenheath. "Most of your mother's family, the Culpepers, are in Kent as you know . . . you will be amongst like-minded people who care for you."

I nodded. I had spent most of my childhood at Oxenheath, and until coming to the Dowager's home four years ago, I had only known Culpeper relations, many of whom were significant Kentish landowners. I tried not to think of my aunt's harsh ways, dwelling instead on my happier memories. For my father's sake, I found some optimism and attempted a smile.

"Yes, father, I shall be well. Do not worry about me."

My miraculous reward was my father's arms passing around me, and an awkward embrace.

Chapter 4

"Friendship makes prosperity brighter,
while it lightens adversity by sharing its griefs and anxieties."

Marcus Tullius Cicero
Roman lawyer, writer, scholar, orator and statesman
(106-43 BC)

I

Oxenheath, Kent
Summer, fall 1533

OXENHEATH IS A LARGE ESTATE on the riverbank with a tall and square manor house of red brick, gardens, an expansive demesne of meadow and woodland and a network of enclosed fields worked by tenants and labourers. In my childhood the manor was home to my grandfather Culpeper and my immediate family, including many of my half-siblings.

My mother's older sister Margaret also called Oxenheath home, and so too did her husband William Cotton and their tribe of six children. My uncle William, who stood at exactly half his wife's height and near to a third of her girth, was most often away on "the King's business", as my aunt would explain with deliberate vagueness. Yet the man was so cowed by his wife that I doubt I would have noticed his presence if he had been there. I also suspect his absences were more likely prompted by distaste for his wife than any duty he owed to our monarch.

The Culpeper relations, particularly a line of distant cousins from Bedgebury, were frequent visitors. Many times, I and three or four siblings would be dispatched to Bedgebury to return the visit. I always requested to be one of those dispatched, being very fond of those cousins, and because my harridan aunt Margaret at Oxenheath loomed as a blight on my otherwise happy existence. The lasting impression of my childhood is of being surrounded always by my Culpeper family, and immersed in constant merry noise and activity.

When I was nine years old, my grandfather Culpeper died, and Oxenheath became the property of Aunt Margaret, thereby—no doubt to Aunt Margaret's annoyance—passing into the hands of Uncle William. Not even that could entice my uncle back to Oxenheath for lengthy periods. Within six months we heard he had died in London of sweating sickness. My mother died that same year and, as my father was often away on genuine King's business, the Dowager Duchess of Norfolk became my legal guardian, while my siblings and half-siblings were distributed to various other family households across Kent. My sister Mary remained at Oxenheath. Aunt Margaret probably lived to regret that display of charity, for Mary was stricken with some breathing malady. My father told me she was often in the care of monks at the nearby monastery, but this care entailed a significant payment to the abbey on top of the usual tithes. As my father was virtually penniless, that expense had fallen upon the grudging and bitter Aunt Margaret.

My father did not tarry long at Oxenheath once he had delivered me there. I didn't blame him, for we were denied a warm welcome. The minute I stepped into the front entrance, Aunt Margaret regarded me with a dour expression, the broken veins on her nose and cheeks vivid with aggravation. She clucked: "So you have been up to your tricks, Mistress Catherine! Tch, tch! See here, there will be no time for that here! I expect you to devote your time to helping with the children and with household tasks. I will drive that Howard mischief from your soul!"

My poor father winced when I turned a look of reproach on him. We followed Aunt Margaret's broad back to my bedchamber, a tiny, dark cavity beneath a flight of stairs near the top of the house. When my aunt stalked from the room, my father turned a pleading expression on me.

"You will try and be happy here, Catherine?"

I crossed my arms and pouted.

"It need only be for two years," he said. "Then you can return to your step-grandmother's home. Indeed, she remains your legal guardian even now, while I am at Calais—your aunt must confer with her regarding your education and general well-being. I do think that at this time of your life you need a stronger rein than your step-grandmother offers."

It failed to console me. And indeed, it proved to be difficult to be happy at Oxenheath.

Overnight, it seemed, a bitter winter closed in, confining me to the house, and to duties not much different from those of a nursery maid. My six Cotton cousins—ranging in age from five to ten years, almost indistinguishable in appearance and behaviour—were in my charge. Of course, my aunt did have servants to attend to the children but, whether through frugality or indifference, she had retained young, dim-witted lasses, incapable of performing even the simplest tasks. They seemed more interested in bedding the uncouth and unwashed male servants than in looking after children. In fairness, after the first few weeks, I understood how the prospect of bedding any man could be considered preferable to caring for the devilish Cotton tribe.

Charles, Isabella, Edward, Margaret, Henry and Elizabeth Cotton! I could hardly tell them apart unless they formed a line, when their heights gave me an inkling of who was who. They all possessed wild black curls, snapping green eyes and short, rotund bodies. And they all shared the ability to make my life a misery.

Every day, it seemed, some fresh mischief was afoot, or there was some new torment to inflict on me. Frequently I found beetles and frogs in my bed. One morning I discovered rents in every child's hose and had to spend the rest of the day, and most of the day after, repairing them. Another day, all six pretended they could not hear me and no matter how much I repeated an order, their faces would remain puzzled as they shook their heads and pointed to their ears: "What say you, cousin? Speak up! I cannot hear you." I gave up repeating myself when my voice grew hoarse.

Yet another morning, I woke to discover all my clothing missing except for one worn gown and a pair of shoes. To be without suitable clothing in winter invited frostbite, chill blains, or worse, so I had to throw myself on the mercy of the seamstress, and several shawls and simple gowns soon came my way. Although it was an inconvenience at first—and certainly I shouted and screamed a few times to the glee of my cousins—in truth this was the one favour they did me. I despised the Spanish farthingale, corsets, heavy skirts and hoods we were condemned to bear, and the prank gave me a perfect excuse to wear them no longer. We rarely had visitors and Aunt Margaret cared little if I ran around like a low-born rustic, and so for the duration of my stay I dressed in light clothing. Even when the stolen garments were mysteriously returned to my bedchamber, I did not wear them. An intense and demanding sensuality consumed me even at that age, and so I luxuriated in the lightness and freedom of wearing few clothes, enjoyed the frisson of rich fabrics close to my skin, and the whisper of a cool, fresh breeze through my hair. I may have regarded this development as a minor consolation for my life of drudgery and discontent, but no doubt it served to cultivate that dangerous sensuality and my ingrained immodesty, which were to cause me untold trouble in later years.

At the first sign of spring, I yearned to explore out of doors and I had the perfect excuse to leave the manor. My sister Mary had remained in the infirmary at the abbey during the winter, and I told my aunt I had an obligation to visit her. Appreciating the opportunity to have me out if sight, Aunt Margaret paid no heed to the impropriety of me travelling alone and gave her grudging consent. Soon thereafter I called for a horse and was on my way.

The Abbey of Saint Bede, which housed a small community of Benedictine monks, could be reached by the road that meandered through pretty Kentish countryside. A shorter path wound along the riverbank, over a meadow and through broad, shady woodland. I chose the latter way, it being the more interesting and offering more reason to linger. Indeed, on that first day I idled beside the river for several hours and took several paths through the shadowy wood, before reaching the abbey demesne.

My first experience of the abbey was not through the gatehouse but by way of the farm and the kitchen gardens, viewed over a low stone wall. I noticed a grey-clad monk at work with a trowel in one garden. I tied my horse to a tree, clambered over the wall and made my way towards him.

He looked up as I approached, and straightened, pressing a hand to the small of his back as he did so. A short, stout man, he possessed a mass of fine white hair, which stood out from his tonsured head like a halo. It framed a plump, rosy and unlined face. His long habit was of natural wool, which gave it its grey colour, gathered around his rotund middle with a leather girdle and worn beneath a scapula of the same fabric. The hood hung down his back.

"Hail! Well met!" he called.

I lifted a hand in greeting. Although he smiled broadly I sensed he studied me carefully.

Months of being deprived of friendship had made my soul heavy; now the heaviness lifted. I sighed and returned the smile.

"Good morrow, sir," I said. "I am Catherine Howard of Oxenheath. I understand my sister Mary has been within your infirmary for the winter. I have come to visit her. Would you take me to the Abbot?"

The old monk seemed startled at my name, so at odds with my being unescorted, my uncovered head and simple garb, but he recovered quickly.

"Of course, you may visit your sister," he said, his beam growing wider. "However, there is no need to disturb the Abbot while he is at his prayers. I shall take you to the infirmary myself."

He dropped his trowel, withdrew a cloth from a fold in his habit and wiped his large hands. He thrust them out at me.

"I am Father Vyncent," he said; eagerly, my own hands reached out and became enfolded in his warm grasp. His fingers were liberally stained with ink.

He held them up with a rueful expression. "The bane of my chief duty here at Saint Bede's," he said.

"You are one of the scribes here?" I asked, as we began a slow stroll towards the grey stone Abbey.

"The only scribe, my dear, apart from a few of my brothers who try hard, albeit with little success!" He sighed. "I am sole scribe, notary and illuminator!"

I cast him a curious sidelong glance. Besides despatching the Abbey's normal business as a scribe, working on legal documents as a notary, and painting miniatures and initial letters as an illuminator, the monk's title of 'Father' also indicated he was a priest; and with his work in the vegetable gardens, and the time he had to devote to prayer, I had to wonder when he had a chance to sleep. Yet he seemed alert, healthy and possessed of an enviable contentment. I found myself wanting to linger with him, as my own dissatisfaction faded in the warmth of his disposition.

Perhaps he sensed my yearning for friendship, for when he delivered me to the closed door of the infirmary within the east wing of the monastery, he turned to me and said in an undertone, "If you should visit your sister again, please also extend your visit to me! We can talk, share some of our fine wine, and I will show you some of our books. I do believe we shall be firm friends!"

I smiled. "Indeed I shall." Father Vyncent looked pleased. As he tapped on the door, a thought occurred to me.

"Does the abbey receive travellers who bear news of the court?" I asked hopefully.

"Aye," murmured the monk, casting me another shrewd glance. "As a Howard, you are of course related to the new Queen."

"She is my cousin," I confirmed with immense pride. "And I long to hear news of her."

We heard the soft tread of approaching footsteps on the other side of the door. I sensed a trace of aloofness steel over Father Vyncent at my words—as a priest, he would not be a supporter of the King's second marriage. Unaccountably, his sudden coolness hurt.

He did not miss my distress. As the door opened, he grasped my hands again.

"Then you must come often to visit me," he said. "I shall keep you informed of how your cousin fares . . . Ah, Brother Ambrose, here is the Lady Catherine Howard, to visit her sister Mary!"

A stooped and gaunt monk standing in the open doorway nodded. "Pray enter," he said in a soft, sibilant voice. "Mary sleeps at present as she was afflicted with a wheezing attack last night, but you can see her for a short time."

I nodded a farewell to Father Vyncent before following the gliding form of Brother Ambrose through a sunlit dormitory. Patients occupied only a few of the beds. The small, thin form of my sister Mary lay in one.

I took a seat beside her, anxious at her wraithlike paleness and the erratic rise and fall of her narrow chest. In her wispy dark hair and heart-shaped face I saw our mother.

"How goes she?" I whispered to the hovering Brother Ambrose.

"She had a difficult winter," he replied, "every cough followed by a wheezing attack.

Now, with the new spring growth in the air, she sneezes and wheezes more often." He sighed. "Perhaps in the summer she will improve."

"My family is grateful to you for her care," I said. I untied a pouch from my girdle and handed it to him.

The monk shoved the pouch into the folds of his habit, nodding. The gift made him more voluble. "I treat her chest with a special rubbing balm and also soak a handkerchief in a tincture which we prepare here," he said. "If she holds it to her mouth and nose during an attack, it seems to relieve her breathing. Last night, as on other nights, I gave her a sleeping potion to ensure she rests. I fear she will sleep through your visit."

"Then I shall not tarry," I said, rising. Waiting patiently and virtuously beside a sickbed is not one of my talents. "You do fine work," I said to Brother Ambrose. "I shall visit again soon . . . please tell Mary I was here."

The monk showed me out of the abbey and I made my way across the tilled vegetable fields to the wall where I had tethered my horse. To my disappointment, Father Vyncent was no longer at work with his trowel, so I had no excuse to linger. However, I promised myself I would visit again soon, to partake of his hospitality, enjoy his friendship—and learn more of the life my cousin the Queen led at the royal court.

II

IT WAS THE FIRST of many visits to the Abbey of Saint Bede and was the start of my prized—and, some would say, odd—friendship with Father Vyncent. In one person, he became for me a father, brother, confidant and confessor. I found in him someone who was able to understand my thoughts and emotions at a glance, someone who issued sound and kind counsel, and someone who did not judge me. In return he found in me unswerving loyalty and devotion, companionship and—I grew to suspect—a source of mirth.

In the summer, Mary's health improved as Brother Ambrose expected, and she returned to Oxenheath. Although I had grown fond of my sister in the intervening months, for she was a bright, affectionate child, her presence at Oxenheath meant a double misfortune for me—I no longer had an excuse to visit the Abbey so often, and she became yet another child thrust into my care. Summer dragged by. My memories of my friends and of Henry Mannox grew dim. No news came our way regarding events beyond our boundaries, and no visitors relieved my loneliness. I confess that when Mary had her first wheezing attack with the turn of the weather, and she returned to the monks, I rejoiced inwardly. Unfortunately, even then, inclement weather kept me from riding out to Saint Bede's on a regular basis. Only when spring crept again over the slumbering land was I able to begin my frequent habitual escapes from Oxenheath to the more welcoming environment of the Abbey, to bask in friendship and gossip.

From Father Vyncent I learnt that my cousin the Queen had given birth twice since the birth of Princess Elizabeth—both boys, both stillborn and deformed. With gloom, I heard of the King's growing dissatisfaction and regret in his marriage. With the birth of two deformed infants, whispers of witchcraft swept the Court and, believing them, the King knew himself to be cursed. Taking advantage of the whispers, her enemies accused Anne Boleyn of being a witch in league with the devil. Her malevolent influence, it was said, had brought down the Roman Church in England, weakened our King and had humiliated the beloved Queen

Katherine in the process; the new Church of England had sprung from her cauldron as she rode her broomstick.

King Henry was now Supreme Head of the Church in England. He was openly condemned for his immoral second marriage and for the break from the Church of Rome. Those who did not support the King's actions were imprisoned in the Tower and executed.

England's revered former Lord Chancellor, Sir Thomas More, who refused to take the Oath of Supremacy acknowledging the King as head of the Church of England, was such a one imprisoned. Father Vyncent would utter Sir Thomas's name with awe, and with relief he would emphasise that, despite Sir Thomas's treasonous behaviour, the King valued his opinions. Indeed, the King soon delivered Sir Thomas from the Tower and certain execution. Presented with this apparent indication of the King's wavering conviction on the subject of his divorce, the Queen grew increasingly insecure in her position. She established a vigorous campaign for Sir Thomas to be arrested again. Anne Boleyn possessed considerable feminine wiles to which the King had long been susceptible, and she used them to her benefit. Sir Thomas was once more imprisoned.

"Even then, the Queen did not relent in her campaign," Father Vyncent remarked to me with some bitterness one day during my second summer in Kent. He always tried not to speak ill of the Queen to me, but sometimes his personal views tainted his tone. "The Queen scolded the King, and denied him all favours, until Sir Thomas was sent to the block. We have heard the saintly man went to the angels two months hence." Father Vyncent bowed his head and crossed himself. "These are anxious and treacherous times, my dear," he said on a sigh.

His words echoed in my ears as I departed the abbey. Of course, I did not urge the mare to speed, even though Aunt Margaret had ordered me to return home as soon as possible. I kept our pace at an amble through the deep coppice and across the sunlit pastures. Ahead, the river glinted its cool temptation. Although I expected my delay would earn me a harsh scolding, I dismounted and set my horse free to graze, and swished through the long, sweet grass to the river bank, fringed with willows and massive oak trees.

Only birdsong, the whisper of the breeze through leaves and grass and the flow of water broke the warm silence. I had become accustomed to loneliness, although I still found merely sitting alone with my thoughts an uncomfortable pastime. Consumed with the urge to so something, no matter how trivial, I removed my gown and my shoes. Clad only in my shift, I waded into the water.

The cool water soothed my anxieties while delighting me with its silken touch. Gingerly feeling my way over the silted riverbed, I moved further into the depths until the water was breast-high. I dunked my head, longing to feel the weight of my hair being lifted from my head and shoulders and relishing it when it occurred. The gentle rush of the current buffeted me and I staggered, one foot unable to find the ground. I righted myself, just as a terrifying memory assaulted me.

A memory of this very river and another warm, midsummer's day. I was eight years old, bathing with a group of my cousins visiting from Bedgebury. Fearlessly, I had pushed out into the depths. One more step . . . and the ground fell abruptly away from my feet. I slipped and plunged downward . . . *down* . . . *down!* Water gushed into my nose and mouth, choking me, and my arms craned upwards, reaching desperately for the rippling water's surface and the glowing disc of the sun far above . . .

Then the silhouette of a hand breaking the surface, fingers splayed like a talon, plunging downwards and locking around my wrist. An enormous strength pulled me to the surface. I surged out of the water, and sucked in gulps of air as the strong arms of my saviour wrapped around me . . .

Seven years later, I shuddered at the memory of my near drowning, and then smiled at the recollection of its outcome. Still smiling, I turned and made my way back to shore.

On the bank of the river, I removed my clinging shift and draped it over an oak branch. Unmindful of modesty, I spread out my gown in the sun and lay down on it. I closed my eyes against the glaring sun.

With the caress of the gentle elements on my skin, I shivered in delight. My body tingled, much as it did when I teased myself with my own touch, as Henry Mannox had taught me. I summoned sweet memories of him by allowing my hands to follow the intimate paths on my body he had revealed to me.

My tickling fingers had slid to my thighs when a shadow passed across the sun. At once, a shiver skated across my flesh. I frowned, trying concentrate on my caresses—but it was no use. I opened my eyes in annoyance and blinked.

I gasped in horror. A man's silhouette towered above me. Yelping, I sprang to a sitting position, snapping my knees to my chest, straining to see who he was, but he remained a dark shape against the sun. He took an ominous step towards me.

"No! Go away!" I cried. Petrified, I rolled over, pushed myself to my feet and took several staggering steps up the bank.

His hand shot out and closed around my forearm. I screamed in mortal terror, tugging, desperate to escape.

"Sweet Jesus, Kate, it's me!"

Now I could see him. His features and his voice rooted me to the spot. Wings of jet black hair framed a pale face, a neat black beard and moustache, cat-like blue eyes.

He grinned with a flash of white teeth, studying my bosom with interest. The grin transformed his plain features, making him wondrously handsome, and the tinkling bell of memory became a clarion.

"Cousin Tom!" With a cry of delight, I hurtled myself against Thomas Culpeper, whom I had always called Tom, my favourite of the Bedgebury cousins. I wrapped my legs and arms around him, much as I used to when I was nine years old and he, my hero, was near twenty. But now I was almost fifteen, a woman—and stark naked.

"Whoa there!" Aghast, it was Tom's turn to stagger backwards, his arms staying resolutely at his sides. He tripped on an exposed tree root and fell on his back with a loud grunt, taking me with him.

"What are you doing here?" I cried, careless of the tumble. "Oh, this is wondrous! Oh, how happy I am—."

The distracted look on his face cut off my effusive exclamations.

"Um, Kate, maybe you should get off me," he muttered.

I frowned, puzzled. As he shifted beneath me with a grimace, I detected against my thighs the manifestation of a quite unchivalrous interest in me.

I think my jaw dropped. Tom laughed and shrugged. "What do you expect?" he said. "You're no child any more, my Kate." He paused. I could feel his warm hands resting lightly on my waist. "Well? Do you intend to remain atop me?"

I swallowed nervously. I knew he had already seen more of me than was proper, but was embarrassed to expose myself again, which would happen if I stood up. I hesitated. With a heave, Tom rolled me onto my back and pressed me into the ground.

"Maybe I should assist you with what you were seeking before my interruption, what do you think?" he said, raising one eyebrow. "Quite an adult pursuit, I must say! And indeed an engaging spectacle."

"No, I think not," I said and pouted, although I didn't attempt to push him off me. The heat into my loins rose to my cheeks, tickled by Tom's swinging hair. "And you ought to have turned away."

"My Kate, there is not a man in England who would have turned away from watching *that!*"

Despite my attempts to feign umbrage, I felt my mouth twitch with amusement. The growing ease between us, and Tom's fond way of addressing me, chased away my pent-up loneliness and anxiety. Watching my reactions, Tom sighed in his good-natured way and rolled off me.

"I think you had better dress," he said, rising gracefully and loping away from me to the riverbank. "I'll wait down here."

My shift was still wet, so I scrambled into my gown and shoes. While I struggled with the lacings, I studied Tom's form. He stood at average height, was very lean, but the uncommon breadth of his shoulders made him appear shorter than he was. That morning he was hatless and dressed simply in a tunic of dark blue brocade and black hose and shoes. His long legs were shapely.

"When you have stared at me enough, do come hither," he called back.

Flushing, I tripped over pebbles to join him. Of its own accord, my hand slipped into his.

"How did you know I was staring at you?" I asked.

"Because if the positions were reversed, I would be staring at you... you and I are cut from the same bolt, you know." He squeezed my hand and nodded towards the river. "Remember when I hauled you out of there?"

I smiled and nodded. "It seems you were always rescuing me from some trouble or other."

"Aye! Let's see now—there was you on a runaway horse, stuck up a tree, being attacked by a magpie . . . oh, and I remember quite a few nights when you were frightened by thunderstorms or nightmares. Tell me, I have always wondered—were all those rescues really required or were they a device on your part?"

"Of course they were required," I said. "Well, maybe one or two of the nightmares were *exaggerated . . .*"

We laughed. Tom lifted my hand and pressed it to his mouth. His soft beard tickled my skin, and the sensations left me tingling long after he lowered my hand to my side.

"You forgot the time when you were defending my honour against your brother," I said with an edge of long-held bitterness.

"Oh, aye!"

We were silent in shared memory. My own was not pleasant. Tom had an older brother, also called Thomas—it was not uncommon for families to baptise two or more sons with the same name, in case one died. Thomas the elder was a solid, dim-witted rake, whose only redeeming quality was his unstinting loyalty to his namesake younger brother. Whether out of envy for the time young Tom always had for me, or from natural instinct, Thomas the elder had delighted in teasing me and generally making my life a misery.

"Roly-poly, roly-poly," he had chanted at me one day in the rose garden at Bedgebury. I ignored him and tried to flee, but he followed me along the narrow path, still chanting. I had seen young Tom on the garden's perimeter, one eyebrow arched in curiosity and, anguished, I headed in his direction. He took a step onto the path, heading towards me. Clearly, Thomas had not seen him, for his tormenting continued.

"Roly-poly, roly-poly!"

Tom had loomed before us, his face flushed dark red in anger. Thomas the elder stopped short.

"I say, brother," he blustered, quailing before Tom's wrath, "I was only teasing . . ."

Tom said nothing but drew back his elbow and soundly boxed his brother on the nose. Thomas yelled, staggered backwards and fell into a rose bush, which occasioned more pained yells.

Tom had then taken my hand and led me from the garden.

Now, he slanted me a look.

"I am sorry all that cuddliness has gone, but nevertheless, you have grown beautifully, I must say."

I blushed. "You would know," I mumbled. "You saw all too much of me a few minutes ago."

"Ah, what a wonderful memory you have given me, for my long and lonely nights! Do not feel embarrassed or guilty about it."

"Lonely? You?" I laughed in genuine amusement.

He merely laughed again and lifted his shoulders in an expressive shrug.

"I have been lonely here," I said. "I hope you intend to stay a while?"

"I am on my way to London. I heard you were here so I decided to come and see for myself the wicked lass who has been seducing all the men of the Dowager Duchess of Norfolk's household. Having viewed your—er—attractions, I am beginning to believe there may be truth to the rumours."

"I did not seduce all the men at Lambeth!" I said, affronted. "There was only one, and even that was perfectly innocent!"

"Was that the music teacher? Horatio something?"

"Henry Mannox," I said. My chin tilted in pride as I uttered his name.

"Hmmm," said Tom, studying me. "Are you in love with him?"

"I—er—no . . . maybe . . . yes—um."

"It's good that you're so certain," said Tom dryly.

"Why does it matter to you?" I retorted. "Are you envious?" Another thought occurred to me. "Are you married or betrothed yet?"

Tom tugged at my hand, still enfolded in his grasp. When I was brought up against his body, he released it and wound his arms around me. His hands stroked my buttocks through my skirts and he blinked in some astonishment. "No," he answered my question in a distracted manner, "although my family has had some mysterious intentions for me for many years, I am led to understand. And no, I am not envious, just curious. I have no need to be envious. I could make you forget Horatio if I wanted to."

My head swam as I became again acutely aware of the shape of his loins, and relished his stroking of my body. My eager hands inched outwards until my fingers touched silk-clad, manly thighs. His face moved closer. Henry could not have been further from my mind.

Tom released me and stepped back. His chest seemed to be rising and falling with some agitation, but when he spoke, it was with cool amusement. "See?" He turned around, scooped up a pebble and sent it skipping across the surface of the river.

Bemused, I watched him hunt for another stone, his face without expression. I wondered why he had not attempted to kiss me—but perversely, I was relieved he had not. But I found his changed manner bewildering.

"So, I am to London," he called back to me casually. He sent another pebble skipping across the water. "I intend to petition the King for a place in his Privy Chamber. My father has said I need only make the request, and the position is mine. The King has long held my family in favour."

"You would be better to return to Bedgebury," I said, also scrabbling around in the dirt for a suitable skipping stone. "I hear the King only likes to be surrounded by beautiful and handsome people."

Tom looked up, a grin battling with an expression of pretended affront.

"Why, Kate, you think the King would not find me pleasing to look at?"

My hand found a tuft of grass. I pulled some strands from the ground and tossed them into his face, declining to answer, rather suspecting that the King would find Tom very appealing indeed.

He sat down, stretching his legs out in front of him.

"I do not understand why you wish to go to court at this time," I said, not disguising my gloom, and sitting beside him, I unconsciously mimicking the way he was seated. Our arms brushed. "I would have thought any person remotely connected with the Howards would rather make a judicious retreat."

Tom slanted me a look. "So you are aware of court gossip then . . . I wondered."

"My friend Father Vyncent at the abbey seems to know everything and he takes delight in regaling me with news about my cousin the Queen, while trying not to hurt my feelings," I said dryly. "It appears she is not in favour at this time."

"Aye, that's true," Tom remarked. "However, I suspect my lineage is sufficiently removed from the Howard clan to count not against me." His tone was teasing so I could not take umbrage. "Besides," he went on, "the prospect of living amongst danger and intrigue arouses me."

"Hmmph," I grunted. "I am sure it does . . . good sense and Tom Culpeper were never well-acquainted." I suppressed a laugh as Tom again pretended to be affronted, the glint in his eyes betraying his own good humour.

"And what do you think of the rumours pertaining to the Queen's adultery and witchcraft?" I asked anxiously. "It's said the current turmoil springs from her cauldron as she rides her broomstick."

Tom pursed his lips thoughtfully. "Whenever a woman appears to have extraordinary hold over a man, witchcraft always seems to be raised as a reason for it—and when the man is our all-powerful monarch—well!" Tom shrugged and glanced at me. "You know what the cauldron and broomstick are, do you not?"

"What?" I said, puzzled. Tom looked away, cleared his throat and scratched his temple. "Never mind," he said, but after several taut seconds, he looked at me again with a mischievous wink, and then his meaning became clear. Unwittingly, my gaze shot downwards to Tom's thighs and then to the corresponding part of my own body.

"Very good," murmured Tom. He cleared his throat again. "As for the adultery," he said with forced casualness, "personally I cannot see Anne Boleyn being so foolish."

His words brought me a measure of comfort. "I would hope that she would not be foolish," I sighed. "Adultery in a Queen is treason, and the penalty for treason is—."

However, Tom no longer listened. He lifted his head and sniffed, a frown beetling his brows. I sniffed also. Smoke!

As one, our heads swivelled around. With growing alarm I saw thick plumes of black smoke rising beyond the nearby coppice, dispersing into placid blue sky.

"What's there?" Tom exclaimed, jumping to his feet.

"The abbey . . . Father Vyncent!" My exclamation ended on a high note of panic as I staggered upright.

Tom did not hesitate. Swiftly he ran past me towards our horses. Trembling, I scooped up my skirts and followed.

Chapter 5

"Minds ill at ease are agitated by both hope and fear."

Ovid
Roman classical poet
(43 BC-17 AD)

I

THICK SMOKE wove choking tendrils through the trees of the coppice. Our horses reared and snorted. Tom grabbed the reins of my mare and dug his heels into the flanks of his own. At a hair-raising gallop and beneath treacherous overhanging branches, we sped towards the burning abbey.

In a small field at the fringe of the monastery land we came to a rearing halt. I cried out in horror. Plumes of thick smoke billowed from all the windows of the abbey, and blackened its grey walls.

On the lawn near the front entrance raged a great bonfire, its orange flames reaching far into the sky, blanketing the scene with acrid smoke, cinders and ash, its intense heat scorching our uncovered skin. As we watched in petrified astonishment, an armoured soldier emerged from the abbey, his arms laden with books and scrolls; he tossed his load into the fire. Behind him staggered Father Vyncent, anguished hands clutching his head, his mouth forming pleas we could not hear. The soldier turned to go back inside, and elbowed the priest out of the way. Father Vyncent went flying, and fell to the ground with a bone-jarring thud.

At once, I made to jump off my mount in furious indignation. However, Tom detained me with a firm grip on my arm. "Wait, Kate, it's not safe."

In distress, I watched Father Vyncent struggle to stand. His bowed his head in his hands as other soldiers added books and manuscripts to the fire.

Horrified, I took in the rest of the scene. A large group of grey-clad monks huddled in the kitchen garden. Brother Ambrose stood amongst them, hovering over the prone figure of one of his patients. I also noticed the tall and austere Abbot, watching the desecration of his home with ill-disguised anger. A small group of soldiers sat in a circle near the front entrance, sharing a tankard of what I assumed was some of the abbey's rich wine; their ribald laughter and cheering could be heard above the crackling of the fire and the dim sounds of smashing coming from within the abbey. Their cheering became raucous as two soldiers emerged from the abbey's front entrance, bearing between them a large chest. They heaved it onto an already laden cart.

"What's happening?" I cried to Tom.

"The King has claimed for his own all the property of the monasteries," he shouted back over the noise. "All the abbeys and convents are being dissolved, their chattels and land sold to fill the King's coffers. I have heard of this happening, but this is my first witnessing of it."

"But . . . what will happen to the monks?" I exclaimed.

"Those that do not resist may be lucky to receive a pension . . . others will have to find an alternative living or be homeless and destitute."

I stared into the depths of the bonfire engulfing all Father Vyncent's labours.

"What of the books . . . the learning?" I whispered to myself.

Tom heard me. He looked at me with eyes teary and bloodshot from smoke.

"Lost forever, it seems," he said. "No wonder some say the Devil is at work in England!"

II

THE SOLDIERS DEPARTED at last with their booty-laden carts. When the crackling of the flames and the noise of destruction abated, we could hear the soldiers carousing as their procession weaved away through the soft and peaceful Kentish countryside.

We secured our horses and hastened to the monks. Tom veered towards the Abbot's group, while I ran to Father Vyncent, who stood apart from the rest.

I embraced him as he wept. He clutched hold of me, and seemed to obtain a measure of comfort from my presence, for his weeping soon all but ceased and when he drew away from me, he summoned a weak smile.

"It appears I shall have a lot of work ahead of me, restoring what has been lost!" he said in a tear-laden voice.

I hugged him, admiring his spirit. "I shall help you," I said impulsively. "I cannot write well, but I can ensure that you receive a suitable living with all the materials you need—there are advantages to being cousin to the Queen after all!"

Father Vyncent regarded me with a fond yet sad countenance before his gaze left me. A glimmer of curiosity appeared in his bleary eyes. I turned to see Tom striding towards us through the thinning smoke. The two men bowed to one another. Tom turned to me. Like Father Vyncent's, his face was streaked black, and I assumed mine was the same.

"Kate, I'll have to ride to the village to fetch some help. The monks will have to be lodged, and we will need horses and carts. Will you be safe here until I return?"

I nodded. "Make sure you detour by way of Oxenheath," I said, "and tell Aunt Margaret she has a moral duty to offer temporary lodgings to some monks, and whatever other assistance she can offer!"

Tom grinned. His teeth were very white in his blackened face. "I'll delight in it," he said. "I'll return soon. Father Vyncent." He nodded a farewell to the monk, touched my elbow in an oddly intimate gesture, and jogged away. I gestured to Father Vyncent that we should leave the vicinity of the bonfire, and led him towards a stone bench beneath an apple tree, on the perimeter of the kitchen gardens.

Shock had rendered insensible all the monks except the Abbot Cuthbert and Father Vyncent. Those two became huddled together in intense conversation as I made the other monks comfortable with blankets and stools fetched from the infirmary, which had escaped significant fire damage.

A chilly dusk had fallen when we heard the sound of approaching horses and the rumble of carts. Tom on his horse led a straggling procession through the gates of the abbey. The Abbot approached him and the two men consulted before Tom began to shout instructions and wave his arms; the villagers who had accompanied him leapt to do his bidding. One by one the monks with their meagre belongings were assisted onto the carts.

Soon, all save the Abbot, Brother Ambrose and Father Vyncent had departed for the village. Aunt Margaret had been persuaded to offer a temporary home to the three who remained. The Abbot told us, however, as we took the road to Oxenheath, that he would depart for a Priory at Canterbury the next day, where he knew the Prior, and Brother Ambrose mentioned a sister in Rochester who would welcome him. Only Father Vyncent made no mention of friends or family, and it occurred to me I knew nothing of the life he had led before joining the abbey, if indeed he had had one; many babies were 'donated' to monasteries at birth, and knew no other life. I wondered if Father Vyncent was one of those, in which case the desecration we had witnessed would be an even worse tragedy for him than I had first envisioned.

Aunt Margaret gave us a stiff welcome and bade me arrange for apartments and food for the guests. When they were resting comfortably, I traipsed to the nursery, heeding the call of duty.

I exclaimed in horror when I stepped inside. A maid slept soundly, sitting upright against the wall, as if frozen in shock. Her legs were splayed out before her, and her mousy hair straggled from beneath her cap, sticking to sweat-slick cheeks. Food stains decorated her clothing and she half-sat in a puddle of what I hoped was spilled ale.

Her regular snores formed a discordant background to the chorus of riotous, childish merriment. All seven children, my sister Mary included, were engaged in a fight with food, cushions, pillows and even with one mattress from a bed. Shouts, screams and laughter assaulted my ears. Feathers and food flew. One child—Edward, I think—saw me hovering, transfixed in the doorway. With a cry of glee, he picked up a strawberry and threw it at me. It landed with a splat on my neck. He yelled in triumph. Whooping with glee, the other children soon followed his lead. Stunned, I could only hold up my arms as an ineffectual shield against the bombardment of fruit, jellies, bread and tarts, while staggering into the chamber, wondering how on earth I could put a halt to all this before Aunt Margaret learned of it. "Stop it, stop it," I cried. The noise and glee only increased in intensity.

"Enough!"

The deep sustained roar echoed through the chamber. At once, blissful quiet reigned, but for the rumbling snores of the maid. Sagging with relief, I looked around.

Tom, ever my saviour, stood in the doorway. For a man of only average height, he had an enormous presence, heightened this time by the fearsome black streaks on his cheeks. The children were frozen still, staring at him with mouths agape.

"You!"

Another ear-splitting holler had the maid snuffling and opening one bleary eye. Seeing Tom, the other eye shot open and she struggled to her feet. She bobbed an awkward, swaying curtsey.

"Tidy this mess and get these children cleaned and to bed—at once!"

"Aye, sir," she mumbled, tottering away from the wall. I doubted her ability to be of much use, and indeed as I watched, she slipped on a squashed strawberry and went flying. I made to go to her assistance, but Tom beckoned me.

"Come, Kate, this is not your place." Glowering, he waved his finger at the children, all now standing meekly in a silent and still row. *"I do not want to hear another sound from any of you, is that understood!"*

The children stared and nodded. Tom took my arm and pulled me from the chamber.

"Cousin Tom to the rescue again," I murmured as he led me along corridors and down flights of stairs.

"Force of habit." He grasped my hand tighter. "Does that little scene I witnessed mean that Aunt Margaret has made you her nursery maid?"

"More or less," I mumbled.

Tom made a sound akin to a growl. "And you a Howard, and cousin to the Queen of England no less." He stopped so abruptly I staggered into him. I did not hurry to right myself. "Where are your apartments?" he demanded, his hands lingering on my waist.

I reluctantly took the lead and soon we stopped outside the hole that was my bedchamber. I opened the door and hastened to the pitcher of water on my side table. Immobile with shock, Tom hovered just inside the door.

"This is your bedchamber?"

I scrubbed at my face, not answering. Tom came to my side and took the cloth from my hand. His mouth was pressed into a grim line.

"I shall speak to Aunt Margaret about this," he said, placing his fingers beneath my chin and wiping the cloth down my cheeks. I cringed at his words.

"Tom, I do not want trouble," I said. "She will just make my life more unbearable when you are gone."

"Then I will stay on until she is persuaded." He scrubbed at something on my hairline. I stayed his hand.

"You will?" I asked hopefully.

He paused and his gaze locked with mine. He shrugged. "Why not? I can go to court any time, and I would like to help Father Vyncent find a suitable living . . . and of course, I must fulfil my duties as your champion!"

I grinned and gave a small jump of delight. "That's wonderful! Oh, we shall have such merriment, Tom!"

"'Merriment'? What sort of 'merriment' do you have in mind? Hide and seek? Leap frog? Some other childish game? Because my idea of pleasure is something else entirely."

"Maybe you can teach me the joys of that pleasure," I said, my mirth making me dredge up the old lessons in provocation that I had mastered at Lambeth. I batted my lashes and trailed a finger down Tom's chest.

I ought to have known they would be wasted on him. His eyes narrowed on my face. Then his gaze dropped. I sensed he became preoccupied. His head loomed closer, his mouth aiming for my neck. I gasped as his mouth locked onto my skin and I felt his teeth and tongue against me.

He drew away and licked his lips. "Mmm, strawberry," he said with a wink. "Now, that's something like my idea of pleasure. What do you think?"

I could only stare, senseless with some deep yearning his mouth had awakened. I was still gaping at him when he laughed, pressed the wet cloth back into my limp hand and kissed me on the cheek.

"Good night, my Kate," he said, backing away, still smiling. "When you are ready for that sort of pleasure, let me know, eh?"

I made a little strangled sound of consent. Tom laughed again, swept a low, mocking bow, and sailed from the chamber.

III

THEREAFTER, my life at Oxenheath was easier and happier. I do not know what Tom said to Aunt Margaret, or how he had said it, but within a day of his arrival, I had new spacious apartments on the manor's top level, and even was given a maid. I no longer had to care for the children—although Aunt Margaret did mumble to me, with an attempt at humility, that she would be grateful if I supervised the nursery maids and laundresses on occasion. Given what I had seen of one maid's negligence, I thought that was a sound request. As I now had little to occupy my days, I had no hesitation in concurring.

Summer reigned. Abbot Cuthbert soon departed for Canterbury, and Brother Ambrose left shortly thereafter for Rochester, leaving instructions with Aunt Margaret's apothecary for Mary's care. Tom tarried at Oxenheath, as did Father Vyncent, the latter of necessity. Tom and I rode every day, and danced, and swam. We lived in blissful ignorance of events at court and beyond our boundaries.

I felt keenly my inability to find Father Vyncent a living. With his assistance, I wrote to various families of the nobility in Kent and surrounding counties, seeking a chaplaincy for him. Replies were slow in coming, and the news was not heartening, despite my name. Whereas some families would consider taking on a chaplain, none could supply Father Vyncent with the time or materials he required to continue his writing—ink, parchment, pens, penknives, pumice stone, awls, and reading frames.

"Perhaps I should write to the Queen," I said morosely to Tom one brisk autumn day as we walked towards the river. It appeared Father Vyncent would remain at Oxenheath for the winter and, although that did not trouble me, Aunt Margaret was becoming increasingly irascible over the matter and never failed to let me know how she resented the extra mouth to feed.

We paused beside the river. Shivering, I turned into Tom's body and wrapped my arms around him. He enfolded me in a comfortable embrace and kissed the top of my bare head. "I think you would have more luck with the Duke of Norfolk—or the Dowager," he remarked.

I stiffened. "The Dowager!" I leaned away, looking up at him eagerly. "Why, what a splendid idea!" I pulled his head down and gave him a smacking kiss on the cheek. His expression became rueful. "I could use the opportunity to remind her of her obligations to me—I have been at Oxenheath for far longer than my father envisioned!"

"Eager to see Horatio, eh?" said Tom.

"Indeed!" I moved out of his embrace, not bothering to correct his name for Henry, so accustomed had I become to its usage. I began to retrace our steps, keen to have the letter written at once. Tom followed with a slow, reluctant trudge.

I was eager to see Henry Mannox. Over the preceding months, I had detected in Tom a manly interest in me. However, the notion perplexed me. Neither virtue nor maidenly modesty demanded I resist him, for I suspect I possessed neither—rather, it was the prospect of leaving my childhood behind forever; it was the images in my mind of simmering cauldrons and broomsticks; it was the strange, deep throbbing, which tunnelled upwards through my body when Tom looked at me a certain way, or when he embraced me or kissed my cheek or neck. Even his habit of kissing my neck and the way I enjoyed it evoked memories of lurid childhood tales of vampyres and angels of darkness. That I found such wickedness alluring only served to agitate me further.

Evil or ecstasy—I knew not which—lay beyond being intimate with Tom. Whichever it was, I knew it to be dangerous. Confronted with the danger, I wanted to clutch hold of the childish, safe friendships I had heretofore experienced. Henry Mannox became a symbol for those.

Perversely, however, I enjoyed testing the self-imposed boundaries, eager to catch a glimpse of what lay beyond. I welcomed it when Tom embraced me, shivered in delight when I felt the manifestation of his desire, and eagerly exposed my neck to his biting kisses. Perhaps sensing my reluctance to go further, and knowing by my chatter how often I thought of Henry Mannox, Tom never kissed my mouth, and declined to give my body anything more than a fleeting caress through my clothes, no matter the provocation from me. For my own part, I kept my hands well away from his fascinating loins and resolutely refrained from looking there, although I believed other women at Oxenheath were not so circumspect.

I had always known Tom was sexually experienced and that women found him handsome. As a child, I understood that he obtained mysterious favours from the maidservants. I had not even given it a passing thought. Now, the suspicion that he might be intimate with someone else, and share with her what I had glimpsed but denied myself, was hurtful to me. I know Tom tried hard to be discreet, and I even hoped for a while that he was not seeking enjoyment elsewhere—until one morning in late summer I discovered otherwise.

After dinner, from which Tom had absented himself, I had gone looking for him. I had taken my time—idly lingering in the gardens to pick roses, listening to the birdsong and delighting in the soft, clean air on my skin. As usual, I could tolerate being alone for short periods, and had headed to the stables, assuming Tom tarried there, for he had been delivered of a splendid new horse the previous week, a gift from his family at Bedgebury.

Tom had been at the stables. However, he was not preoccupied with his horse.

A woman had his attentions. He was taking her, up against the wall of one stall, her plump legs wrapped tight around his waist, her little moans bursting from her in time with Tom's thrusts. The roses tumbled from my limp fingers. Perhaps I made a sound, for the woman—a pretty, buxom chambermaid—looked over Tom's shoulder at me. She smirked and said something to Tom. He stopped moving and his head turned. His expression froze.

I uttered a little cry, picked up my skirts, and ran from the scene.

I avoided Tom for the rest of the day. When I next encountered him, he behaved as if nothing had happened, and without speaking only handed me my abandoned roses, now limp and dying. We never spoke of the incident. For a time, I discovered I could drive the memory of the occasion from my mind, by resolutely turning my attention from it—like the slamming of a door, a reliable device of self-protection I was to hone in future years. Eventually, however, I would have cause to remember it in unguarded moments, and it did not cause me pain. Tom's intimacy with the maid, and any other like it, meant nothing to him. This I knew, because I understood Tom . . . and I understood Tom because he was more myself than I was ever permitted to be.

IV

THE LETTER TO THE DOWAGER was dispatched at once. However, it was not until after Christmas that a response was received, addressed to Aunt Margaret.

She called me to her chambers to receive the news. The Dowager had asserted her rights as my legal guardian and had insisted, once the weather improved, that I make my home at Horsham in Sussex where the bulk of her household now currently resided. The Dowager herself would soon be returning to Sussex from court, and expected me to be there on her arrival.

By postscript to the letter she granted Father Vyncent a living as one of her chaplains and claimed her estate could supply him with all his writing needs.

It was decided Tom would escort Father Vyncent and me to Horsham in the spring, and from there he would travel back to London where he would petition the King for a place in his household. This plan left me feeling strangely bereft.

"I do not understand why Tom wishes to go to court," I grumbled to Father Vyncent one day as I watched him at work on a manuscript.

He dipped his quill in ink and glanced at me.

"What do you expect him to do instead?" he asked mildly, although his expression was shrewd. "Master Culpeper thinks of his prospects as his family expect of him—and he has better prospects at court than anywhere else."

I cupped my chin in my hand. "I—well, he could stay on at Horsham," I said with a shrug.

"And do what? What are his prospects there?" he probed. When I shrugged again, Father Vyncent scratched for several seconds on the parchment, then he murmured, "I am sure with some encouragement from you, he would consider staying."

I absorbed the implication of his words.

"I cannot," I whispered. "There is Henry . . ."

Father Vyncent studied me and nodded. "Aye, child," he said. He sighed and returned to his work. His murmured 'child' seemed to resonate in the silence, long after he had uttered it. He looked up again and smiled. "I am sure Master Culpeper would be the first to admit that he did not spend a goodly part of his life rescuing you, only to hurt you by introducing you to emotions and sensations you are not ready to experience," he remarked with startling insight.

I departed, troubled. The Tom Culpeper I knew was not renowned for his noble foresight and judgment, so I wondered at the accuracy of Father Vyncent's statement. I doubted Tom's reluctance to be intimate with me was born of noble reservations for my well-being . . . perhaps it was simply because he could gain his ends with little bother elsewhere! I feared he would forget about me as soon as a suitable woman of good rank looked his way with interest, and that was bound to occur at some time when he was at court.

As the milder weather ushered out the winter, in the flurry of preparing for our journey to Horsham, I could forget such anxieties. At last my banishment was over. For four days, Tom, Father Vyncent and I travelled along quiet country roads, breaking our journey at dingy inns in small villages. Too often, we passed the smoking ruins of monasteries and encountered rattling carts laden with treasure, heading for London.

When we passed through the gates of Horsham and the rambling red-brick manor house—constructed in the shape of an "H"—came into view, glowing in the evening sunlight, an intense anticipation consumed me. Even Father Vyncent appeared moved. Tom, however, when I looked at him to share our sentiments, seemed morose. Without the animation that had so frequently possessed him at Oxenheath, his features appeared ordinary. Disheartened, I sighed and turned away from him.

One of the Dowager's stewards met us, and we separated as Father Vyncent and Tom were shown to their quarters. I hastened at once to the communal bedchamber where I knew I would find my old friends.

When I stepped inside, I paused unnoticed for several seconds, happily absorbing the scene. Except for slight changes the passing years had made to my friends' appearances, nothing had changed. The cavernous chamber mirrored the one at Norfolk House, with its large curtained beds amidst a jumble of furniture, abandoned musical instruments, platters of leavings, groups of chattering girls at work on tapestries and other sewing works.

As I studied the scene, Joan looked up from her sewing and glanced in my direction. She shot to her feet.

"Catherine!"

At once my friends swarmed around with excited squeals and chatter, swamping me with enthusiastic hugs and kisses. I was bundled, laughing, to the centre of the chamber and pushed onto a chair, feeling like the Dowager before she regaled us with tales of court, as the girls gathered around me.

"Oh, Catherine!" said Agnes. "We have missed you! I do hope your stay at Oxenheath was not too lonely?"

"Not all of it . . . my cousin arrived from Bedgebury in the summer . . . in fact he tarries here now."

" '*He*?' " asked Katherine Tylney, at once alert. She had blossomed over the last years into a pretty and buxom young woman, and had clearly developed an interest in menfolk as well.

I nodded. "Thomas Culpeper," I said. "Tom . . . but he is on his way to court, Katherine, so do not waste your charms on him."

Katherine pouted, then brightened at once. She looked at me slyly.

"Henry Mannox is still here . . . he'll be pleased to see you."

The other girls tittered as I flushed.

"There have been festivities here on the eve of each week's end—which is tomorrow!" said Alice Restwold. "Gentlemen come from the school and there is much dancing and feasting."

I clapped my hands in delight. Perhaps on the morrow I would also see Henry! Oh, it was good to be back!

V

HOWEVER, I did not see Henry at all the next day, or during the following night's festivities. I reached the uncomfortable conclusion that he was avoiding me.

I tried not to reveal my disappointment and perplexity. Tom, however, noticed it. He cornered me in the Great Hall after supper, amidst the riotous dancing beneath smoking torches. The gentlemen from the school had arrived, as anticipated, along with several guests from surrounding noble houses. I trembled when Tom loomed over me with glittering eyes and teeth bared in a grin, his body pressing me back against the stone archway. When he had no hesitation in trailing his burning mouth down my neck, in full view of anyone who cared to see, I assumed that he, like me, had imbibed rather too much.

"So where is Horatio?" he said against my ear as I sagged against him, barely able to hear him above the music. "I have noticed you looking out for him all day."

"I do not know," I mumbled. At that second, I didn't much care either. I arched my neck, rubbed it as a cat would against his soft beard and I shuddered as his fingers brushed over my bosom.

I hoped Tom would at last kiss my mouth, when someone clapped a hand on his shoulder. It was a young gentleman, swaying drunkenly.

"I say, old man," he slurred. "A group of us are heading down to the lake. Why not join us?" His bleary eyes settled on me and he leered. "And bring your beautiful woman . . . you can continue your pursuit down there...I am sure there will be many who will be doing the same."

As he lurched away, I was reminded of the extent of Tom's charm, that he effortlessly and swiftly attracted both men and women to his presence even after a short acquaintance.

"Come on," I said to him. "It sounds like good sport."

On the terrace, a group of my friends swept me away, and Tom joined a rowdy and drunken faction from the school. Someone gave a shout and held up a tankard of wine over Tom's head; he tilted back as the wine was poured over him to the cheers and laughter of all; he drank and spluttered, although most of the wine splashed over his shoulders and to the ground. He ripped off his doublet. The girls around me squealed and clapped.

Already, many flocked at the lake, skulking in pairs in the bushes or splashing and yelling in the freezing water. It was a clear, still night. A blanket of stars sparkling in a cloudless sky; a sliver of moon and a few torches provided the only light.

Tom joined most of the others in stripping to his undershirt and diving into the water. He emerged from the dive, his hair streaming with water, shirt clinging to his body. I hesitated, enjoying the view of his back and buttocks . . . then he turned to look back at me.

"Come on, Kate!" he called.

His appearance rendered me speechless and immobile.

The wet, clinging undershirt was almost translucent. It seemed to cling lovingly to every sinew, slope and crevice of his lean chest and belly. It revealed a thin shadow of hair, low on his belly, which drew my eyes inexorably downwards. And it moulded the generous swell where my gaze stopped, transfixed. Even in the dim light, it was a more erotic sight than any nakedness could have been. Shaking, I dragged my attention away and fumbled with my clothing, until I had stripped to my shift. I picked my way across pebbles to the water. It was freezing almost beyond bearing. I hugged my arms around myself, stopping when the water was thigh high.

"Just dive in, Catherine!" someone called.

I looked at Tom. Experiencing a wave of inner heat, I sank beneath the surface of the water.

I emerged, gasping and spluttering. When I dashed my hair of my face, I saw Katherine Tylney wading towards Tom, her loose black hair fanning out on the surface of the water behind her. Now frozen with more than chill from the lake, I watched as she curled her arms around Tom's neck and kissed his cheek. One of his arms went about her and patted her on the shoulder. He still looked at me.

I turned and pushed my way back to shore.

Shivering, I sank onto grassy ground between two bushes. I hugged my knees to my chest and tried to stop my gaze returning to the lake . . . to Tom . . . but it was no use.

He had abandoned Katherine and, to my deep shock, was wading to shore. As he approached me, the heat began to creep from my loins, outwards through my body, until I thought the water on my flesh must be simmering. Unable to stop myself, I watched his languid approach with mouth agape.

He thumped down on his knees before me, grinning. He laid his hands on my upraised knees and easily parted them, my weakened muscles providing no resistance. He moved between my thighs until I felt the shape of him against my groin.

Lost, I sank back onto the ground. He moved with me until his chest rested on mine, and his wet hair swung forward until it slicked against my cheeks. His gaze was intent, his top teeth biting into his bottom lip as he studied me.

"I leave at first light," he said at last. "Do you have a parting gift for me?"

My gaze flicked to his lips. "A kiss?" I managed to suggest. "We've never shared a proper kiss."

"Well, that is the ultimate intimacy, is it not?" he said. I tilted my head in curiosity. Tom laughed. "That and because I knew I would not be able to stop at such a kiss," Tom said, staring at my own mouth. "Bearing that in mind, if that is your gift, I have no objections."

I slipped my hands around his neck. I savoured at the growing heat and hardness pressed against my body. I lifted my head to meet his.

"*Woo hoo!*" came a ribald yell from above us. A stream of wine seemed to pour from the heavens, splashing onto our heads, followed by laughter and cheers. Tom was hauled off me. Stunned and spluttering, I struggled to sit.

A group of scholars hoisted Tom on to their shoulders. Someone shouted, "I say, methinks you need some cooling off, old man!" and more laughter, whoops and cheers rang out. Young faces were bright with merriment in the flickering golden light thrown by the torches. A grin forming on his face as he was carried to the water, Tom looked at me and shrugged.

I gave a bemused smile, then with a frustrated sigh raked my fingers through my hair as Tom was tossed into the water with a loud splash and to more cheers. It would be impossible to share any intimate moments with Tom tonight. I resolved to see him off the next morning—with the promised kiss.

However, when I returned to my bed that night, the excess consumption of wine ensured I slept long and deep. When I finally opened my eyes, the sun had risen to its peak in the sky. And Tom was long gone.

Chapter 6

"I should have no compassion on these witches; I should burn them all."

Martin Luther
German Priest and Scholar.
(1483-1546)

I

Horsham, Sussex
Spring, 1536

RAIN BATTERED the windows of our ladies' chamber and thick mist shrouded the green parks of the manor. The roaring fire in the grate did little to dispel the chill of the room or the bleakness that had settled upon me since discovering Tom had departed Horsham. The cold grey light of day had banished the excitement and boisterousness of the previous night's revelries. I shivered on the window seat, accompanied by the cook's cat, which had earlier slunk into the chamber and was now curled on my lap, and by two hound puppies smuggled in by the groom. I stroked the cat's soft black fur and found solace in the creature's deep purring, and nudged at the puppies when they threatened to chew my shoes.

Katherine Tylney stood in the other window embrasure, whispering and giggling with the groom. Margaret Morton and Alice Restwold dozed on one bed, and in the centre of the chamber the pinched, cold hands of Joan Bulmer, Agnes Ap Rhys and the other ladies were working a tapestry of a glorious hunting scene. Low murmurs of conversation rose from the group, and stifled yawns were plentiful. Disinterested and too idle, I did not question why Joan cast the occasional speculative glance in my direction. However, I became instantly alert when she at last raised her voice.

"I think that cat is your familiar, Catherine!" Joan taunted loudly. "Next you will be copulating with the Devil like your cousin the Queen!"

A ripple of shock swept through the chamber. Katherine and the groom drew away from each other and stared at me, Katherine's hand flying in alarm to her mouth; the other ladies gasped, and someone gave a quavering wail; Margaret Morton and Alice Restwold arose from their slumber and struggled to sit up.

Inwardly I recoiled. Joan's taunting provoked fears that had long been my unacknowledged companions—the fear that witchery was shared in families and that, like my cousin, I too was a witch, and the equally dreadful fear that such speculation was entertained by others who might do me harm.

I summoned all my ability to dissemble and laced my next words with an impressive scorn.

"Are you calling the King the Devil?" I asked. "That must be treason, Joan Bulmer. I would watch my tongue if I were you."

A blush of shame suffused Joan's round face while several of the ladies dissolved into giggles. Conversation resumed, more cheerful and animated than before, and Katherine and the groom returned to their whispering. Margaret and Alice both smiled at me in a display of support before sinking back against the pillows and entwining their arms about each other with deep sighs.

The chamber door grated open, and the pointed face of chambermaid Mary Hall peered around it, her small eyes darting. This was Mary Laschelles, the maid Henry and I had long ago watched in the deserted chamber at Norfolk House. She had married John Hall, her partner on that occasion. It had seemed to me since my arrival at Horsham that Mary had displayed a curious attitude to me that was quite improper for her station: blatant disrespect, with barely veiled animosity. Both were now present on her countenance as she sidled up. Perhaps detecting the aromas of supper, the cat leapt off my lap, bounded across the chamber and slunk through the door, the puppies scampering boisterously after it.

Bristling at Mary's manner, I raised a haughty eyebrow as she bent to whisper in my ear.

"Ma'am, I have a note for you from Master Mannox," she said. She pulled a folded piece of parchment from the folds of her apron and, darting a glance over her shoulder, passed it surreptitiously into my hand.

I slid the note at once into my sleeve, a rush of excitement tripping my heartbeat.

"Thank you, Mary."

Mary did not at once heed my firm dismissal. It was only when I jerked my head imperiously in the direction of the door that she stalked away.

I turned my back to the room and unfolded the note. I frowned to decipher Henry's hand:

> My Lady Catherine,
> Pray come to me at the chapel at midnight for then I shall best be
> at leisure to be at your convenience, and caution begs for cover of
> night. I long to see you and speak with you. It doth comfort me to
> know that the time is soon.
> I am, my Lady, your
> Henry Mannox.

My smile was one of delight and relief. I understood now that Henry sensed a need for secrecy; heeding this, he had avoided me the previous day, preferring to arrange instead a secret and romantic assignation! Thrilling anticipation banished the weariness and dejection that had afflicted me since Tom's departure.

Unaware of my rendezvous, and weary from the previous night's activities, the ladies were asleep long before midnight. I lay in my shift on the bed I shared with Joan, listening for the bells of the table clock as they rang the passing hours. When sleep encroached, I would force myself to stare at the single burning torch in the wall sconce and summon whatever thoughts would keep me awake.

My reflections turned to the previous evening's revelries . . . to Tom, at the lake. I shifted in unsatisfied yearning. What might have happened if we had not been interrupted before we kissed? Possibly nothing, as we were exposed to public view, but it was exciting to imagine . . . I could still feel the heat of his groin next to mine, and I stifled a moan . . . I am lying in the grass, waiting for him to emerge from the lake, his undershirt clinging and revealing his body. Joan appears before my eyes . . . she is holding out the squirming cat to me with a taunting smile, and her silent lips form the word, "witch." I turn my head away, and she is gone. I close my eyes, seeing only swirling colours, hearing nothing but my breathing. I do not start when at last I feel hands caressing and exploring my body, nay, but I smile and sigh in surrender. The hands roam my form, evoking delicious shivers that ripple over my skin. When the stroking arrives at my thighs, my legs open of their own volition as the dully painful pulsation awakens in my loins. I gasp and arch at gentle probing fingers. I am shocked by the wanton yearning the ache induces, yet I crave for it to be assuaged.

The swirling colours part, and another form appears before me—a silhouette against a blazing torch. The form looms closer and the features I recognise are ones I know well . . . a fine body covered in a wet shirt, a sweep of black hair, glittering blue cat-like eyes, white teeth bared in a lecherous grin . . .

My body convulses wildly. I groan his name. The vision dissipates to the chimes of midnight.

My eyelids sprang open. My heart thudded erratically and my hoarse gasps rent the silence of the chamber. Beside me, Joan stirred but did not awaken.

My shocked gaze went from the torch to my body. My shift had worked its way upward and was now twisted beneath my arms, my torso exposed to the chill night air. One of my hands gripped a thigh, the other, gleaming with slick moisture, rested against the throbbing join of my legs. My entire body below my waist still seemed to be convulsing.

Confused and shaking violently, I swung my legs over the side of the bed, my shift tumbling to my thighs. My head fell into my hands and hot tears sprang from my eyes and coursed down my cheeks.

What was this depravity that had overwhelmed me? In my visions, Joan had called me a witch and had handed me the cat she had earlier called my familiar . . . worse, I had then plunged eagerly into wicked yearnings that the Devil himself must surely have incited—*and satisfied!*

I was indeed a witch . . . a heretic! Possessed by the Devil!

Insensible with fear, my gaze searched the walls for a crucifix. Finding none, nevertheless the notion connected with an image of Father Vyncent. I seized upon it with frantic relief. Father Vyncent would deliver me from this mortal sin!

I jumped off the bed, possessed only of sufficient sense to grab a cloak from the armoury and throw it around me before I ran from the room.

The cat skulked in the dark gallery. Muffling a terrified scream and pressing myself against the wall, I skirted around the creature and sped away through the darkness, my cloak flaring behind me.

To reach Father Vyncent's quarters, which adjoined the vestry, I had to cross the inner courtyard and enter the chapel through its large, heavy doors. The cloying scent of incense cloaked the interior of the chapel, and a small lamp on the altar provided the only light. My gasping breaths tore the silence as I hastened down the centre aisle toward the altar and the door to the vestry beyond it.

An arm slid roughly around my waist. The chapel rang with my petrified scream. An engulfing hand across my mouth cut it off.

"Shush, my lady. It's me!"

Henry!

Trembling, I turned in his embrace. In the dim light of the altar lamp, I absorbed his familiar features, unchanged from three years before.

I barely registered his kiss and his crushing arms. My heartbeat still tripped and fear shook my body; Henry seemed to take this as a sign of ardour and increased the intensity of his kiss. With weak fists I flailed at his shoulders, and at last he drew away from me.

"You are right," he whispered huskily. "We must exercise restraint. I have no wish for tattle of our relationship to meet the ears of your step-grandmother when she returns! She dealt me quite an ear-boxing after you departed Norfolk House. Tis a wonder I was not dismissed!"

"You were not the only one she cuffed," I managed to whisper, my hand going to my cheek in memory.

The door to the vestry swung open and light blazed into the chapel. Henry sprang from me as the stout form of Father Vyncent filled the doorway.

"I heard a noise," Father Vyncent said mildly, rolling into the chapel and coming to my side. The light behind him lit up his fine hair like a halo.

Henry bowed. "My apologies for disturbing you, good father," he stuttered, backing away. "I shall leave you in peace." Father Vyncent watched with some amusement as Henry hesitated before turning and running from the chapel. "I presume that was young Master Mannox," he said, turning to me.

I nodded. "Father Vyncent—oh, I must talk with you! You must help me!"

He cupped my elbow in his hand. "Of course, child. . . . Come in here. We can share some mulled wine while you tell me what troubles you."

The warmth and brightness of the vestry welcomed me. I sank onto a chair before a table littered with parchment, quills and inkpots. I took a large gulp of malmsey, wondering if my friend would feel so kindly towards me once he heard of my heresy. Tears blurred my vision.

"Child, what ails you?" Father Vyncent drew up a stool before me. It creaked beneath his weight. He took one of my hands and pressed it between both of his.

"Oh, Father Vyncent, I fear I have committed a grave sin!" I exclaimed with a loud sob. "I—I have copulated with the Devil, and I—I obtained intense, lustful enjoyment from it!"

Father Vyncent dropped my hand as if it had burnt him and almost fell from his stool as he swayed from me. His face drained of all colour as he scrabbled at the crucifix that hung from his neck. My chin dropped to my chest and I sobbed pitifully. It seemed an eternity before he took up my hand again. I looked up. Through my tears, I saw Father Vyncent battling with confused thoughts, scrutinizing me with intelligence and perception as the colour returned slowly to his cheeks.

"Why do you say such things, child?" he asked at last.

With heat sweeping into my face, I lowered my eyes and made my confession. I spoke of desire that stirred cauldrons, and the ache which seemed fixed on images of broomsticks; I mumbled about angels of darkness, then launched into a detailed description of my dream . . . the burning desire, and the incubus which had come to me to relieve it.

Father Vyncent dropped my hand and rose from his stool. His broad back to me, he walked to a nearby table. His large form seemed to shudder as, with one finger, he stroked a large tome resting on the table. He lifted the heavy cover and let it drop again before finally turning to face me. Deeply flushed of cheek, he pressed his mouth closed as if quelling some thought. Unaccountably, the atmosphere seemed to have lightened, and I frowned in confusion.

Was that merriment I detected in Father Vyncent's countenance? And was he suppressing laughter?

"Father Vyncent, I have *amused* you?" I asked, deeply hurt. "You find it *amusing* to be in the presence of a witch?"

"Ah, child!" Father Vyncent bowed his head at my remonstrance. He resumed his seat and took my cold hand. For several taut seconds he continued in his deep reflection.

At last he cleared his throat.

"Child, you are not a witch or a heretic," he assured me. "You have not copulated with the Devil. You must not entertain such notions!"

"Then, what—?"

He passed his hand across the grizzly stubble that covered his jaw.

"Would that Master Culpeper were here!" he muttered half to himself. "He could explain this much better than I . . . My Lady, tonight you merely had a dream. The—er—physical effect of the dream was something every young woman should know, although doubtless many do not, or perhaps they simply ignore it." He smiled brightly, leaned back and laced his hands across his chest. "There are no cauldrons and no broomsticks in your soul, and no incubus claimed you this night! It was an awakening of your womanhood. Do not doubt it, but welcome it and enjoy it!"

I stared at him. A tentative ease crept over my tortured soul. I saw no difficulty in relishing what had occurred to me a short time before, if it were not witchcraft. Yet, what would a celibate monk understand of the ecstasy that had claimed me, so powerful that surely it could not come from within? Moreover, if what had happened to me had its roots in something more earthly than witchcraft, what could a monk understand of my finding the figure of a man so desirable that all reason was lost?

Perhaps Father Vyncent understood more than I gave him credit for.

He cleared his throat. "However, Mistress Catherine, I do feel the need to counsel you," he said firmly. "It is written in Scripture: to avoid fornication, let every man have a wife and every woman a husband. If an unmarried woman cannot contain her lust, then let her marry, for it is better to marry than to burn with passion."

So I was right to doubt my lusts. If not witchcraft they still placed me in danger. "Then I must marry," I whispered. "Henry Mannox wishes to marry me. . . . I could—."

Father Vyncent straightened at once, gripping my hand. "No, no, you misunderstand." He wiped his forehead. "Regardless of the fact that your family would never sanction such a match, you must only marry Master Mannox if it is he who is the object of your passion. I am sure Saint Paul understood that marriage to the wrong man does not deliver a woman from the desire to fornicate with the true object of her desires. Tell me, given that it was not an incubus, was it Master Mannox who came to you in your dream?"

A wave of fresh heat swept into my face. I shook my head but said nothing as concern smote me: he who had shown himself in my dream was now gone. If I could not then marry, what trouble would my desires inflict upon me?

"Ah!" Father Vyncent beamed as if satisfied. He patted my hand. "Child, rest easy," he soothed. "These feelings you have—they will not urge you to take the cook or the groom to your bed, God bless them. And if you were so urged, I am sure that you have the necessary mastery of your passions to resist such folly! Rest easy, child, and have no fear!"

I looked into Father Vyncent's kind face and trusted him. Consoled, I laughed at the notion of the cantankerous cook in my bed and finished my wine with enthusiasm.

Father Vyncent walked me to the chapel doors and I embraced him thankfully before slipping out into the night. The rain had long since passed, and I was drawn to the fresh spring breezes swirling on the terrace. The moonlight glowed its silver light, and the sweet scents of wet flowers and grass created a potent intoxication. I drew a deep breath as the silken breeze lifted my hair and snaked beneath my cloak and shift, tingling against my bare legs. Contentment and pleasure shivered through me as I dwelt on my dream, and on him who had come to me at the pinnacle of desire.

II

THE PLEASANT SPRING of 1536 slid into a blazing summer. Outdoor activities filled my days—bowls, hawking, following the hunt—and feasting, dancing and festivities occupied my nights. We heard nothing of activities at Court. I was lulled into a sense that all was well with the Queen and with my family.

Henry wore my handkerchief about his wrist and I slept with his many notes beneath my pillow. Passion was kept to a minimum, yet that was not disappointing. Already, my thoughts had started to wander from Henry; for it was not he that came to me in my dreams, and nor was it his image I summoned to participate in my waking fantasies.

The whispered tales of coupling that Joan Bulmer often related fascinated me anew. Joan was one of the few ladies in the Dowager's charge who was married, although her husband was a tyrant and her family had imposed a separation within weeks of the marriage. She now waited for her husband to die or for an annulment from the Pope, so that she would be free to marry again. Despite the short duration of her intimate association with the tyrant, Joan had a wealth of salacious information concerning activities in the marriage bed. Her tales held me enthralled, as they heightened my awareness not only of my sexuality, but also of what I now recognised as the splendid attributes of men folk.

The idyll ended one midsummer's afternoon. With a clatter of many hooves, the shouting of grooms and the rumbling of coaches and carriages bearing the Norfolk crest, the Dowager Duchess of Norfolk returned to Horsham.

III

I KNEW THE DOWAGER DUCHESS OF NORFOLK would regale us with news of Court at a time of her choosing. However, a mere three hours after her arrival, servants were huddled in whispering groups, and I detected about them a mounting air of agitation. Dread settled over me.

"I am going to see my step-grandmother," I announced at last to the ladies. I had just witnessed Mary Hall and a chambermaid from the Dowager's household in a whispered consultation in the gallery; both had clamped shut their lips upon seeing me and had scuttled away, Mary with a knowing gleam in her eye. I knew then that action was required on my part. "There's some important news of Court, and I intend to find out what it is. Who will accompany me?"

At once, the ladies appeared busy with their activities. "We shall leave that pleasure to you," Agnes said dryly, strumming her lute, "but be sure to return quickly with the news," she added with an ingratiating smile.

"You shall be lucky if I do. Cowards," I muttered, marching from the chamber.

The Dowager's quarters occupied the same level of the manor house as ours, in the opposite wing. My uneasiness rose with every step as I hastened along the gallery beneath portraits of my ancestors.

The great oak doors of the Dowager's receiving chamber were closed. I lifted a tentative hand and knocked feebly. One door creaked open and the face of Jane Percy, one of my step-grandmother's ladies, peered through the narrow gap. She frowned when she saw me.

"Her Grace is resting," she said primly before I could speak. "The journey has wearied her and she is not receiving company."

Despite my apprehension, I would not be thwarted in my attempt to speak to my step-grandmother. A firm push against the door sent Jane stepping back and I slipped inside before she regained her balance.

"I shall not stay long," I called back over my shoulder as I strode across the empty chamber to the closed doors of the sleeping quarters.

"Lady Catherine, this is an outrage! You cannot—!"

With Mistress Percy's shrill exclamations ringing in my ears, I burst into the bedchamber—and stopped short.

It was dim and quiet. Other ladies moved about, tending to the old woman's vast wardrobe. A large four-poster bed stood on the dais in the centre of the chamber. Filmy curtains of white lace hung from the carved cornice, shielding the interior of the bed. At my abrupt entrance, a rumble from the depths of the bed set the curtains fluttering.

"What's that noise? Who disturbs my slumber?"

The ladies glared at me. Ignoring them, I walked on unsteady legs to the bed and swept the curtains aside.

The ancient woman on the bed, half covered by a rug of ermine, lay propped against large cushions and pillows of gold and crimson satin. She wore a dressing-gown of midnight blue velvet, but no cap, and her sparse grey hair hung in limp strands to her bowed shoulders. Her once alert eyes were dull, the lined skin of her face and neck looser and more sallow than of yore. She had contrived a weak glare at my intrusion but when she identified me, her annoyance dissipated and her shoulders sagged. She sighed, closed her eyes and sank back against the cushions.

My nervousness was now mixed with compassion. I stepped closer to the bed so that the curtains fell behind me, hiding us from curious stares. I laid a tentative hand on one of hers, amazed at the contrast between my white, smooth skin and the blotched, claw resting on the ermine. To my surprise, the claw turned, and gripped my fingers with surprising pressure.

"Sit," the Dowager Duchess rumbled, not opening her eyes. "I suppose you want news of your cousin." Sinking onto the bed, I winced from the crushing of my fingers. To my horror, a lone tear squeezed from beneath one shrivelled shut lid and trickled down the side of the her beak-like nose.

"Step-grandmother, tell me! What has happened?"

The Dowager drew a wheezing breath and exhaled a gust of hot, evil-smelling air. Her eyes opened, her face contorting with anger and shame.

"The Queen's brother—your cousin—Lord Rochford, was arrested for treason," she snapped brutally, "along with Mark Smeaton, Sir Henry Norris, Francis Weston and William Brereton. All were charged with adultery with the Queen and all were found guilty!" The old woman's venomous countenance and her terrible pronouncement had me drawing back with shock. "Only Mark Smeaton confessed to the crime—*on the rack* of course! But all were executed."

Although the news had set my head spinning, I managed to whisper the next frantic questions burning on my tongue. "And the Queen? What of the Queen, step-grandmother?"

The Dowager struggled to a more upright position still gripping my hand. Amidst my fear, the pain of it went unnoticed. She thrust her face closer to mine. Stale breath wafted over my face.

"Anne Boleyn went on trial before a panel of twenty-six peers, presided over by her uncle—." The old lady's voice wavered and she closed her eyes. "*Your* uncle . . . *my stepson* . . . the Duke of Norfolk," she whispered. "She was found guilty of incest, treason and adultery—*naturally!*" Despite her sarcastic emphasis, the old woman clearly battled with shame over her divided loyalties. "As a token of special favour, the King agreed that she should not have to suffer the butchery of the axe man." Renewed, surging hope drew from me a loud gasp. The old eyes opened to transfix me. "Instead, he brought over from France an expert executioner." She paused. My free hand convulsed into a fist and flew to my mouth, stifling a wail. The Dowager sighed. "Anne Boleyn's head was struck off with a sharp French sword," she whispered hoarsely. "She denied all charges to the end."

I swayed. It was only my step-grandmother's firm and painful grip that kept me from tumbling to the floor in a faint. She thumped me on the shoulder with her other hand, forcing my head downwards until my forehead rested on the mattress. Gradually, my dizziness abated but in its wake came tears of anguish.

I felt the old woman's hand stroke my head whilst the other mercifully released its grip on my fingers.

"You must not cry, child. Nay, neither of us should cry! It does not bring back the dead or right evil wrongs. We must look to the future, indeed we must!"

Lifting my head, I wiped my sleeve beneath my nose. I sagged with intense loss.

"What future is there for the Howards now, step-grandmother?" I asked bitterly "Why, I remember once you said nothing would bring us down—except the executioner's axe. We've gone one better—not only an axe for one Howard, but also a French sword, no less, for another! The Howards are finished!"

"That we are not!" The bellow throbbed in my ears. "I will not hear such words from a Howard! Two may have been destroyed, but there are other Howards—*better* Howards—untainted by common Boleyn blood!" The old woman brandished her fist in my face.

I stared as, in the abrupt pulsing silence, her index finger rose from the fist—*and pointed at me.*

I gazed from the finger into my step-grandmother's now fever-bright eyes. Her fervour and enthusiasm were seductive. The tears dried on my face and a smile twitched my lips. She nodded slowly. "Aye," she murmured, "we remain the greatest name in all England—and shall be greater still, I know it. Now, be off with you, child, for I am weary." As if drained of spirit, the old woman sank back once more against the cushions. Her eyelids fluttered closed and her face turned from me in dismissal.

My grief struggled briefly with my pride before succumbing. I slid off the bed and swept the curtains aside. Ignoring the curious expressions of the ladies, I walked to the doors, my chin held high. As I left, a guttural shout rose from the bed.

"Do not forget who you are, child! You are a Howard! And we shall rise again!"

IV

ON THE VERY DAY OF ANNE BOLEYN'S BEHEADING, King Henry VIII was betrothed to the Lady Jane Seymour. As the Seymours and their Protestant allies entrenched themselves in the King's favour, I did wonder how my step-grandmother's prophecies for my family could possibly be realised, and grief overcame me as my doubts were renewed. Anne Boleyn had been a great source of family pride, and for me an example and inspiration. With her demise, and the manner of it, disillusionment and humility were mine, and it was only the recollection of the Dowager's confidence in my worth that averted despair.

Young minds heal quickly, however—passionate minds quickest of all.

Oft times, I found myself staring dreamily at Henry's elegant hands as they played the spinet or virginals; too often I noticed how his hose moulded his long legs, the swing of his arms when he walked, how his fair hair curled at the back of his neck. Even his kisses I began to anticipate with pleasure. However, there was a part of me he did not stir—the object of my deepest desires was not Henry. Knowing this, I was able to resist temptation, ably assisted by a surge of pride, which forbade me to think of ignoble Henry Mannox as a husband.

Such difficulties did not dominate my reflections for long. The frivolity of King Henry's Court—largely encouraged by Anne Boleyn—had touched us all, and it attained a new intensity with the news that the new Queen was with child. Although it was not news that was received with great rapture at Horsham, we wanted the kingdom to be secure and our King to be happy, for it could only benefit us all; with all his subjects, we hoped the child was the longed-for healthy boy and so we waited in breathless anticipation of the news.

On 12 October, 1537, the King's ten-year battle with the Papacy had its intended result. Queen Jane, in the palace of Hampton Court, was delivered of a healthy baby son.

To ensure safe delivery of the infant Prince Edward, Queen Jane had been cut open by barbaric Tudor surgeons. Twelve days later, she died of puerperal fever.

Once more the King was in search of a wife.

Chapter 7

"Three things are necessary for the salvation of man: to know what he ought to believe; to know what he ought to desire; and to know what he ought to do."

St Thomas Aquinas
Scholastic philosopher and theologian
(1225-74)

I

Horsham, Sussex
1 May 1538

"LET US RIDE TO THE VILLAGE TODAY," I cajoled Henry one morning the following spring when he arrived for my music lesson and, finding us alone in the music chamber, shut the door behind him. "Wouldn't it be wonderful to see the May Day celebrations?" I slipped my arms around his waist and deliberately brought my body closer.

Henry's initial reluctance gave way to a flushed eagerness to please. "As you wish," he concurred. "Maybe you'll give me something in return?" he suggested, stroking my jaw.

"Maybe." I dropped my arms and skipped away. "Come, let us call for horses now!"

The prospect of being part of the May Day festivities had enticed me to distraction for several days. Last night and that morning, much of the population of all the parishes would have ventured into the woods to gather tree branches which would become the village Maypoles, each one the centre of dancing and rejoicing. Of course, there was a secret, dissolute undertone to the festivities—rarely did men and women emerge from the forests unsullied by sexual adventures. However, to me, that was an intoxicating addition to the air of exhilaration evoked by the festivities.

A short time later I entered the village on horseback, accompanied by Henry. At once we were swept up in the large crowd surging to the green, just as some twenty oxen entered the village centre from the opposite direction, dragging the long Maypole behind them. Each ox wore a nosegay of bright flowers on its horns, and the Maypole itself was decked in a glorious array of flowers and herbs, kerchiefs and flags. With a roar from the crowd, the pole was raised and planted in the ground; eager hands threw straw about its base and set against it spring boughs and yet more flowers. I clapped in rapture as Morris dancers entered the village to the sound of the bright, jangling bells.

"Let us dance, Henry!" I called above the noise, my legs twitching to join the dancing throng.

There was then a distant thunder of many wheels on the wooden bridge to the north, accompanied by a deafening clatter of hooves and the excited barking of dogs. The crowd noise became a murmur and all heads turned.

Two liveried horsemen entered the village, their banners bearing a crest I knew well— a shield divided into quadrants beneath a golden lion. Following the horsemen came a legion of armoured knights on horseback, an uncovered chariot and a line of many wagons, litters and more riders, simply garbed. Barking dogs weaved between prancing hooves, barely escaping being trampled.

Silence settled over the crowd. Hampered by the hundreds of people in the narrow village streets, the advancing procession lost its orderliness, its sweating horses rearing and snorting.

"Make way! Make way!" shouted the leading horsemen. Like the slow parting of a sea, the crowd divided.

When the open chariot drew level with me, I was able to see who rode inside, although I had already guessed his identity. As my gaze fell on the figure of a man reclining against cushions of cloth of gold, my breath froze in my lungs. I recognised the leonine grey hair beneath a black velvet cap, the lean torso clad in an embroidered and jewelled doublet of emerald brocade. His arrogant countenance turned indolently in my direction and black Howard eyes fell upon me—and seemed to see me for the first time since I had come to know him as a child. As I stared at him, a thick, grey eyebrow rose in haughty remonstrance at my apparent impudence, and the eyes glittered with a new, curious awareness.

I dropped my gaze. Thomas Howard, third Duke of Norfolk—the most ambitious peer in the realm, the man who had presided over the trial and execution of his own niece—had come to Horsham.

II

ALTHOUGH ALL ENJOYMENT had gone from the day for me, I delayed our return to Horsham manor for as long as possible, arousing Henry Mannox's ire. I insisted that we return by the long way of the road. We rode in heavy silence.

When we arrived at the gatehouse to the estate, only a wavering moon above the mist relieved the darkness of night. Henry shouted our arrival to the gatekeeper and the gates yawned open.

I glanced warily at Henry's scowling countenance. "Thank you for accompanying me today," I said with forced cheerfulness. "I shall have to think of a suitable reward."

"Do not trouble yourself," Henry snapped. "That which I really want from you, you have no intention of giving. I am sure of that now."

"What you really want . . . ?"

He shot me a baleful glance. "After all these years, you still have no wish for us to be wed, is that not so?"

I squirmed in discomfort. "Henry, you know my step-grandmother—nay, my whole family—would not countenance a marriage between us. Why, you yourself have urged discretion in our meetings."

Henry's jaw clenched. "I know, but I thought in time your family might consent. After all, you have nothing but your name. Neither do you know any suitable men, and the Dowager has done nothing to find you a husband—and you are well into marriageable age."

I nodded with misery at the indisputable facts. A life as an old country maid, lonely and bitter, seemed to stretch before me.

"You also gave me to understand that you too thought we would be wed one day—you encouraged my embraces and my caresses, sought my attentions," Henry continued his bitter tirade. "But I see now that I merely amused you and was useful to you. I should have taken you to my bed in the beginning, rather than treat you as someone whom I would eventually call wife."

I felt ashamed. In silence, we dismounted in the forecourt and a groom led the horses away. Sullenness and pain contorted Henry's countenance.

I gave a cry and threw my arms about his neck.

"Oh, Henry, I am sorry! Pray forgive me."

He gripped my forearms and put me firmly from him.

"It is finished," he said, agitated. "I shall see you tomorrow for your lesson, Lady Catherine. Be sure we are not alone."

III

THE LADIES' CHAMBER lay dim and silent, the ladies asleep, when I returned to it. Thankful to be alone in darkness with my shame, I tiptoed to my bed and began removing my clothing.

My solitude was not to last, however. As I fumbled with the fastenings of my corset Joan poked her head through the bed curtains. I turned my back, tugging at my wretched garment.

There came a rustle and a pad of feet, and Joan brushed my awkward fingers aside to undo the corset's fastenings. I breathed a shaky sigh of relief when my torso was freed from its constriction.

Joan slipped her arms about me and rested her chin on my shoulder. Grateful for this comfort and display of friendship, I grasped her arms and leaned back against her with a sigh.

"We welcomed some new arrivals today," Joan murmured against my ear.

"I know. The Duke of Norfolk. The manor must be filled to the rafters," I commented dryly.

"Oh, aye, but I did not mean him." Joan's heart beat an excited tempo against my back. "Two gentlemen arrived with the Duke's household. They are to leave his service and join the Dowager's household as her stewards! I waited up to tell you this news!"

"Mmm?" There was clearly more to the tale and Joan continued in breathless animation.

"Yes, they are well-bred gentlemen, of handsome countenance, and appear to be of virtuous nature. After supper, I danced with one of them—Edward Waldegrave—and I am to walk with him on the morrow!"

I turned. Joan's round face was prettied with a beaming smile. I embraced her.

"How thrilling! Come, let us get to bed, and you can tell me more about this Edward!"

However, when we had climbed into bed, Joan at once buried herself beneath the bedcovers and was asleep almost as soon as her head touched the pillow. I was left to thoughts that whirled as fast as Morris dancers and which, combined with the warm and stifling atmosphere of the chamber, robbed me of all prospect of sleep. Finally, I rose from the bed. In an old gown and a cloak, I stole from the chamber.

I longed to speak with Father Vyncent. Many an evening I had spent in the vestry in his company, mulled malmsey loosening my tongue. He would sit in the chair opposite me, fingertips pressed together and raised to his mouth, shrewd eyes never leaving my face, silent as if hypnotised by my speech. His consolation was always forthcoming when needed and his counsel always welcomed, if not always heeded. In Father Vyncent I knew I had a friend—perhaps my only friend—who truly loved and understood me.

However, he was away in Bath, taking the waters for his failing health, leaving me alone to wrestle with my dramas. Tonight, I wandered unhappily to the inner courtyard, where many sleeping forms snored beneath the archways amidst the clutter of armour. Several dogs lifted their heads at my entry, eyes gleaming in the dimness; a few clicked across the stone flags to snuffle at my skirts. The scent of roasted meats, ale and body heat hung heavily on the air. I made for the freshness of the terrace.

A single torch burning on the outer wall was the first sign that I was not alone. Then came the sound of muted conversation. I recognised the Dowager's voice; the other belonged to a man, but I did not at first know its deep, authoritative tone. I slipped behind a large stone lion, and strained to hear.

"The young Prince is a frail lad," the man remarked. "The King desires more sons to secure the Tudor succession and keep the Plantagenet claimants at bay." There was a sarcastic lilt to the man's words and the Dowager snorted.

"He could always trump up some charge against such as they, and send them to the block to be rid of them. Forsooth, he is doing a good job of that already."

Shivering in delight at such treasonous talk I sidled closer beneath the shelter of the statue. I peered around the lion's forelegs, to see the light of the torch flames licking their faces.

"Be that as it may," my uncle the Duke of Norfolk conceded, "the King prefers to secure his throne through legitimate means."

"What of the Princesses Mary and Elizabeth?" said the Dowager. I silently applauded my step-grandmother for championing the claims of the women.

"Now bastards by law, both."

"The King could still name them as his successors should the Prince die . . . for that matter, he could also choose his bastard son—your own son-in-law—the Duke of Richmond!"

"Henry Fitzroy is dead," my uncle said, "as I have good reason to know. The lad died a natural death, and the King had me bury him in secret, to forestall alarm and intrigue against the Princesses. I wrapped his body in lead and hid it beneath a bundle of straw in a wagon, and thence to Thetford where he now lies."

There was a silence. I hoped for more, but the Dowager's next words froze the blood in my veins.

"If the King seeks another wife, I have the perfect candidate here in my care," she said in a low, fervent tone.

"Oh?" The Duke rubbed a weary hand over his face, only mildly curious.

"Aye, your brother Edmund's daughter Catherine!"

An astonished roar of laughter from my uncle echoed through the night.

"Stepmother, you must be mad! One of my nieces was Queen of England and went to the block, and you have the gall to thrust another at me for the role? You must think them easily dispensable indeed—or me insensible."

"Listen to me! I know these things. I have watched her for many years. Catherine Howard is no arrogant scold like her cousin—she is both winsome and compliant!"

"Bah! A Howard woman has to be more than 'winsome and compliant' to win the King's trust. Let me not hear more of this folly."

He turned to go, but the Dowager gripped his arm.

"She is comely," she insisted in a rasping voice. "Better than that—she provokes the lecher in a man."

The last comment stirred the Duke's interest. As I watched this exchange with growing horror, clutching the stone lion with shaking fingers, the Duke's eyes narrowed as he regarded the old woman and dwelt on her words. He grunted. But then he shook his head. "Stepmother, I know of your household's reputation. This Catherine—it would be a miracle indeed if she were—untouched—and living here. To win the King's regard, any woman must also have the innocence of Jane Seymour."

"She is still a virgin, I am sure of it." Indignation spiked the Dowager's pronouncement, although I knew her well enough to detect uncertainty. But the Duke did not perceive it, his lips pursed in deep thought. "And not betrothed or promised either. There was a foolish mishap some years ago with the music tutor but it came to naught—I made sure of that. Catherine Howard is proud of who she is, she would not promise herself to one of such low rank without her family's consent."

The Duke of Norfolk rubbed his jaw. "It seems I must meet this paragon of virtue," he remarked meditatively. "Arrange for it on the morrow." He retrieved the torch and held out his elbow; the Dowager clutched it and together they turned and stepped toward the inner courtyard. As they passed by me, unaware of my presence—or of the torment they had inflicted upon me—I shrank back into the shadows of the statue. "However, it may be of no consequence," the Duke continued, his voice fading into the distance. "The King contemplates a political marriage. England has many enemies . . ."

Much of the Dowager's rumbling response was inaudible to me: ". . . look at Catherine and the King will forget all politics . . ." The two conspirators burst into ribald, echoing laughter.

Alone in the dark, my trembling knees gave way and I slid down the statue to the ground. Clutching my drawn-up legs, I lowered my head.

Wife to the King? How could my relatives contemplate such a diabolical plan? As wife to King Henry VIII, my life would be in constant danger. Displease him, innocently or not, and I would surely be sent to the block. If I carried his child, it would be cut from me with no regard for my life. As my uncle had said, I would be dispensable.

In icy desperation for comfort and deliverance from this fate, I longed for Father Vyncent. He had never failed me. Without him I must seek my own solace and salvation.

I struggled to my feet, staggered across the terrace and down the wide stone stairs to the gravelled pathway that traversed the gardens in a neat, straight line. The mist was lower and thicker now, illuminated to an eerie weak candescence by the moon above it. The only sounds were my stumbling steps, the steady drip-drip of water from the trees, and my tremulous breathing.

The path ended and I found myself in the park. It was darker here, full of menacing shadows. With relief, I burst from the cover of the coppice to the lakeside, where I sank weakly onto the soft grass.

Rarely alone, I was accustomed to being able to seek out and find company when I needed it. My predicament reminded me of the long and lonely days at Oxenheath, before

Tom had arrived to liberate me.

Tom . . . Tears, which had been frozen with fear, now sprang to my eyes. His image and memory were now so clear, not only as the subject of my lust, but as a childhood companion, staunch ally and champion. Had he known of my present plight, I knew he would help me.

However, he was far away in London. I had to help myself . . .

I heard a small splash from far out in the lake. Looking up in surprise I dashed the tears from my eyes and peered through the mist that hung over the water's surface. I gasped aloud in shock. A man stood chest-high in the water, his naked back to me. He appeared to be washing, and his wet, dark hair hung to shoulders that gleamed pale in the moonlight.

Tom?

I scrabbled noisily to my feet, but he gave no impression of being disturbed in his ministrations. I would have cried out to him but for my pounding heart and breathless lungs. Joy overpowered me and without thinking I removed my clothing and ran, naked, to the water.

I waded silently through the mist toward the depths of the lake, guided only by the small splashes ahead of me. The water was cool, but not cold, a silken caress on my skin. When the mist parted again, I saw the man was just beyond touching distance, still oblivious to my approach. I stopped—already the water was at the height of my chin. Gingerly, I stretched out a toe, finding nothing but a frightening memory.

Tom . . . rescuing me in the river at Oxenheath . . .

. . . To win the King's regard, any woman must also have the innocence of Jane Seymour
. . .

He now immersed his head to rinse his hair. Emboldened, I kicked off from the pebbled ground beneath my feet and glided on the surface of the water toward him. When he burst from the water, I was there.

His loud shout of alarm was muffled by the mist as my arms slipped around him from behind.

"Peace," I whispered, close to his ear, allowing my legs to float about him. I lowered my mouth to a hard shoulder, as my hands roamed him in a delicate caress. I tasted clean, wet skin, felt smooth flesh over hard sinew and strong bones, and a rapidly thudding heart; hoarse breathing lifted a brawny chest.

When I sensed my words and touch had soothed him, I drifted around, still lightly holding him with hands and legs. I closed my eyes tightly and shuddered as large, ardent hands began to explore my flesh, and, with a throaty growl, a fervent mouth closed over mine.

I claimed my salvation, amidst silence and mist-laden moonlight, and bathed in the peaceful waters of the lake.

IV

I LAY BETWEEN TWO CLOAKS. The chill before the dawn lay on my cheeks and nose and I opened my eyes to see the mist dissipating in a fresh breeze, revealing a silvery sky. I turned my head slightly to the left, seeing golden dandelions dancing in long green grass. To my right
. . .

A man's form half lay on me. Steady warm breaths exhaled against my ear, a heavy hand lay on my ribcage, a leg thrown across one of mine. I turned my head further, seeing not the black, straight tresses of my long-held fantasies but soft brown curls touching a swarthy shoulder. Tentatively, I slid my hand up a torso that was not whip-lean, but large and solid.

I pulled the edge of the cloak over my face, stifling a shocked gasp. In the cold, stark light of a new day, the truth that I had so blithely ignored in the previous blissful hours struck me as a bludgeon.

Of course, within seconds of touching him in the lake, I had known this stranger was not Tom. But by then, pleasures of the flesh—so long denied me, it seemed—had consumed. Furthermore, this stranger had not come with sway on my heart, mind, or memory. Immersed only in desire and its gratification, my emotions and thoughts dormant, it had been easy to disregard everything but how his flesh and his touch felt against my skin . . . and simple to pay no account to anything else once my body had attained the joys of its ultimate surrender.

Now, tingling at that memory, I inched the cloak down and peered over it at the man beside me.

He possessed a handsome manly countenance. I knew from the previous night that he possessed a tender and considerate touch. Moreover—as another truth hit me—he had delivered me from the doom my relatives planned. I could not be wary of him, or regretful of what had occurred.

In gratitude and renewed desire I pressed into his warmth, turning towards him so that our breathing mingled.

He stirred, exhaling a deep sigh, before his eyes snapped open. They were green and startled. Struggling against sleep, he raised himself on one elbow and stared at me, wariness taking the place of disorientation in his expression.

A neat beard enhanced his features . I felt a thrill of warm appreciation.

He cleared his throat but I spoke first.

"Who are you?"

Now he softened. His lips twitched with amusement.

"Francis Dereham," he said in a low, refined timbre. His voice raised the fine hairs on my arms for it had uttered earthy invocations in my ear during our love-making. "I am newly employed at the Dowager Duchess's household . . ."

He was one of the new stewards Joan had told me about! My interest heightened.

". . . And you? You are in the Dowager's service?" he asked.

"Er, no. The Dowager Duchess is my step-grandmother and legal guardian. I am Catherine . . . Catherine Howard."

Francis Dereham's lips parted as he absorbed my introduction. His chest jerked in a silent laugh of astonishment. His chin dropped and his eyes lowered in a mocking acknowledgement.

"My Lady . . . I am at your service."

Laughter surged in my chest and burst forth unrestrained. At my mirth, he looked up, an eyebrow raised in question, a crooked smile forming on his face.

"You have serviced me thrice already," I explained merrily.

"Aye, that I have." He shifted to lie fully on me, nudging my legs apart with his own. "And I shall do so again." His soft beard tickled my face and his mouth against mine raised a tremor through my body. Acknowledging gladly that I was no Jane Seymour, I entwined my arms about his neck and drowned willingly in shameless pleasure.

V

WE RETURNED TO THE MANOR through a golden dawn. If I felt any regret or dissatisfaction, it was quelled by my admiration of Francis Dereham's impressive form beside me, and by the secret knowledge that I was now an unsuitable wife for our King.

However, I acknowledged with a grim, cold determination that if I required deliverance from the plan being formulated for me, I required more than a loss of my maidenhood. Being got with child would be an adequate, albeit possibly temporary, measure. Marriage, or at least betrothal, would be better . . .

When we reached the inner courtyard, Francis drew me into the cold shadows of an archway.

"You may be with child," he remarked in a low voice, watching carefully for my reaction.

"It matters not," I murmured. "Except that I would be happy."

Francis, exhaling a long sigh of relief, smiled at me.

"How is it that a man's life can change so in a matter of hours?" he mused, pushing a lock of hair from my face, tucking it beneath the hood of my cloak. "You must be a witch."

I stiffened. Francis tilted his head in puzzlement at my reaction. A gentle smile curved his mouth. "I am teasing," he said, touching my nose.

Relaxing, I laughed. I raised myself higher to kiss his mouth.

At the sound of footsteps descending the stone staircase, we drew apart. Some sleeping forms were stirring and two dogs commenced a growling tussle nearby. Francis put his lips to my ear. "We will meet anon," he murmured. I nodded and watched him slip away into the shadows.

As I began my ascent the Duke of Norfolk rounded the turn in the staircase.

His black eyes were heavy-lidded, his nose long. He was not overly tall, nor of powerful physique. His two saving graces were his sensual Howard mouth and his thick, leonine hair. Yet, somehow I had never hesitated in thinking him attractive, even handsome, and knew that other women who encountered him felt the same. I assumed his allure rose from his power and his reputation for being a skilled lover, as well as his bravery and skill in surviving in even the most difficult circumstances.

He stopped when he saw me. I hesitated, but then continued my climb until I stood on the same level as he. His narrow-eyed stare flickered from my ruddy hair barely hidden by the cloak's hood to examine my face.

"You are Edmund's daughter," he pronounced, curiosity sharpening his gaze. "I have heard much of you."

"Uncle," I greeted him, clutching before me the invisible shield of my union with Francis Dereham.

With a rough movement, my uncle reached out and pulled at the neckline of my cloak. Its silver fastening snapped and the garment tumbled to the ground. I gasped.

He noted my bosom rising from the bodice of my simple green gown, inspected the shape of my legs outlined against my skirts. I prayed that Francis's beard had left its marks upon my skin and that the scent of our copulation was upon me.

However, if I bore any such evidence, my uncle did not appear to notice. On the contrary, he smiled in satisfaction. "It appears my stepmother was right about you," he murmured. "Tell me, niece—do you wish to go to court?"

I swallowed my despair. "I am but a simple country woman, uncle," I said, "with simple needs and wants. I have no yearning for the great world of the court."

He laughed in astonishment. "A Howard happy in obscurity? I think not!" He passed a thoughtful hand across his mouth, and then waved it in dismissal, recommencing his clattering descent. "We shall talk again."

Frozen, I stood there long after his footsteps had faded away. At last, with fumbling hands I retrieved my cloak and drew it about my shoulders.

"As God is my witness," I whispered as I returned to my bedchamber where my friends still slumbered, "I will not be Queen of England." My teeth grated. "There will be no other will but mine!"

I collapsed onto my bed and somehow I slept. However, in my turbulent dreams I fled before waves that threatened to engulf me.

Chapter 8

"Some defeats are more triumphant than victories."

Michel de Montaigne
French essayist
(1533-92)

I

"COME, CATHERINE, WAKE UP!"

I surfaced through a fog of deep sleep and disturbing dreams. Blinking, I saw the bright sun of late morning streaming through the open windows, Joan's flushed face close to mine and Agnes bouncing jovially at my feet. I pulled a pillow over my face with a groan.

"Go away," I mumbled.

A whispered exchange ensued and the mattress heaved as Agnes got up.

"We shall just make your excuses at the Duke's tourney, then," Joan said airily. "Tis a pity that you will miss this surprise celebration. Come, Agnes, let us depart and leave Catherine to her slumber."

Tourney? That single excuse for sport, pageantry, music, dancing and feasting! I pushed the pillow from my face and struggled to sit up, sleep and irritation gone at once.

They grinned. They were simply dressed in light kirtles with square cut bodices and no overskirts or gowns. Better still, instead of French hoods, they wore spring flower garlands and gossamer veils.

Joan, perceiving my excitement, hastened to the armoury. I swung my legs over the side of the bed. The abrupt movement pulled tender flesh; at once, I recalled the events of the previous night. Confused emotions—fear, pleasure, triumph, regret—prompted a pause, interrupted when Agnes grabbed me away.

The sun had risen to its peak by the time we left the Manor and made our way on foot to the field beyond the parkland. A soft breeze, which set our skirts and veils swirling, relieved the unseasonably warm day. My simple kirtle of dove-grey satin was embroidered with silver *fleurs de lis* and a matching veil, hung from a garland of white roses, caressed my neck and shoulders.

We crested a hillock beyond a coppice of elms, and I paused with a gasp. The site of the tourney was spread before me like a banquet for the senses. The multitude thronged across an emerald field and over the makeshift wooden platforms and stands. From all directions streamed lines of people, on horseback, in carts and on foot, to see the magnificent war-horses in their bright caparisons[*] and gleaming chanfrons[†] and atop them the knights, in mail and armour that flashed like burnished silver. The fresh spring breeze fluttered pennants of every hue, set billowing the red velvet canopies of covered stands and presented to me the intoxicating scents of roasted hog, sweet trampled grass and fresh flowers. My soul rejoiced to hear the cries of the marshals, the heralds' clarions, the thud of lance against target and the

---

[*] decorated covering for a horse, especially for a warhorse
[†] medieval plate armour to protect a horse's head

cheers of the crowd above the rumbling of hooves.

Agnes scooped up her skirts and ran on ahead, entered a covered gallery, and emerged followed by the rest of the Dowager's charges. Their laughter and gay talk carried to us on the breeze.

"What are the rules?" I asked, when they had gathered around.

"It's a tourney of peace," announced Katherine Tylney, "and any man of reasonable jousting reputation is welcome!" A tourney of peace was one in which the wooden lances had been deliberately weakened and blunted to prevent serious injury. When the lances were sharpened it was called a tourney of war. The rank and reputation of the combatants also varied.

"All strikes in the joust must be on the shield," Margaret Morton added.

"The Dowager will be Queen of the Joust," someone said; the ladies burst into giggles.

"That is if she awakens—she sleeps in her chair now and her snores are fit to wake the dead!"

"The Duke will be competing—he wears his mistress's token already."

"I hardly think he needs to win the joust to earn her favours," Joan said, to more giggles.

I gave a delighted skip. "Come," I called. "Let us tarry no longer, ladies!"

As I swept ahead, my shimmering skirts billowing, the chattering ladies fell in behind me. Heads turned and there was a lull in the clamour as we approached. As I enjoyed the attention, the words my uncle spoke the previous night returned to me and I had to acknowledge their truth: "A Howard happy in boring obscurity? I think not!"

At the head of the lists was a platform draped in deep red velvet, with an elaborate and voluminous chair at its centre. Once the jousting started, that chair would become the Throne of Honour for the Queen of the Joust. She would award a prize to the victor of the tourney, usually a piece of jewellery or a veil that she wore, and would also lead with him the first dance of the night.

At present the Dowager Duchess, she who would be Queen of the Joust, slept in the deep shade of another covered platform. She lolled heavily in her chair, deep snores flapping her lips; about her hovered Jane Percy and her other ladies. We tiptoed past them and took our seats on wooden benches commanding an uninhibited view of the lists.

Joan nudged me. "Look, there goes your uncle."

I followed the direction of her gaze. The Duke of Norfolk was mounted on a massive grey destrier*, the caparison embroidered with his crest. He stared at me unwaveringly. My skin prickling, I looked away.

Another knight drew my attention. His black stallion was covered by a blue caparison embroidered in gold stags, and his armour dazzled. He also appeared to be watching me through the slit in the visor that covered his face.

This knight nudged his horse with silver spurs and steered it through the throng towards me; all the other ladies watched as he came alongside the platform. The horse pranced and pulled, the firm grip of mailed hands on the reins barely restraining him. The knight nodded at me. When he spoke, his helmet muffled his voice.

"My lady, may I have the honour of being your champion in today's joust?"

_____
* a warhorse or charger

His words brought from me a blush of pleasure and a tremulous smile. I lifted my arms and removed the veil from my flower garland. The knight held out his wooden lance and I tied the veil around the weapon. I looked, searchingly, into his covered face. He bowed and tugged the stallion's head around; with a snort and a tug at the bit, the horse sprang into a trot and the two departed in a cloud of dust.

The ladies emitted sighs and exclamations as I resumed my seat.

"I hope for your sake he wins," said Katherine. "I wouldn't mind bestowing my favours on such a one!"

"The Church has long frowned on the favours you think of, Katherine Tylney," retorted Joan. "Besides, the Blue Knight is unlikely to be the victor—the Duke of Norfolk is the best jouster in all of England."

The Blue Knight? The name aroused my curiosity. For a knight to be given a jousting title meant he had some reputation in the sport. The speculation was forgotten as to my discomfort, I saw the Duke continued to regard me intently. He beckoned to the scarlet-clad Chief Herald who hastened to his side. My uncle bent down and spoke to the Herald, who then glanced at me and nodded. My uneasiness intensifying, the Herald ran to the centre of the tiltyard and lifted his clarion to his lips; it blared, and an expectant silence settled on the crowd.

"Hear ye, hear ye!" the stentorian voice rang out. "The position of Queen of the Joust shall now be assumed by the Lady Catherine Howard!" He gestured to where I sat, and the crowd roared and flags waved as my friends gasped and embraced me.

Joan and Agnes tugged me to my feet; they fussed over my skirts and gestured towards the Throne of Honour. With dragging steps, I made my way towards it. I was conscious of the intent behind the Duke's action. Frustrated, I realised I was now subject to a will far greater than mine.

I sank into the Throne of Honour while Joan and Agnes took seats on either side of me, eager to bask in my glory. Waiting at the tilting-post, the Duke smiled in satisfaction.

The bright figure of the Blue Knight near him was a welcome distraction for me, and for a reason I could not fathom, another recollection assailed me . . . at the lake . . . Francis Dereham . . . and how I had made myself ineligible to be our sovereign's next wife.

I shook myself out of my reverie. No matter how dearly my uncle wished to draw me from obscurity, now or in the future, his schemes would come to naught. The previous night had been but a first step in exerting my will.

I whispered a repeat of my previous night's vow. "No other will but mine."

"What did you say?" said Joan.

"Nothing." Relieved, I expelled a long breath, smiled into Joan's curious face, and turned my attention to the events before me with a new eagerness.

On each side of the partition that split the tiltyard, riders were practicing at the tilting-post and riding at the ring. The marshals watched carefully to determine if all combatants were skillful enough to compete in the joust without endangering each other or their horses. Injury to a knight in the joust of peace was always regarded as unfortunate, and an injury to a horse unforgivable. A knight with brass spurs urged his charger into a gallop at the tilting-post, lance brandished. With a weak thud, the lance met the target and did not break; the sandbag, suspended on the other end of the horizontal pole, swung around; the horse was not swift enough or, more likely, the knight's horsemanship was poor; with a *clang*, sandbag met armour, and the knight tumbled to the ground. A groan rose from the multitude as, with one foot still encased it its stirrup, the charger dragged him away.

On the other side of the partition, another knight galloped towards a ring suspended by a rope from a long pole held aloft by a nervous page. The knight drew closer and with an energetic thrust of his lance, attempted to spear the ring. He galloped beneath it, the ring barely moving on its rope. The page gave a visible sigh of relief and laughter rippled around the arena.

It was then the turn of the Duke of Norfolk at the post. A green veil fluttered on his lance and he was unhelmeted. His destrier stood four-square and still, neck arched, but its nostrils flared red and its teeth were bared around the bit.

Gold spurs plunged into flanks. The destrier surged into a gallop and approached the target with thundering hooves, the Duke's lance at the ready. With a strong thrust of the arm, lance met shield with a thud and broke—the essential indication that the strike had been a good one. The sandbag swung around on its pivot and passed within a hair's breadth of the Duke's departing back. An appreciative roar erupted from the crowd.

The Blue Knight on his prancing and impatient charger, waiting at the start of the run, drew my enthralled attention. As the pages rushed to clear the debris, foam dripped from the black stallion's mouth and it pulled ferociously. When the run was clear, the Knight loosened his grip on the reins.

The stallion leapt forward. Cantankerous when restrained, the animal clearly relished its freedom. Like a black and blue streak, man and horse thudded towards the target.

The hit was clean; the lance shattered; unseated spectators scattered before the advancing stallion; the sandbag swung through empty air. I rose to my feet with the crowd, cheering and clapping until my hands stung.

As all knights returned to their tents and the tilting-post was dismantled, jugglers ran into the arena and minstrels began to play. Breathless from excitement, I resumed my seat to enjoy the intermission.

My enjoyment was brief. From the opposite side of the arena, a fair woman in a green gown and French hood watched me with pursed lips and a hostile countenance. She occupied a central position on the platform and clearly others deferred to her. I looked away.

"Joan," I said, "who is that woman in green?"

Joan cast a covert glance before responding with animation.

"That's Bess Holland, the Duke's mistress. She was a servant girl when she caught his eye!"

"She accompanies him openly?"

Joan smirked. "Lust can make a man forget all sense of decorum." We giggled.

"She doesn't appear to like me," I commented.

Joan inspected me shrewdly. With no apparent connection to the previous exchange, she remarked, "Henry came by the chamber this morning. He told us not to wake you for your lesson."

I debated with myself whether to confide in her about the end of my dalliance with Henry Mannox, and even about Francis, when something drew her attention.

"Oh, look! There is Edward Waldegrave!"

I watched a simply garbed, stout young man striding towards us through milling spectators. Fair and curly hair sprang from beneath his cap and his ruddy face was illuminated by a smile. With pride, Joan leant forward over the barrier as he stepped up to it, and the two began a low-voiced conversation. As Joan savoured the envious attention of her friends, I decided to keep my news to myself for the present. I sat back to enjoy the joust.

As the shadows lengthened and the tents and recets** filled with the injured and exhausted knights, the number of combatants was quickly whittled to the final two.

At opposite ends of the tiltyard and separated by the central partition, the Duke of Norfolk and the Blue Knight faced each other. The Chief Herald strode into the arena to repeat the rules.

"Brave Knights! Ye must strike thy opponent's shield or be disqualified! Ye shall have however so many passes as may be required to attain a victory! Fight on!"

This surprised me. Usually, in an individual joust, there would be three passes, or encounters; if no victor emerged, the competition would continue on foot with swords, and then with daggers. However, this was to be the ultimate test of mettle and skill on the part of horse and knight. It would be an enthralling combat.

The Chief Herald lowered a red flag and waited as the crowd stilled. I clutched the armrests of the Throne with damp hands. The snorts of the black stallion rent the silence; as usual, the grey destrier was poised, though its hide quivered beneath its caparison.

The flag was raised. Spurs dug. The horses burst forward to the deafening roar of the crowd, powering at a stretch towards the encounter.

With an ear-splitting *clunk*, lances crashed into shields; both knights swayed back on impact, splinters of shattered lances showering upon them. The impact failed to unseat either one, and their mounts thundered to the ends of the run. My silver veil and Bess Holland's green one fluttered to the dust amidst pandemonium in the stands.

The Blue Knight was now close to my position. When a page had once more fastened my veil about a fresh lance, the Knight looked up at me and raised his weapon. I sprang to my feet.

"Fight on, brave knight!" I shouted with exuberance. My words were lost amidst the din of cheering and stamping.

The combatants, armed with their new lances, again faced each other and the Herald lowered the red flag. Clasping my trembling hands together and pressing them to my lips, I waited.

The flag was hoisted high with an audible whoosh. The black stallion's deep snorts resounded and the crowd roared as the horses sprang forward.

Another solid impact shattered both lances. The knights remained seated, if shaken. They returned to their positions as the dust settled and the pages scampered onto the run to clear it of debris.

Thrice more the combatants met, with the same result. After the fifth encounter, the tension and excitement of the crowd had risen to fever-pitch and the commotion was deafening; I trembled with exhilaration. Joan and Agnes were on their feet and red-faced with excitement, their hoarse yells lost in the din. The two splendid horses showed signs of fatigue; their necks were bowed, froth dripped from mouths, and their caparisons were dark with sweat. All of us knew the knights' full armour was heating their flesh as effectively as an oven; it was not unusual for a knight to die of heat exhaustion, and this was a very real possibility today. The marshals began to look anxious for a result.

* the enclosure where knights rested and rearmed

For the sixth time, spurs dug into flanks when the flag was lifted. With no discernible decrease in speed, the gallant horses stretched towards each other, dust and clods of earth flying beneath their hooves.

With a crash, lances met shields and splintered. Both knights swayed; the Blue Knight was quick to right himself, continuing his ride to the end of the run. The crowd gasped as one. The Duke of Norfolk swung forward but his momentum carried him too far, so that he was lying against his mount's neck, frantically clutching it. It was in this ungainly position that he reached the end of his run.

A chant arose, to stamping feet and clapping hands: "Blue Knight, brave Blue Knight! Blue Knight, brave Blue Knight!" The pages prepared the combatants for the next encounter, arming them with new lances, retying the tokens. The Duke was now closest to me; I could clearly see his angry gestures as he examined one lance and threw it aside, waving for another. At the other end of the field, the Blue Knight sat relaxed and still mounted, waiting for the signal, unperturbed by the commotion that raged around him.

With the raising of the flag the horses again sprang forward. The thrill of the crowd could no longer be restrained; stamping feet beat time to the galloping hooves. Breathless, I watched for the impact.

It did not occur as expected. Rearing grey hooves sent into the air billowing dust that obliterated the detail of the encounter. I saw a flash of shields, flailing arms, heard the crash of a lance over the frightened neighs of horses. The pieces of one lance tumbled to the ground, my silver veil fluttering to the debris. In what was probably only a matter of seconds but seemed an age, the horses emerged from the melee and galloped on. The Duke of Norfolk was upright in his saddle, the Blue Knight bowed low over his mount's neck.

I waited anxiously as Knight and horse came to a halt just beyond my position. Slowly, the Blue Knight straightened and I sighed with relief. A fresh lance was placed in his hand and he looked directly at me.

He raised his lance. He wobbled, feet slipping from stirrups. He tumbled to the ground in a loud clang of armour.

With the ensuing uproar, more deafening than anything that had preceded it, cawing blackbirds in the surrounding elms burst into the sky. Weakly, I sank to my seat as the Duke of Norfolk raised his lance in victory. Several pages gathered around the prone and still form of the Blue Knight, and hoisted him onto a trestle. He was carried away to the recets, another page leading the placid black stallion.

The Duke trotted his charger around the perimeter of the lists, acknowledging the thunderous accolades of the crowd and the vigorous waving of flags and veils. Sweat matted his hair and perspiration cascaded down his face. When he came alongside the platform where his mistress waited, he drew his horse to a halt. To rising whistles, Bess Holland approached the barrier and the Duke laid a heavy mailed hand on her neck in a startling intimate gesture, before turning and riding towards me.

When he had dismounted, he paused, regarding me with triumph. I was enough of an Englishwoman to appreciate the skills he had shown, enough of a Howard to be proud of his accomplishments. I smiled as he slowly approached with dragging feet, and reached up to remove the flower garland from my head.

When my uncle knelt before me, I pressed the garland onto his wet hair.

"I bestow on you this garland as a reward for chivalry," I murmured. "Never has there been a knight more worthy of one such prize!"

The Duke raised his head. We smiled at each other in genuine rapport.

"You assume the role of royalty so well," he said in an undertone only I could hear. Detecting his implied meaning, the smile fell from my face.

"Then it is well that I have the chance to play it, for I shall never be royal in reality," I retorted.

He laughed briefly and mockingly.

"We shall see," he said.

Surrounded by his minions and to riotous cheering, the garlanded Duke of Norfolk led his grey destrier down the centre of the field, and disappeared into the thronging spectators beyond the lists.

II

THE ARRIVAL OF WRESTLERS into the arena at the fall of dusk distracted the attention of Joan and the other ladies and I was able to make a hasty disappearance, unobserved.

The area behind the stands where the tents had been erected bustled with activity; horses were being groomed, watered or walked; pages hurried about bearing bowls of steaming water, and cloths, pails and platters of food for the injured or resting knights. Many spectators had gathered, eager for a glimpse of their heroes. I weaved my way through the throng, unsure of what I was looking for—until I spied the black stallion.

The magnificent animal stood secured to a pole outside a closed tent, a page brushing its quivering hide. The caparison with its gold stags on blue was draped over the page's shoulder. I stopped short, staring at the garment in growing comprehension. With an excited leap of my pulse, I approached with a determined stride.

"Is the Blue Knight within?" I asked the page.

The grubby lad regarded me with a lascivious gleam in his eye. He nodded. "Aye."

I felt warmth in my cheeks. "He is well?"

"Well enough." The page grinned.

I lifted the tent flap and lowered my head to enter.

"I shall see ye ain't disturbed," remarked the impudent lad as I disappeared into the tent.

It took several seconds for my eyes to adjust to the dimness. A single candle burned in one corner of the tent. The scents of balm and melting tallow mingled in the warm and close atmosphere. My gaze was drawn to the opposite corner.

There, propped against cushions on a trestle bed, was Francis Dereham.

A beaming smile wreathed his face when he saw me. Because I had recognised—though tardily—his insignia on the caparison, his identity did not startle me, but I gaped speechless at him nevertheless.

He was naked but for white cloths bound about his ribs and another thrown casually across his loins. His flesh gleamed with a damp, ruddy tinge. A drop of perspiration trailed from below the bound ribs, down his taut belly, to disappear beneath the thin covering. My avid gaze followed it to where it disappeared

"Are you going to come closer and speak with me?" Francis asked, amusement giving a lilt to his tone. "Or will you stand there silent all night?"

I shook away my daze and laughed. As I stepped alongside him, the meaning of his bound ribs came home to me.

I frowned.

"You were hit?"

"So it seems," he murmured.

"The Duke did not have a weakened lance!" I gasped. "He caused a distraction with his rearing horse and deliberately smote you in the chest with an unweakened lance!"

"I do not know . . ."

"He is proper-false!" I exclaimed, bristling. That a kinsman of mine should resort to such unsporting tactics was shameful. Francis took my hand.

"Tis of no account, Catherine. Tis just a bruising of the ribs. Jousting is a mere sport to me that I play when my other duties permit. And a simple flower garland from you would not satisfy me, so victory is of no import."

I regarded him thoughtfully.

"So in effect you were the victor in the joust, for the Duke disqualified himself with his actions," I mused. "And you were my champion, competing for my favours. It seems to me then, that I have some favours to award."

His hand found its way beneath my skirts and slid up my leg. "Is that so?"

I reached down and with one fingernail followed the path the drop of perspiration had taken, twitching aside the cloth that did little to hide what lay beneath. Francis sucked in a sharp breath.

Emboldened and overcome, I lifted my skirts and swung one leg across his body.

"Methinks the Pope would not approve," murmured Francis Dereham against my mouth as he grasped my hips.

"The Pope must understand the temptation," I gasped as I sank into spine-tingling delights.

III

BLAZING TORCHES relieved the darkness of the warm night when I emerged from the tent.

The page had gone. The black stallion was blowing into a pail of water, and lifted his head to regard me with placid, bloodshot eyes and dripping muzzle. I patted his neck and slipped into the mill of intoxicated revellers.

The arena had been cleared for the dancing and many minstrels had gathered at the perimeter. I stepped up to the Dowager's platform where many of her household now mingled, ingesting great quantities of ale and food; good cheer was plentiful, and my step was light as I weaved through the gathering to where Joan and the other ladies were grouped.

The Dowager had awoken and now sat upright in her chair, clutching a goblet of wine in one hand, regarding the spectacle around her with barely suppressed delight. The satisfaction heightened when she noticed me and she beckoned; clearly, being usurped in her role as Queen of the Joust had not annoyed her.

"Catherine! Where have you been? You are to lead the first dance with the Duke!"

I groaned inwardly. I had forgotten that part of my role as Queen of the Joust. I glanced towards the opposite platform; my uncle was now striding across the arena towards us, clearly well-recovered from the joust. He wore regalia suited to his noble rank—a bejewelled doublet of cloth of gold, and a cloak of red velvet trimmed with ermine. In my simple kirtle, with my bare head, and remembering how I had spent the previous hours, I felt too plain and dissolute to partner him.

He stopped at the platform, bowed and held out his hand to me. I hesitated. The ladies gently pushed me towards him, and silence settled on the gathering crowd.

Aware of many appreciative and expectant stares, I laid my hand on his and he led me to the centre of the arena. There, beneath the blazing torches, I experienced a thrill of accomplishment and an odd surge of power. My uncle smiled at me in triumph.

The minstrels lifted their instruments expectantly.

"Players—*La Regina*, if you please!"

I could not miss the significance of my uncle's choice of music. However, I could think of nothing but the prospect of a wonderful dance before an admiring, eager audience. As my uncle clasped one of my hands, we faced the musicians. The tune burst into life and I became absorbed.

My uncle was as fine a dancer as he was a jouster, and it delighted me to watch as he turned and weaved around me. My own saltarello steps were precise, my turns accomplished in an exalted flourish and swirl of shimmering skirts. When we resumed our handholding at the re-start, to the sound of rapturous applause, I could not restrain my smile of pleasure.

"You move well, niece," my uncle remarked as he circled around me again. "It's a shame that such talents as yours are hidden away in Sussex."

"I do not find it so," I said as I commenced my own circle. Emboldened, I continued. "I do hope you are not going to spoil this evening by further extolling my virtues as a Queen, uncle. After all, I am quite unsuited for the role."

The Duke took my right hand in his and we did a complete circle around each other. "I disagree," he remarked. "Not least because you are a Howard, and every Howard would make a suitable monarch. However—," our left hands grasped and again we turned about each other, "I shall not talk of it, if you so wish—for the moment. Instead, shall I describe to you life at court?"

Through the subsequent chorus and as we again resumed, he spoke to me in a low, seductive tone that parted my lips and enthralled my soul—he spoke of fine clothes, extravagant jewellery, pageantry and revels . . . of sophisticated women and lusty men . . . and embracing it all, the glittering figure of our great King.

My beguilement had commenced with the fine music in my ears, the rejoicing of my spirit in the moving to it and my appreciation of my partner's skill; it was completed as my uncle shrewdly laid before my mind's eye the glorious tapestry of King Henry VIII's court.

The saltarello came to an end too soon. The musicians burst into a merry bransle, drawing more people into the arena. My uncle leaned closer.

"Think of it," he murmured into my ear. Then he was gone, slipping through the crowd. As I was swept along into the Washerwoman's Bransle, there was a new spring in my heels and new warmth in my cheeks.

Chapter 9

"The art of war teaches us to rely not on the likelihood of the enemy's not coming, but on our own readiness to receive him; not on the chance of his not attacking, but rather on the fact that we have made our position unassailable."

Sun Tzu
Chinese general and author of The Art of War
(ca. 500 BC)

I

I ADMIT THERE WAS A FEELING OF RELIEF when, two days after the joust, I learnt I was not with child.

Francis, too, was thankful, although he tried hard not to show it.

"Perhaps that's fortunate," he suggested. I told him the news whilst we walked in the orchard one evening. Cold and blustery conditions had usurped the warm weather of the joust; the fruit trees swayed and scraped against one another and leaves swirled about our ankles. "I have do believe we should exercise some caution and concealment," Francis added.

I whirled to face him. "Why? You are ashamed?"

"No!" Hot colour flooding his cheeks, he grabbed both my hands. "Catherine, my intentions towards you are honourable, you know that."

"You have voiced no intentions," I said in a sulk, striding on ahead. "I cannot read your mind. And I must doubt your intentions now that you talk of *caution* and *concealment*. Fie, Francis!"

My ruse worked well. Francis grabbed me from behind and spun me around. With the ardour to which I was now accustomed, he crushed me in an embrace and kissed me frantically. I allowed him his way for several pleasant minutes before dragging my mouth away and pushing at his shoulders.

"We should desist—someone may see," I said with sarcasm.

"No one is here," Francis muttered seeking my lips again. "Catherine, I like to think we are—promised."

My heart gave a leap but I kept my expression stern. "Are you promising we will be wed?" I pressed.

"I—aye. Aye!"

I relaxed. A promise of marriage was as binding as marriage itself. There was no more certain way to ensure my Uncle Norfolk's plans for me to marry the King would come to nothing. I could not suppress a smile of glee that I had bettered my cunning kinsman.

"You seem pleased." With an expression of relief, Francis took one of my hands and pressed a hot kiss onto my fingers.

"Mmm." My thoughts raced. "And, thinking on it," I murmured, "Your suggestions of secrecy are well bethought." I spoke cautiously, for my motives were self-interested: although I wished to ensure I could never marry the King, my Uncle Norfolk had successfully seduced me with his talk of life at the royal court, and I now longed for such an experience. Yet, I knew my uncle would do nothing about finding me a position there if he knew I was promised to be wed, or with child—I was worthless to him in those circumstances. Yes, secrecy was vital. "Aye, let's take care and keep this matter between ourselves for the foreseeable future," I said.

"I am pleased you agree," Francis replied. "I have no wish to rouse the ire of your family so soon—I am conscious of my low rank and that I have no property. I would like us to keep our secret until I have inherited a portion of my uncle's estate."

I shrugged. That was in the distant, uncertain future. I could think only of present pleasures. And present pleasures were delicious, I realised, as Francis kissed me again.

II

TAKING THE CAUTION that Francis and I agreed upon meant some inconvenient intimacies, until discreet enquiries of the cook's wife earned me a vial of a foul-tasting tincture and other remedies against conception. I seized upon them gratefully and Francis relegated the pig-gut sheaths to the bench-hole.

We ladies generally retired early to our chambers. There we awaited the arrival of our male admirers at the midnight hour, after the Dowager had retired. We now counted Francis and Edward Waldegrave amongst the lovers who would slip into our communal bedchamber, laden with delicacies—strawberries and apples and, of course, wine. From clandestine feasting, it was an easy step to lovemaking behind the bed curtains; often, Francis could not even wait to remove his hose before he would fall on me with enthusiastic zeal.

Henry Mannox had maintained an icy distance from me since May. His anger turned to bitterness when he heard tell of the friendship between Francis and me.

However, tattle amongst servants did not easily get to the ears of the Duke or Dowager, and they would likely disregard it if it had; furthermore, Francis had yet to refer to me as "wife" to anyone but me. The secret of our promise remained safe. In my contentment, Henry Mannox's manner did not perturb me unduly: the summer of 1538 was the happiest I had known. To reinforce our union, Francis bestowed on me a shirt of fine linen, some velvet and satin for a gown, a quilted cap of sarcenet and an embroidered friar's knot to symbolise our love. I had the security, love and intimacy my soul craved. Even better, plans were in hand for the Dowager's household to move to London in the spring. With that glittering prospect on the horizon and the promise it held for me of a life at court, I looked forward to my future as never before.

My Uncle Norfolk departed for London at the end of the summer. He had said little to me during his stay, appearing preoccupied, and had spent much time away in London on the King's business. When he was not there, he was often calling on the Fitzalans at Arundel. My uncle had a new grandson, much doted upon, and I suspect was angling for a match between the infant boy and a daughter of the Fitzalans.

He was not long gone when the Dowager required Francis to travel Portsmouth to see a cloth merchant from Flanders. He would be away for three days. When he asked me to accompany him, I had reason again to be grateful for the Dowager's poor supervision, and did not hesitate. We left early one morning, I riding pillion behind Francis, the first days of autumn lending sharpness to the clear air.

We made excellent time, for the roads were in good repair. Beneath the soft sky, labourers made hay in the meadows, its sweet scent wafting to us on the fresh breeze. I rode with my arms loose about Francis' waist and my cheek resting against his back, the steady gait of the horse and the warmth of Francis' body lulling me into a pleasant doze.

We broke our journey at an inn in a tiny village. Francis referred to me as "wife" to the innkeeper, and I found it wondrous that here I was not Lady Catherine Howard but Mistress Dereham; I wasn't certain I enjoyed the charade, and liked it even less when, after we had eaten, the innkeeper showed us to a tiny, rudely furnished room directly above the noisy tavern.

I stood amidst old rushes and looked in shock from the one warped armoury to the narrow bed with its threadbare sheet thrown over a straw mattress; my fingertips rested on a rocky table on which stood a cracked ewer and basin. I realised I would have no woman to help me with my toilet or dress, and no maid to empty the chamber pot. It was also unlikely the inn would provide hot water or a privy.

Francis, however, bounced around the room like a puppy, removing his clothing and tossing it on the bed.

"Is not this agreeable? And to think, I do not need to steal from your bed in the early hours!"

Stripped to his undershirt, he turned to face me, and sobered at once. He strode across the room and pulled me into his arms.

"What ails you, my love?"

Despite my wretched mood, an involuntary quiver at his near-nakedness passed through me. My fingers splayed over his chest, feeling the warmth of his flesh through the thin fabric of his shirt. I fought the urge to wrench off my own clothing and feel his shape against mine. He, watching my face, drew a sharp, anticipatory breath. My ever-seething desire battled with the inclination to sulk, and won.

"Help me disrobe, quickly," I muttered, reaching around to my back with desperate hands to undo my bodice.

He tugged off my hood. When my heavy gown fell to the ground, he fumbled with my corset fastenings.

"Marry! What manner of garment is this!" He finally tossed it to the ground while I giggled and scrabbled to pull his shirt over his head. When at last my shift joined his shirt on the floor I pressed myself to him eagerly, and felt the wooden edge of the table against my thighs as Francis urged me backwards.

I rather suspect revellers in the noisy tavern below could hear the subsequent frenzied thumping of the unsteady table and the crashing of the ewer and basin to the floor.

III

"WE'LL STAY ELSEWHERE ON OUR RETURN," Francis said the next morning, sitting up in bed and scratching his arms vigorously. "This mattress is home to several creatures, I think."

I refrained from making a sarcastic reply. I had already risen and was scrubbing at my shivering body with a coarse cloth and cold water from the replacement ewer. Outside, rain pattered against the window and roof, and there was a steady drip of water from a leak onto the foot of the bed.

A ride in the rain was more attractive to me than extending our stay at the inn, so we made a hasty departure. We endured a miserable ride for the duration of the morning. The horse floundered in the mud, and cold rain penetrated my cloak and soaked me to the skin. However, as we approached the coast, the sunshine burst through the parting clouds, and the downpour ceased all at once. The gentle breeze tingling my cold nose held a distinct tang of sea salt.

As we rounded a bend in the road, I sensed a tensing of Francis' muscles and a straightening of his spine. Curious, I peered around him.

On the left side of the road, a deep ditch stretched across a fallow field. On the other side, several dozen men and women were digging another ditch, some of them knee high in thick mud. They looked up as we passed, their dirty faces grim.

"What are the ditches for?" I asked Francis.

Francis hesitated. I concluded at once that he knew or suspected their purpose but did not wish to alarm me. "I am not certain," he muttered. He was staring up ahead and I again craned to see what had attracted his attention.

A line of about six horse-drawn carts, each one heavily laden with stone, was proceeding slowly along the muddy road. Francis nudged the horse into a canter.

As we came alongside the cart last in line, he pulled our horse to a walk. The cart's driver—a bent, grizzled old man— glanced at us with no interest.

"Good cheer to you!" Francis greeted. The man lifted a finger to his cap in reply.

Francis gestured to the carts of stone. "There is building afoot?"

The man issued a nasally *hwark* sound; I watched in appalled fascination as he inclined to the side as if to spit. Fortunately, on catching my eye, he seemed to think better of it; he swallowed before answering.

He nodded. "Aye," he mumbled. "The King's buildin' a castle at Portsmouth with them there stones from the abbeys."

"A fortification?" Francis asked, further confusing me. The old man nodded and looked away, as if we were no longer there.

Francis drew the horse to a halt and the cart rumbled ahead. The carts were taking up much of the road, making passing impossible or dangerous. Nearby, a narrow, muddy path wound across the pastures towards the distant cliffs. Francis pulled the horse's head around and urged it through the roadside ditch. We cantered along the path to where the land fell away to the sea.

Where the path veered down the hill to the cove, Francis dismounted and lifted me down. Absently, he left me standing as he strode to the edge of the cliff.

I wandered to his side and at once forgot the discomfort of my damp clothes. Struck by the beauty of the shimmering sea, I lifted my face to the sun and breeze with a contented sigh.

When Francis had been silent for several minutes, I glanced at him, and then followed the downward direction of his gaze. I gasped in amazement.

Below us sprawled the town of Portsmouth, its clutter of dark wooden buildings hugging a bustling harbour. In the harbour idled two tall warships, with 'castle' battlements at bow and stern; a third was moving slowly into the cove, its white sails and pennants whipping in the wind, its deck swarming with men bearing guns and bows. Emblazoned on the pennants was the red Tudor rose. As the ship approached the dock, cheers rose from the citizens crowded on the shore.

I saw along the shoreline what appeared to be a barricade; on the hill opposite, several stone structures were being built: two looked like towers, the third a low castle. I remembered the ditches. I plucked at Francis' sleeve.

"What's happening?"

His expression was taut.

"Invasion," he said bluntly. "England is preparing for war."

IV

WHILE FRANCIS HURRIED through his business with the cloth merchant, I wandered the streets of Portsmouth. I turned my mind from the threat of war and was blind to the filth in the narrow streets and the even filthier vagrants. Fascinated, I inspected the wares displayed in the open shop windows and watched the players in the crowded square. The riotous noises and pungent smells of a busy town left me exhilarated rather than repulsed.

On our return journey, Francis rode in silence. That night at another inn—this one less primitive and dirty—he appeared lost in thought and alternately grim and excited, his lovemaking accomplished in an absent-minded, mechanical manner rather than with the unbridled passion I had come to expect. I assumed he had learnt more of the invasion threat, but he said nothing of it. In my wish to remain ignorant of things unpleasant, I did not press him for details.

The next day was fine weather for travelling. We made good time, and dusk was falling when we arrived at Horsham. In the inner courtyard, Francis' kiss was quick and stealthy before he hurried off to his quarters. Aimlessly, I wandered out to the terrace to watch the last of the sunset.

I was lost in an agreeable daydream, where I danced at court in a glittering ruby necklace and gown of gold brocade, when there was a shuffle behind me. I turned.

Father Vyncent stood there, a wide smile on his round face.

"Father Vyncent! You've returned." I ran to him and embraced him warmly. When we drew apart, he patted my shoulder.

"How goes you, my child? I have missed you greatly."

"I am well. I have much to tell you. How is your health?" I examined him carefully. Before leaving to take the waters at Bath, he had experienced flutters of the heart and dizzy spells; now he looked no less stout, but his colour was better.

"I am much rested, my dear. Come, let us share some wine while you tell me your news."

I followed his shuffling figure through the chapel to the vestry.

He sat opposite me after he had poured the wine.

"I saw you with a young man when you came in," he said. I felt the beginnings of discomfort beneath his probing—how would he receive the account of my liaison with Francis? Something told me he wouldn't be pleased. I took several fortifying swallows of wine.

"That's Francis Dereham," I mumbled. "He arrived with my Uncle Norfolk's household in May and is now the Dowager's steward."

"The Duke of Norfolk was here?" For a moment, the news distracted Father Vyncent from Francis. I finished my wine and refilled my cup.

"Aye, although he spent much of his time back in London and with the Fitzalans at Arundel . . . Oh, Father, I must tell you what I overheard while he was here. It concerns me and—and Francis Dereham."

Father Vyncent frowned in concern at the agitation in my voice.

"Tell me, child."

I drew a deep breath.

"I overheard my step-grandmother and my Uncle Norfolk discussing the possibility that I should become our King's next wife." As Father Vyncent blinked in astonishment, I laughed, the sound carrying an edge of panic. "Aye, it's ridiculous is it not? I am obscure and untutored in court life . . ."

Father Vyncent shook his head. "That's not the reason for my surprise. Child—."

"Father, I do not wish to marry the King! The notion frightens me!"

"I do not blame you, my dear. Any woman in the realm would prefer to cut her throat than consider the marriage bed of our sovereign. However—."

"So when I heard my uncle's opinion that the King's next wife must be as virtuous as Queen Jane, I—I—." I stopped in mortification. Father Vyncent stared at me in growing dismayed comprehension.

He broke the heavy silence.

"You committed fornication," he whispered. "With Master Dereham!"

He needed no affirmative response. I threw back my wine in agitation.

"Although we have been discreet and have told no one of it, we are promised to be wed," I mumbled, anxious for his approbation.

If anything, his dismay intensified. He closed his eyes and rubbed his temples. The florid colour returned to his face. "I have failed him," I heard him murmur to himself.

"Failed whom?"

He looked at me with a bleakness that wrenched my heart. "Master Culpeper."

"Tom?"

Father Vyncent emitted a hoarse sigh before refilling his cup from the jug. In silence he drank deeply. He did not clarify the reason for his disturbance, except to mutter, almost inaudibly, "I should have been here to prevent this calamity!"

He finished his wine and regarded me sadly.

"The irony of this, my dear, is that your actions were for naught. I have no doubt that what your uncle wants he usually gets, but in this instance—." Father Vyncent shook his head. Seeing my puzzled expression, he continued. "France and Spain are in alliance, and are angry at the abuse of Mother Church in England," he explained. "It is said they are mustering their troops. England is preparing for war."

"Aye, we saw signs of it in Portsmouth. But—."

Father Vyncent held up a hand.

"King Henry realises he must make a marriage alliance to protect England," he said, "and is intent on doing so. I understand he is considering one of the Duke of Cleves' sisters. My dear, you never will be Queen of England!"

I stared at him, at a loss for words. So, all I had done had been for naught! And what had Father Vyncent meant when alluding to Tom? As I grappled with it all, deep loss and regret overcame me and I lowered my head to my hands.

V

IN THE WINTER, word came that the King of France and the Emperor Charles V had made their alliance official. Having expressed a common alarm and revulsion at our King's attacks on the Church, the two erstwhile enemies made a pact. This meant neither would enter into any relationship with England without the other's consent. It was in effect a declaration of war. The long-threatened Catholic crusade was about to begin. War panic in England intensified. The planned sojourn in London for the Dowager and her household now became a necessary retreat from the more vulnerable south.

England needed an ally. Father Vyncent told me that a royal marriage alliance with Cleves, a Duchy that straddled the lower Rhine, would be a mortal blow to the Emperor. The Emperor struggled with the revolt of the German Lutheran Princes, and leader of those was the Duke of Cleves.

We heard of the Duke's two beauteous sisters. By early spring, when the Dowager's household began its journey to London, there was but one name on the lips of all.

Anne of Cleves.

Part 2: Passion

"Subdue your passion or it will subdue you."

Horace
Ancient Roman Poet
(65—8 BC)

Chapter 10

"The wine urges me on, the bewitching wine, which sets even a wise man to singing and to laughing gently and rouses him up to dance and brings forth words which were better unspoken."

Homer, The Odyssey

I

Norfolk House
South Bank, London
Spring, 1539

I HAD KNOWN the Dowager's London estate of Norfolk House as a child; now, at eighteen years of age, I viewed it with new eyes. I did not see the dark corners and the back stairs as excellent places for childhood hiding games, but as perfect for secret assignations with Francis Dereham. Formerly, Westminster Palace across the river was an unreachable Camelot of childhood fancies; now it was a reality to which even such as I could aspire. At eighteen, I viewed the tall gates at the estate's entrance as a means to welcome the world in and not as a comforting barrier keeping it out.

My uncle, Lord William Howard, became a frequent caller, as did my aunt Katherine, the Countess of Bridgewater. The Countess's first visit to Norfolk House was also the first time in three years that she had seen her daughter, Agnes Ap Rhys. As always, the Duke of Norfolk was a constant presence at the estate.

Remarkably, the threat of war faded as spring became summer. The Emperor Charles V decided an alliance with his old enemy, the King of France, was too high a price to pay to punish England for its crimes against the Church. The Emperor instead turned his religious fury on the Lutherans, whilst King Francis sighed with relief that costly warfare had been diverted.

However, Lord Cromwell persuaded our King to continue with his marriage plans, for even though England was safe for now, she remained isolated, and a marriage alliance remained a politically strategic move. By all reports, having seen Anne of Cleves' portrait, the King was besotted, and he agreed to the suggestion. The two married by proxy, and Anne of Cleves was to arrive in England in the winter to make the marriage official and take her place as Queen of England.

The summer months crept by in peaceful apathy. Nothing was said to me of a position at the royal court and the Duke of Norfolk paid me no heed. I drew the unhappy conclusion that mine was, after all, to be a life of insignificance and dreariness.

I FOUND IT EASY to love Francis Dereham. He was handsome, kind and dashing; moreover, he loved me and was adept at showing it. To my discomfort, however, when he inherited a small Norfolk property on the death of his uncle, he began to press for a public acknowledgement of our union.

"I know I have no title, but my family name is respectable, and now I have property," he said late one night as we embraced in the shadows of the gallery outside the ladies' chambers. "Surely, your family wouldn't disapprove of our marriage now."

It was difficult to be annoyed at his naivety and challenging to disavow words spoken from such an alluring and talented mouth. I pressed my lips to his and my head swam when his tongue touched mine.

"What is the meaning of this!"

The strident exclamation of the Dowager echoed down the gallery. Francis and I sprang apart as she stalked towards us followed by a smirking page bearing a torch.

However, she did not reveal the same furious embarrassment she had displayed in similar circumstances with Henry Mannox. When she stood before us, her gaze went to me and she frowned and shook her head with a resigned sigh, before she turned her regard to Francis.

"Well? What do you have to say for yourself, young man? Why do you consort in this manner with my granddaughter?"

Francis stood relaxed in the face of the Dowager's displeasure. To my astonishment, he stepped closer to me and I felt his hand on my shoulder. The Dowager's eyebrows shot high into her forehead.

"Cannot a man kiss his own wife?" Francis asked.

The Dowager spluttered, a patchy red blush invading her face.

"Wife? *Wife*!" If the old woman had been merely annoyed before, she now trembled in indignation. I cringed before her stare.

Francis continued undaunted.

"We are promised, and we have been—intimate," he said. "In the eyes of the Church, we are married."

"Church? *Church*!" Despite the dire predicament, I felt an overwhelming urge to dissolve into hysterical giggles as the Dowager expostulated ineffectually. Perhaps detecting my ill-timed mirth, the Dowager stepped forward and slapped me hard on the cheek.

Francis gasped and his arms went around me.

"Though we do love, this was my passion and Catherine yielded to it," he said, his voice rumbling with anger. "Pray dismiss me if you have the desire, but do not vent your anger on her!"

I listened in appalled fascination with my throbbing face pressed against Francis' doublet. His words surprised and shocked me. He had taken on the blame for our intimacy— when we both knew where the blame really lay—and had defied the Dowager with arrogance and imprudence. Surely, he would not survive such folly.

I felt Francis' arms loosen as he relaxed. Curious, I moved out of his hold and glanced at my step-grandmother.

She was smiling—an appreciative, lustful smile.

"Argh, why would I dismiss you, young man? You are the best steward I have ever had . . . and truly handsome and lusty! Such heart!" She gave a loud hoot of laughter while Francis and I gaped at her and the page giggled. "You please me, young Dereham! You please me! Would that—."

I suppressed a choking laugh. I thought Francis went pale. The torch swung in the page's grasp as he shook with mirth. The Dowager sighed, her contemplative gaze sweeping Francis, before she shook away her reverie.

"Hmm, so we have a predicament," she rumbled. "You say you are married in the eyes of the Church, but we all know the Church has no authority in England now." She winced at her weak argument before continuing. "You are not officially married, and will not be. Young man, Catherine is the niece of the highest peer in the land. She is a *Howard*. She has known all her life that she must marry in accordance with her family's wishes! Marriage for love? Bah! Let me hear no more of this."

Muttering, the old woman swept her skirts aside and turned to retrace her steps.

"Swounds, children!" she grumbled, "do keep at least an appearance of righteousness! I do not wish to see such displays of lust again. This is not King Henry's court!"

As the Dowager disappeared into the distant gloom of the gallery, the grinning page following, I realised she had ventured to our chamber with intent, although it was well past the time when she usually retired. I wondered at the reason when I noticed at our feet a crumpled piece of parchment.

Francis had also seen it and picked it up between two fingers, regarding it with uncertainty.

"It appears to be a letter," he said. "Should we return it to her?"

I snatched it from him, and had no compunction about unfolding it and moving to the window where wavering moonlight provided some illumination. I read the note while Francis hovered at my shoulder.

Your Grace,
Your household be dishonoured with activity of your gentlewoman, the Lady Catherine Howard, and your steward, Francis Dereham esquire. For if it shall like you, half an hour after you shall be abed to rise suddenly and visit the ladies' chamber, you shall see that which shall displease you.

It was unsigned.

Francis took the note from my hand and reread it, his jaw clenched in anger. "Spies!" he rasped. "What blackguard has written this? Of course, that whore, Mary Hall, she constantly watches you with spite—I have observed it."

"Hush! Mary Hall cannot write," I said. I turned my back and faced the window. I knew who had written the note. I had kept many in the same hand.

Francis crumpled the note and laid his other hand on my shoulder.

"It has upset you. I shall hunt down who wrote this and run my sword through him!"

"I am not upset, Francis." I said. "And there's no need for you to hunt anyone down. I know who wrote this."

"Who?"

I sighed and said the name with reluctance. "Henry Mannox."

In the ensuing silence, Francis urged me around to face him, a perplexed frown on his face.

"The music tutor? Why would he do such a thing?"

I rubbed my eyes to avoid looking at him.

"We were—he was enamoured of me—once. I expect he wished for us to marry one day. And now, of course—." I shrugged. "Francis, he is merely jealous," I urged as Francis' lips pressed together in anger. "You must leave him be. I—I will talk to him."

Francis grunted his annoyance, and became thoughtful.

"Of course, I remember now!" he said. "Many months hence, I overheard him talking with that—with Mary Hall. She said, 'She is come of noble house and if you should marry her some of her blood will kill you.' The knave responded, 'Hold thy peace, woman, I know her well enough.' I did not think further on it, but clearly they were speaking of you!"

I drew a long breath and exhaled a weary sigh. So, Mary Hall and Henry Mannox were close enough to engage in intimate, candid discussion. Instinct told me that, despite her marriage, Mary Hall had an unrequited love for my music teacher and former lover. It accounted for her offensive and hostile manner towards me, and if I cared enough, I would feel sorry for her. I waved my hand in dismissal. "Aye, it seems I have a habit of attracting unsuitable men," I said wearily to Francis.

Too late I realised my mistake as a pained expression passed across his face. I struggled for a way to console him and drew on the only method at which I excelled.

"Come," I whispered, taking his hand, pressing it against my bosom and tugging him to towards the door of the ladies' chamber. "I have a need for you." As he willingly followed, I added even as I recognised the untruth of the words, "and for only you, my love."

III

THE NEXT DAY, I sought out Henry Mannox and bade him accompany me in a walk in the orchard. He agreed with an eagerness that smote my heart.

"I know that you informed the Duchess of…of my…association with her steward," I began as we picked our way between the rows of apple trees. I glanced at Henry and saw a flush sweep into his cheeks. He did not look at me. He stopped, plucked a russet apple from a tree and regarded it this way and that as if it fascinated him. I paused beside him.

"Henry, it was you who put an end to our courting," I said in a mild accusing tone. "You knew that we could never marry. I do not understand now why you take such a jealous action."

"I am so far in love with you," he said, "that I know not what I do."

Memories of long ago assailed me: happier times, when my family were at their zenith—a Howard was on the throne of England, and another was in the royal cradle. Through those times I loved this man with a light-hearted, childlike gaiety, and with just awakening hungers. We had danced and loved with an unparalleled merriment. My memories of Henry would always be fond for those reasons, and I would always have a place for him in my heart. But now I was capable of a deeper love and my rapacious physical needs were such that not even Francis could completely assuage them. Regardless of Henry Mannox's unsuitability as a husband, there was no place for him in my life now, other than as a pleasant reminder of happier times.

He watched as I stood silent with my thoughts. His mouth curled down, he looked at the apple in his hand and let it drop to the ground.

"I know it's hopeless," he said, his voice cracking. "I shall accept another position I have been offered . . . but if I could ask for one last thing from you?"

I looked at him warily. In full view of some windows of the house, I hoped he would not ask for a kiss. Henry's mouth moved in a sardonic twist.

"Do not fret yourself, I shall not ask for something you've no wish to give," he said and I winced at the pain in his voice. "I ask only that you think of me sometimes."

"Oh, Henry, I will! Of course I will!"

He bowed and turned on his heel. As he left me standing there amid the fruit trees, my promise seemed to hang on the sweet-smelling air.

Had he possessed the gift of foresight, it is sure he would have asked instead for every trace of his existence to be wiped from my life.

IV

I ASSUMED the Dowager's tacit acceptance of my intimacy with Francis, if not of my promise to him, was further proof that she knew I would never marry the King. It no longer mattered that I was not chaste. The advent of the new Queen must also have accounted for the Duke's disregard of me when he visited Norfolk House. It was as if the events of the Horsham tourney had never occurred. It did not matter to me that I would not be Queen, but the thought of never joining the royal court had me seething with frustration.

Towards the end of the summer, the Duke of Norfolk, with Lord William Howard and the Countess of Bridgewater, their families and households, were all in residence at Norfolk House. Meals in the Great Hall became crowded, riotous events. While they three occupied the high table with the Dowager, the rest of us were aligned along trestle tables around the perimeter of the hall. At night, beneath hot blazing torches, the tables groaned with food, rich aromas hung on the thick air and the house rocked with merriment. In the centre of the hall, minstrels and gaily-garbed jesters entertained us, though the music was all but lost in the din of laughter and shouting.

I sat between Joan and Agnes, eating little but drinking too much. In those days, I too often imbibed wine to the point of intoxication, seeking freedom from dissatisfaction and frustration. Such is the bane of wine that it also gave too much rein to the liveliness of my nature.

Through blurred vision, I saw my cousin, Henry Daubeney—the Countess's son and Agnes's stepbrother—vault over the table opposite us and head in our direction. He was several years younger than I, uncouth, pock-marked and gangly, yet with a charming nature. I grinned at him when he stopped before us.

"Ladies! Tell me if I have got the steps of this dance, the Galliard."

He took a step back and gave a few inelegant hops and wild arm waves. We roared with laughter.

"No, you have it wrong, brother," shouted Agnes. "If it please you, let me not ever partner ye!"

"Why, I am quite hurt, sister! Here, let me try again." He repeated the moves. This time, he hurtled backwards into a passing maid bearing a trencher of sweetmeats. Both tumbled to the ground and the platter went flying, falling with a clatter onto the stone flags. There was a short lull in the clamour as dogs scuttled from beneath the tables and pounced on the food; then raucous laughter surged and the din rose to new heights.

Henry helped the maid to her feet, patting her on the rump before approaching us with a grin. He held out his hands beseechingly. "So, someone must show me! I must not disgrace myself with this dance!"

"Catherine knows how to do it," said Joan through a full mouth.

I was throwing back another cup of wine. As all faces turned to me in expectation, I thumped down my cup in delight. Always eager to dance and now freed from what little inhibition I possessed, I sprang to my feet and stepped back from the table. There were excited claps from the ladies and Henry whistled. I waved my hands before me, attempting to dispel the fog of intoxication, and took my position.

"No, no! Here!" With a wild sweep of his arm, Henry cleared the table before him. There were squeals and astonished laughter as plates, food and cups went flying. Dogs barked in excitement. Henry leaned across, holding out his hand.

I took his hand, lifted my blue tinsel skirts, stepped onto my chair and then to the cleared table. I grinned and lifted my arms just as the minstrels with no bidding began to play.

"Wait!" Henry yelled, interrupting again. The minstrels stopped and I placed my hands on my hips in mock annoyance. "It's a dance with a bare head is it not?"

I laughed. A bare head for men, perhaps; nevertheless, I tore my hood from my head and tossed it aside. Whoops and cheers rocked the hall. I was aware of Francis across the way, grinning in appreciation and clapping. Everything else was a colourful blur, the cacophony of sound a dull roar, splintered by the music of the minstrels who resumed playing.

Intoxication could not suppress my enjoyment of that dance, in full view of all; nor did it inhibit the ease with which I performed and improvised on the steps. The Galliard is a zestful, energetic dance, and that night it provided an outlet for my simmering frustrations and passions. When the music ended with a flourish, applause burst forth, with shouts and the thumping of cups on tables. Laughing and out of breath, I curtseyed low.

As the uproar began to subside, Henry helped me to my seat and someone put another cup in my hand. I lifted it to my lips and my gaze wandered to the high table.

The Dowager, Lord William and the Countess were inclined close to each other in deep consultation and from the way their heads turned to me, I knew I was the topic of conversation. At the head of the table sat the Duke of Norfolk, still and silent, staring at me as if seeing me for the first time since the joust. When my eyes met his, he nodded and lifted his cup in salute.

Two days later, whilst I sat in our chamber working on a tapestry with the other ladies, a maid from the Duke's household entered the chamber and scuttled over to me.

"Ma'am, the Duke of Norfolk wishes to see you. He waits for you now in the gardens."

Chapter 11

"We are ever striving after what is forbidden, and coveting what is denied us."

Ovid
Roman classical poet
(43 BC—17 AD)

I

WHEN I EMERGED FROM THE GREAT HALL into the gardens, I saw my Uncle Norfolk standing at the fountain, his hands clasped behind his back, his stance meditative. As I approached, he turned. Despite my heavy brocade gown and hood, I felt exposed beneath his scrutiny.

"Ah, niece," he said. He held out his elbow to me as I came to his side, murmuring a greeting. I slipped my hand into the bend of his arm. "Come, walk with me."

In silence we strolled along the straight pathways that sliced the gardens into symmetrical manicured and fertile patterns. My uncle seemed lost in thought, although intent on leading me somewhere. With my hand clamped close to his side, I could feel his sinews and the heat of his body. At last we came in sight of the river and we left the path to walk across damp grass to the low stone wall surrounding the estate.

Nearby, upriver, immersed in low fog, gleamed Lambeth Palace, residence of Archbishop Thomas Cranmer; across the water, the breath-taking vision of Westminster Palace, with its lancet arches and flying buttresses, wavered through the swirling mist. The pungent smell of the river twitched my nostrils and the fog laid icy fingers on my skin, but could not diminish the thrill I felt when I regarded the view. I gripped my uncle's arm and his attention was drawn to me at last.

"Do you remember we talked of court at the Horsham joust, niece?"

"Yes, uncle, I remember it well."

The Duke grunted in satisfaction. "As I do. However, I also remember you expressed a desire for a simple life, and said that court held no attraction for you. Is it still so?"

I spun to face him.

"Oh, no! Uncle, I was mistaken. I long to go to court! For all these long months, I have desired nothing more. Yet, you—."

He raised his hand to interrupt me.

"I was busy with the King's matters," he said. "However, I do apologise that you have lived in uncertainty and disappointment all these months. I should have been more attentive to your needs."

My head spun with the enormity of my uncle's admission. Here was one of the greatest men in the realm, apologizing to me! I stared at him in awe.

My uncle regarded Westminster again.

"I am glad that you desire a position in the royal court," he said. "You may know that the new Queen is due to arrive in England in a few months, and she will require an English household. With that in mind, yesterday I sought an audience with the King." He stopped.

The tension building, I swallowed a nervous lump in my throat and attempted to still the erratic rise and fall of my chest. My uncle turned back in my direction, and his black eyes bored into me. "I petitioned the King for a place for you as maid of honour to the Queen. He was pleased to grant it."

"Oh!" I could not suppress my cry of delight. If not for my uncle's austerity, I would have thrown my arms about him in gratitude. Instead, I pressed my trembling hands to my lips and gave several joyous jumps. "I thank you, thank you, uncle!"

"Hmmph." He seemed uncomfortable with my exuberance and stepped closer to the wall, and placing his hands on it, leaned to contemplate the view once more. I stood beside him. If ever a heart sung, mine did at that moment. What pleasures now lay before me!

"You do know," said my uncle, cutting me a stern glance, "that when you are at court, you have a duty to maintain our family name and reputation fresh in the King's mind. You must advance members of your family whenever possible and move His Grace for whatever favours our family requires."

"Yes, yes," I replied. I could not see how a mere maid of honour could have such influence. I imagined little contact with the King himself.

I soon understand the nature of the influence my uncle planned.

In an abrupt movement, he turned to me and took my face in one hand, his fingers grasping my jaw. My breath caught in my chest as he scrutinised my features. When his hot thumb passed across my lips then slipped between them, I gasped with shock and swung my head away, the taste of his skin burning my tongue. His hand dropped, brushing against my bosom.

I staggered away from him, wanting to flee. It was the view across the river that stopped me . . . that, and the surge of some dangerous, forbidden thrill that I both abhorred and—I confess—embraced.

There was a small, knowing smile on my uncle's mouth. In a languid manner, he leaned back against the wall and crossed his arms.

"You are by far the most comely woman in the family," he remarked. "The King has always had a weakness for Howard women. There was your cousin, Anne, of course." The Duke sighed then smiled briefly with bared teeth. "And," he murmured, leaning towards me in emphasis, "Your cousin, Mary Boleyn."

Mary Boleyn, sister to Anne. Mary Boleyn, so easily overlooked, yet a woman who had been one of the most influential women in the realm. Mary Boleyn, the—.

"*The King's mistress,*" said my uncle in a low, ardent tone, leaving me in no doubt about the role he really wished for me at the royal court.

I gaped at him in horror. Many rumours had come to my ears since arriving at Norfolk House, of the King's physical condition—the King was so fat, it was said two large men could fit into his doublet with room to spare. His stench announced his arrival into a room long before he entered it. His ulcerous thigh oozed green pus or, when the wound closed over, turned black and swollen. And then there was his nature: bad-tempered, violent, and unreasonable. Yet, my uncle wished me to share a bed with this man? My belly churned with distaste.

The Duke left the wall. His large hands went around my neck, but gently, almost a caress. Hypnotised, I watched his face loom closer.

"I am not one to bestow a lover before savouring the offering myself," he said.

His breath fanned out across my face as his head lowered towards mine.

I had imagined his attentions as a child, in innocent fantasies hugged secretly to my heart. He had been my hero, who held for me a potent allure with his power and maturity. But I had not imagined this . . . and could never have anticipated the devastating effect the prospect of the Duke's intimate, forbidden touch had on me. At once frightened and excited, I gasped.

The Duke's hands dropped from my face. His own countenance bore circles of colour high up on his cheekbones, but his otherwise cold impassivity told me his attentions had been an inspection, nothing more. I staggered away from him, a lump of fear and disgust in my throat, tears stinging my eyes. With a sob, I picked up my skirts to hasten across the grass. If going to court meant more of this sort of confusing encounter, I would rather remain obscure!

I heard pants behind me, then the Duke grasped me by the arm and spun me around.

"How much do you want this position, Catherine?" he said, his face tense. "How much do you long for beautiful gowns and jewels, for dancing and excitement . . . for *life* ?"

How much, indeed! I wanted it so much I would not think of unpleasantness . . . not now.

"I want it," I whispered. "I want it more than I can say."

His gaze swept my face, lingering on my mouth.

"Good," he said through gritted teeth. "Prepare yourself for changes, Catherine."

He released me, and strode away, back to Norfolk House, now veiled in eddying fog . . .

II

WITH DESPERATE DETERMINATION, I turned my mind from the Duke's alarming manner and acknowledged my first pressing tasks in preparing for my new life: I must tell Francis and also Father Vyncent of the development. The former was not a duty I looked forward to and, typically, I ignored the unpleasant prospect for several days. I visited Father Vyncent at once in the vestry.

He was cautious with his congratulations.

"It's what you have wanted, child, so I am pleased for you," he said, adding, "I shall pray for you." I detected anxiety in his manner.

Francis appeared not to notice the activity that now surged around me: the fittings for many new gowns, the attention of the Dowager as she attempted to instruct me on the finer points of being a maid of honour, the envy of my friends. He appeared distracted, and I suspected he was avoiding me, although he still stole into my bed every night to take his pleasure.

Three nights after my uncle's announcement, I decided to relate my news. Francis and I lay on my bed, the curtains shielding us from the sleeping forms of the other ladies in the chamber. A single candle burned on the wall above our heads, and we were naked and entwined amidst tangled bed covers.

I opened my mouth to speak when Francis sat up. He retrieved his doublet from the foot of the bed and rummaged through its inner pockets.

"What are you doing?" I asked, running an idle finger down his spine and idly admiring the way his smooth, brawny shoulders tapered to his hips. He stopped searching and began to toss something in his hand. I rose to my knees and moved alongside him, my hair falling over my nakedness. He was lobbing a leather pouch, which clinked as it flew through the air and landed in his palm. "What's that?"

Francis picked up my hand and pressed the pouch into it. It felt heavy and I discerned the shape of coins.

"It's money," he said unnecessarily. "My money. I want you to keep it for me."

I blinked in surprise. "Why?"

Francis did not meet my eyes and delayed answering. Distracted, he scooped my hair back over my shoulders. I forgot the pouch as he began to caress me.

I moved closer on my knees to nuzzle his neck, the pouch falling from my weakened fingers. As it fell to his thighs, it roused Francis from his abstraction. He stopped the delicious attentions and placed the pouch back in my hand, holding my fingers closed around it.

"I am going away," he said with a grimace. "I want you to keep this for me until I return."

When I gaped at him, he continued with a rush, his grip tightening on my hand. "The Dowager came to me two days ago," he said, with an earnest expression. "She said the Duke of Norfolk is seeking young, healthy men to assist him with—some business in Ireland. She asked me if I would be interested."

He swallowed as I continued to stare speechless at him. "Catherine, I would have said I was not interested, but then the Dowager said it was a fine opportunity for someone like me to earn great riches! I began to think how wonderful it would be for us when I returned in a year or so, richer than our in wildest imaginations! So I said I'd like to go. I—er—go tomorrow."

I reeled with shock.

"*Tomorrow?*" I exclaimed. Francis shushed me and gestured in the direction of the sleeping ladies. "And you accepted without talking to me?" I whispered. "And what sort of business in Ireland? I never knew my uncle had business in Ireland."

Francis' gaze slid from mine. "It's—er—trade, I understand," he said with vagueness. I scowled at him in suspicion. Piracy was rampant off the coast of Ireland—could it be this that had tempted Francis, this in which my uncle was somehow involved?

"Oh, Catherine, it doesn't matter what manner of business it is, does it?" he said eagerly. "Just think of what the money could mean to us—a large estate, a beautiful house! And the sooner I go, the sooner we can have those things!"

If I were the sort of person to whom distant future comforts meant more than the pursuit of more immediate gratification, Francis' ambitions would have gladdened my heart. All I felt was deep bereavement. Being able to have him visit occasionally while I was at court was better than not seeing him at all.

"Catherine, do not look like that." He took the pouch, laid it aside and grasped my hands. "It will only be for a year. Why, you'll be too busy to miss me!"

"You know about me being maid of honour to the new Queen?" I asked.

"Aye, the Dowager told me. I was waiting for you to tell me yourself." His fingers entwined with mine. "You are sweet to delay giving me your news for fear of upsetting me, but now, you see, I shall be happy, for I will be working hard for our advancement!"

His enthusiasm and devotion were poignant. Pushing away the thought that they were misguided, I loosened my hands, wriggled closer and straddled his thighs to face him. I ran my fingernails lightly through the sparse hair on his chest.

"But I shall miss you," I said tearfully. "Is it possible to die from unsatisfied lust? For if so, I surely will."

Francis grinned. "I would rather you saved it all for my return, rather than die from it," he said. "However, if you believe you are in such peril . . . nay, if we are both in peril . . . I have some suggestions."

A reluctant smile broke through my misery. "What suggestions?"

He grasped my thighs and pulled me closer. The hair on his chest tickled my skin as he recommenced the caressing of my bosom. "You need a good imagination," he said. "First, we must close our eyes and imagine ourselves here, just like this." I shivered and closed my eyes. "Then we must imagine my fingers doing just *this*—." He blazed a light circular trail down my body, arriving at my inner thighs where his fingers paused. When I grunted and wriggled, his teasing fingers moved inward and I exhaled a sharp hiss. I writhed in response to the exquisite torment he inflicted, fearful that I might scream. Overwhelmed, my hand rushed downwards to detain his gifted fingers—and was distracted by a satisfying development at his loins. "And your hand—well, doing what it will . . . aye, that will do it." Francis' whisper was lost in my mouth.

Later, he asked, "Do you think such daydreams will forestall your demise?"

I was leaning against him in trembling weakness. At his question, I roused myself.

"I have a poor imagination," I said, straightening. I touched his mouth in fascination. "However, I have a good memory. Perhaps you would like to provide also a memory of what your mouth can do to me?"

Francis grasped me beneath the arms and laid me down on the bed. "Gladly," he said. "The memory of delectable flavours will serve me well in my own loneliness."

III

RAIN FELL FROM LOW GREY SKIES the next day when Francis departed—a cold, sleeting downpour that transformed the forecourt to a large puddle and heightened my melancholy. I stepped out into the torrent as a stablehand brought a horse to the front entrance and waited whilst Francis loaded the saddlebags with the few belongings he needed for his adventure. The rain soaked my cloak in seconds and needled my face.

When Francis finished his loading, he turned to me. Uncaring of observing eyes, he drew me into a tight embrace. I clung to him.

"I shall never live to say you have swerved," he whispered in my ear. "Remain true to me, Catherine."

"Oh, Francis!"

His arms tightened and it was only a delicate cough from the shivering stableboy that ended the embrace. He took the reins and was mounted before I could reach for him again. When he wheeled the horse around and spurred it to a gallop, I picked up my skirts and ran after him through ankle-high water. In seconds, he and his mount were a dark shape in the mist, the horse's galloping hooves a fading echo. I slowed to a walk, then a stop, and remained standing until I could no longer see him and there was no sound but the pounding of the rain.

I turned and slowly retraced my steps to the house. As I did so, a movement at a window on the top level caught my eye. I glanced up. Through the gloom, I discerned the watching figures of the Duke and Dowager Duchess of Norfolk.

IV

ONE NIGHT, shortly before I was to leave Norfolk House for Greenwich Palace, the Dowager came to me as I prepared for bed. The ladies fell silent as she entered the chamber and approached me, leaning on her page. Her face was grey and drawn.

"Child, I have news for you . . . unpleasant news."

I stared at her, sickening fear surging within my chest. The Dowager lowered her gaze.

"The Duke of Norfolk has had word . . . the ship on which your—young Dereham sailed was set upon by pirates. They plundered the ship and attacked all on board. There were no survivors."

She still did not look at me before turning and walking slowly from the room. I sank to the bed, mute with shock, not noticing when Agnes sat beside me and placed a tentative arm around my shoulder.

Francis . . . dead!

Images of him swam before my eyes . . . my saviour at the misty lake . . . honourable and strong at the joust . . . near-naked and alluring in the tent, and at the decrepit inn . . . my champion in face of the Dowager's wrath . . . selfless and skilled on that last night . . . his tight embrace in the rain before he left.

No more would I see his handsome face and his smile; never again would I feel the warmth of his body, the thrill of his touch—or bask in the safety of his love.

A sob of loss burst from my lips and I lowered my face to my hands.

As I did, the oddity of the Dowager coming to me with this news struck me. Was it a tacit acceptance of my marriage? Or was she making absolutely certain I knew Francis was dead?

And why did Mary Hall's warning to Henry Mannox persist—echoing in my mind: "She is come of noble house and if you should marry her some of her blood will kill you"?

V

I LEFT NORFOLK HOUSE by canopied barge early on the first day of 1540, escorted by my uncle the Duke of Norfolk. My paltry belongings had gone by road to Greenwich Palace the previous day, so nothing but a shared melancholy encumbered us.

The Christmas season had been wretched. Not only had Francis' death left me reeling, but word had also come that my father had died in Calais. And at Oxenheath, Mary had finally succumbed to her breathing malady. I wept over Mary's sad demise. Although I had seen nothing of him in recent years, my father's loss heightened my sense of vulnerability, and I grieved for him more deeply than I could have anticipated. I didn't expect the forever-detached Duke of Norfolk to lament the loss of his youngest brother, even though the two had fought valiantly and successfully together at the Battle of Branxton* twenty-five years previously; yet my uncle's appearance all through Christmas had been grim and pained, making me ponder the unthinkable. That morning, sitting opposite me on the barge, he seemed sunk in dark reflections, which did little to lighten my own ill-humour.

I had not encountered him since the day on the riverbank when he had given me news of my appointment to the royal court. I told myself I was glad of it. After Francis' departure, the Duke had left Norfolk House for Kenninghall, returning just before news came of Francis' death. Now unfashionably clean-shaven, the Duke was one of the few men who, in my opinion, looked better with facial hair than without, and he suffered for the alteration. He was a man whose strong face cast itself without effort into a vibrant, charismatic expression; yet now I found him plain and aged, with deeply etched grooves between his nose and mouth, and slack, wan cheeks. Shoulders bowed, his dull, heavy-lidded eyes remained riveted on the passing dreary scenery. Only the green velvet and ermine trim of his cloak and the silver Lord Treasurer's staff in his clutch bore the magnificence that usually accompanied him.

The dead of winter had silenced the birds and other creatures, the only sound being the gentle sough of the river's brown ice-slicked water as the barge slid through it, the rhythmic muted splash of the barge poles and the occasional murmurs of the bargemen. The canopy overhead did little to shield against the cold, which lay as blades of ice on my cheeks and nose. My breath formed puffs of white around my face and I huddled closer into my own cloak in a futile attempt to keep warm.

A movement from my uncle drew my reluctant attention: as he gazed at the scenery, lost in thought, his hand drifted to the neckline of his cloak and tugged at it and the doublet beneath, a brief grimace distorting his face. I gave a start of shock. Against the skin of his neck I glimpsed the harsh fabric of a hair shirt.

Confused, I looked away before he noticed my stare. Of course, the Duke upheld the conservative Catholic faith and traditions, but never would I have thought that he possessed scruples or humility. Yet, in his wearing of the hair shirt, I saw a conscience at work, pitiless chastisement for some weakness or sin, and a display of character. When the loss of Francis and my father left me feeling unprotected, with lifting heart, I embraced this indication that in my uncle could be, after all, a powerful refuge amidst my defencelessness and uncertainty.

With this wondrous inference, my attention shifted back to him. Perhaps feeling my gaze, he looked at me. He straightened, animation replacing the dullness in his countenance.

I wondered how I had ever thought him plain.

"The King doesn't like women who are pale and lifeless, Catherine," he snapped. "Be of better cheer!"

At once disheartened by his acerbity, I lowered my gaze. My heart gave a leap at his reminder: I was to meet the King at Greenwich Palace this morning. The King would then make haste to Rochester where he planned to surprise his Queen, Anne of Cleves, newly arrived on English soil. In three days, the King and Queen would return to Greenwich Palace when their marriage would take place and I would assume my new role as one of the Queen's maids of honour.

"I hope you are cognisant of the honour the King does you and our family by agreeing to meet with you before he goes to Rochester." The Duke glared at me, leaning forward and pressing his fists on his knees.

* Flodden Field

"Yes, uncle," I murmured. Indeed the influence my uncle must have exerted to arrange for an audience at such a time did impress me. Why he saw a need for such urgency, I could only guess. And my guess ensured my cheeks grew colder and prompted a nauseating churn in my belly—I must be presented to the King before he set eyes on his German wife!

As I quailed at the realisation, my uncle bit out an annoyed mutter: "I will put colour in your cheeks!" I looked up in apprehension. In an adroit movement—how had I ever thought him aged!—the Duke rose from his seat and, in one stride, crossed the small space between us to stand before me.

His cloak swirled opened. Of its own wanton volition, my enthralled gaze dropped to the level of his loins, and my skin began to prickle. Like a sufferer of dizziness who sees the world tilting wildly and must cling to something solid until the faintness passes, my mind latched onto the masculine allure before me, and all that it spoke of in terms of power and security. This I could cope with; beyond it, turmoil raged.

"Stand up," ordered my uncle, gesturing with his staff.

I did as bid, and a harsh grip spun me around to face the riverbank. The slightest hesitation, and the grip left my arm and his arm passed—in a sensual caress, I imagined—about my waist, pulling me back against a hard, sinewy body. My mind in disarray, even through my voluminous skirts I thought I could feel every outline of the Duke's form. Heat swamped my face, but it was the vision on the riverbank, now sliding into view, which drew a loud gasp from my lips.

Wondrous Greenwich Palace, England's largest palace after Whitehall!

The vast rambling structure of red and black-patterned brick with white mortar joins leapt out of the bleak landscape. Filling my field of vision with its vivid and warm splendour, its gleaming carved battlements of gold beasts holding painted poles and gilded veins dazzling my eyes, it struck me with open-mouthed awe.

The hold around my waist seemed to grow tighter and the Duke's breath feathered my cheek. But was it his own passion and arousal that set me trembling wildly—or my own?

"Just think on it," he whispered. "All that could be yours, Catherine. Recall what I told you on the riverbank before Christmas—and just think of that being yours!"

I nodded, speechless. Beholding Greenwich Palace, being held by and against the strength of the Duke of Norfolk, I could forget my fears. My long-held belief that court life was cruel, dangerous and savage seemed but childish folly. The design of holding the King in the palm of my hand, and all the advantages it could bring with it—not only for me but also for my family—enchanted me.

Overwhelmed, I turned in the Duke's hold and smiled at him when his dark gaze met mine. For an instant, a deep rapport bound us. A rarely seen smile cut his usually sombre features, and his hold around my waist tightened.

The shouting of the bargemen as our vessel came alongside the dock broke the reverie. The Duke dropped his arm from me and I staggered backwards. Grimacing in some deep fury, he tugged at his neckline and rubbed at his reddened skin with a shaking hand.

I do not generally dwell on other people's thoughts and emotions, but I knew at that instant why my uncle wore the hair shirt. The reason lay in his tormented and guilt-ridden expression when he regarded me, and in the grit of his teeth and white-knuckled fists when he dropped his gaze to his feet.

Whatever battle waged within him, and while I waited in tense confusion, his continuing with the present course of action proved to be the ultimate victor. As soon as the barge ground against the dock, he raised his head and, without looking at me again, leapt ashore with the vigour of a man half his age, leaving a bargeman to help me disembark. As for me, the startling interlude and the splendour before me provoked a trancelike state that persisted until we passed through the gatehouse of the Palace and across the small outer courtyard. The Duke walked before me with long, swift strides, his cloak billowing and his form bristling. I had to rouse myself from my daze and run to keep up with him.

We entered the inner courtyard and the bustle of the palace. Servants scurried about on their various tasks, and courtiers ebbed and flowed like a colourful tide from every direction. Many of them stopped and bowed as the Duke passed, and curious eyes followed our progress. As I attempted to ignore my sickening nervousness, my uncle, with fists clenched, displayed calmness and control.

"The royal apartments are on the first level," he said, as we ascended a flight of stone stairs. "The King's overlook the river, and the Queen's, the gardens. Try to remember the way," he added sarcastically.

Greenwich Palace was huge, containing rooms for royalty and hundreds of courtiers above a labyrinth of servants' quarters. We proceeded in haste down a wide passage. Cold and damp draughts lifted my skirts and gave me goose flesh. I gripped my cloak around me with pinched fingers made colder by my growing apprehension.

"You must change your clothing before seeing the King," the Duke went on. "Your belongings should be already installed in your chamber. I hope your grandmother equipped you with suitable gowns?"

A servant rounded a corner in the passageway and scuttled towards us. "Here, lad!" The Duke shrugged off his cloak. "Take this to my quarters. I'll be there anon." The servant scampered away with the cloak and we rushed onwards.

With every step my awe and trepidation heightened. I longed for my uncle to provide some reassurance. As we entered a wide gallery with portraits along the walls, I summoned enough courage to reach out and touch his arm. He stopped, turned, and studied me with little interest and great impatience.

I quailed before him. Unable to express my need to connect with him again, instead I gestured to the portraits. "Who are these people?"

After a second, the Duke turned to the nearest painting—it featured a plain, dark-haired man with a mild expression.

"The late King Henry, this King's father." He waved at the next portrait of a beautiful fair woman. "Our King's late mother, Elizabeth of York."

I followed him as we proceeded down the gallery. "Prince Arthur, the King's late brother . . . his sisters, the Princesses Mary and Margaret."

We stopped before the second-last portrait, this of a plain woman with a meek expression. "Queen Jane," said my uncle. He pointed to the last portrait—an infant boy. "Prince Edward."

For a second we stood in silence. I dwelt on absent portraits: of Queen Katherine and the Princess Mary. When I perceived the Duke's sudden sardonic expression, I knew he reflected as I then did on the absence of portraits of our Howard kin—Queen Anne and the Princess Elizabeth.

The tension between us abated. The Duke spun on his heel.

"Come, niece," he said quietly, "We must be quick."

The many doors on the main gallery, and the numerous smaller passages leading from it, indicated the vast size of the Queen's apartments. However, we encountered no one. I understood most of the Queen's 130-strong household would establish itself over the next few days, and then this part of the Palace would be bustling like a small village.

My uncle threw open two large doors at the end of the gallery and strode inside. As I followed, I knew at once I had stepped into the Queen's chambers. Hand-knotted red carpet— a rare luxury—covered the floors and rich tapestries adorned the walls. A large four-poster bed stood on a plinth in the centre of the room with coverings of crimson silk and ermine. A velvet curtained alcove stretching along one side of the chamber indicated the sleeping quarters of the Queen's ladies-in-waiting.

Open casements had cast a chill on the chamber. My uncle muttered, strode to the windows and slammed them closed before beckoning me to a doorway in the far corner.

Through the doorway rose a flight of narrow stairs, and another descended into hollow darkness below. The Duke ascended the steps two at a time and opened a single door at the top. Muted light penetrated the stairwell.

I climbed the stairs and stepped into a small, clean bedchamber with several large windows through which cold daylight poured. Three beds, several heavy chests and two armouries made up its only furnishings. My uncle strode to an armoury, opened it and began to sort through the garments inside. I stepped closer and saw my own clothes. Bemused, I waited while he extracted a white brocade gown trimmed and embroidered in gold and tossed it onto one bed.

"Wear that," he said. He waved towards my head. "And whatever goes with it."

I regarded the gown in doubt. I had a generous bosom and the bodice of the gown was low cut. I wondered if it was an appropriate garment to wear for one's first meeting with the King.

My uncle clicked his fingers in exasperation and glared at me. "Make haste, niece! This gown will do, I know the King's tastes! I'll fetch a woman to help you."

Before he left the chamber, he paused, and then he turned and looked at me.

"You have lost your father, and your—." He stopped, for an instant pinching the corners of his closed eyes. I thought he grimaced, yet when he spoke again, severity had reoccupied his features. "I know that you are looking to me for support at this time, and . . . ," he paused, while I clasped my hands together in hope, "I fear that at times I may miscalculate the best way to provide it." As he looked into my face, gentleness and regret passed over his own, prompting him to place an agitated hand across his mouth as if to wipe such feelings away. "I know not how to best deal with my attractive—and talented—nieces," he muttered.

Compassion overwhelmed me. "Uncle—."

He threw up a hand to silence me, drawing a deep breath. Composure restored, he said, "No matter what I do, I hope you will remember, niece, that as you are a Howard, I have your best interests, and our family's, uppermost in my mind at all times."

I dropped my gaze to my feet and nodded.

"Also remember this," he went on with restored acerbity. "I will be your champion and protector, Catherine, if you do the right thing by me. If you do not—for instance, if you openly indulge in wanton behaviour as appears to be your weakness—I shall show you no mercy."

He did not wait for my response, which was well—for I was too stunned to make one. He swept from the room. I listened for the clatter of his feet on the steps and the opening and slamming of the door to the Queen's bedchamber, before I sank onto a bed, my knees shaking. I blinked away the tears, trying desperately not to cry, for it would not do to have the marks of tears on my face when I met the King.

The sobering prospect settled me and I drew a calming breath. The silence and solitude opened the door on unpleasant thoughts, provoked by my uncle's criticism of my behaviour. Although I tried in typical fashion to slam it shut, on this occasion I could not. Words once spoken by Father Vyncent during one of our many midnight discussions drifted into my mind, easing it at once: "A conscience thrives in self-reflection, my child; and if you should forsake your conscience for the sake of pursuing pleasures of the flesh, you will be on the short road to chaos."

For the first time in my life, I suspect, I then paid heed to my conscience.

Indeed, I had been wanton, as my uncle probably knew or strongly suspected—with Henry Mannox, with Francis, and no doubt I would gladly have been with Tom Culpeper if the right moment had presented itself. I relished the company—and physical appeal—of men, and enjoyed wielding over them the feminine power I possessed, even while I obtained an intense sensual delight in it. I had pursued pleasures of the flesh and, if I believed Father Vyncent, chaos would be my lot as a result, unless I confronted my failings and did something about them.

In my defence, having been raised in the permissive environment of the Dowager's household, on attaining womanhood it had never occurred to me to question my physical reactions to sexual provocation, much less abhor them or deny myself satisfaction, despite whatever minor qualms of conscience and thoughts of witchcraft would smite me. My fault had been in allowing my impulses and my conscience to be ill-matched, so the latter could be easily disregarded.

But, no more, I vowed then and there.

Virtuously, as my head ached with this unaccustomed examination, I imagined I had now taken the first step towards a safer and more peaceful life.

Safe.

I am not clever as my cousin Anne was, but her fate taught me that there was a very practical reason to behave well at the King's court. There were eyes and ears everywhere and I could trust no one. Now that I was at Greenwich Palace—and especially if my uncle's plans for me were realised—it would serve me well to constrain my inclination for licentious behaviour. I had no wish to end my life on the block!

I hastily resolved to be virtuous and chaste until such a time as I married.

I pictured myself as demure, serious, dignified and pure. Then—perhaps because he had just now been in my thoughts for the first time in many a month—I at once envisioned a laughing Tom Culpeper. Giggles bubbled to my lips in response, before all my dread, confusion and fear washed away on a tide of intense merriment.

It was well that I could find humour in the situation, for otherwise no doubt I would have fled without a second thought from the dreary life that now, with my vow of chastity, I had set before myself.

A STOUT, rosy-cheeked woman in servant's garb helped me with my gown and matching French hood. I stepped out into the gallery where my uncle waited. He said nothing, but turned and walked ahead of me down the gallery. Struggling with my new demure guise, I followed.

I knew we had entered the King's apartments by the hushed atmosphere and the ostentatious décor. Ornate, gleaming tables, and plush upholstered chairs lined the passageways, and glittering trinkets adorned every available table space. Most of the priceless tapestries on the walls depicted religious themes. I recognised a scene of Christ in the Garden of Gesthsemane, another of Daniel in the Lion's Den. These vast furnishings also kept out the draughts, so here it was warm, as well as quiet, our hurrying footsteps on the polished plaster floors the only sound.

The dim hallway ended in two large and gleaming doors, firmly closed and guarded by two armoured knights bearing flashing halberds. With a clink and a swish the halberds crossed as we approached. My uncle stopped and waited for me to come alongside him.

"This is the King's receiving chamber," he said. "Keep your eyes lowered at all times and do not speak unless addressed. Is that clear?"

My composure deserted me. I pressed my fists to my pounding chest and licked my lips. To my surprise, my uncle smiled.

"You shall do very well," he said in a low voice. "Be as your nature dictates, it will be your main asset."

The Duke turned to the guards and nodded. The halberds swished apart, and one guard pounded the floor three times with the hilt of his weapon. The doors opened a crack and a small bearded face peeked through it; my uncle leaned forward and I heard him murmur my name. The face retreated.

The voice within boomed: "My Lord Treasurer, the Duke of Norfolk and the Lady Catherine Howard!" The doors yawned open and I blinked as bright daylight poured down on us. As one, the Duke and I moved forward into the presence of our mighty King.

Chapter 12

"To be a king and wear a crown is a thing more glorious to them that see it than it is pleasant to them that bear it."

Elizabeth I, Queen of England (daughter of King Henry VIII)
(1533—1603)

I

DESPITE THE DUKE'S ORDER to keep my eyes lowered, I disobeyed it from the instant I stepped into the receiving chamber, for at once a gathering at the end of the long room drew my rapt attention. Two men stood before a dais, shielding from our view him who sat there. One of the men, tall and thin, wore clerical habit—a black doublet and skirt. The other, taller and stout, wore a full, wide-sleeved gown of black silk, bordered with bands of gold and trimmed in sable, over an underdress of fig-brown. With heads together in intense consultation, neither one turned at our approach.

"The gentleman on the right is Bishop Stephen Gardiner," said the Duke in an undertone, referring to the tall, thin man. "The other is Lord Cromwell." I detected a barely constrained note of derision.

The chamber possessed a stark, austere magnificence: the white polished plaster floors bore a mock-marble effect, and ensconced in the dark, gleaming wall panelling were three genuine marble fireplaces. Apart from four pillars of carved gold on either side of a central aisle, the chamber had no decoration. Silvery sunshine, devoid of warmth, poured through the large glass-paned windows uninhibited by drapes. The chamber attracted attention to the dais, and kept it there.

As we proceeded down the aisle, our echoing footsteps splintered the silence. Bishop Gardiner glanced around. He straightened at once. Lord Cromwell—heavy of jowls, with a large, bulbous nose—directed his attention a second later and also stared. They separated. In the split second before I remembered to lower my gaze, I perceived a glittering colossus of a man perched awkwardly on the edge of a large carved chair on the dais.

Willing myself to remain calm, I walked on, seeing only my skirts and the white floor beneath my feet. No one spoke. I stopped when my toes reached the red velvet-covered dais and lowered myself to my knees before my King, clasping my hands before me. I could feel the heat radiating from him, and my nostrils twitched at his aroma: heavy, spicy perfume over a pungent natural scent. He had thrust out before him one yellow, silk-clad leg; the other, bearing most of his weight, was bent beneath the chair. He sat as if poised against pain. Of his clothing, I noted a pleated skirt of deep blue silk and a sleeved doublet of the same material, braided with silver, and set with emeralds in gold mounts. Over this, he wore a surcoat of white velvet, embroidered with gold and lined with sable; square-toed, white silk shoes were the only other item of clothing my dazzled lowered gaze could perceive.

I started when he spoke, the hairs on my arms rising with the deep contralto rumbling from depths of a vast chest.

"Who do we have here, Norfolk?"

My uncle replied with a subtle deference in his tone. "Your Grace, this is my niece, Lady Catherine Howard."

"Ah, yes. Yet another niece of yours, eh, Norfolk?"

There ensued some discreet sniggers of amusement from the other two men. I sensed annoyance radiating from the form before me, and for the first time the sheer brazenness of my uncle struck me. I held my breath, wondering if we would be dismissed without further ado. The King's hand came into my line of vision after several tense seconds, during which time my skin prickled as the King subjected my features to intense inspection. Large and fat, with bejewelled rings imbedded in pink flesh, the hand went beneath my chin. Hot, clammy fingers exerted an upward pressure. At last, I looked into the face of England's revered and feared monarch.

Beneath a bonnet of black velvet embellished with a large, curling red feather, small, half-closed eyes of an indeterminate colour scrutinised my face. As my eyes met his, patchy colour appeared beneath a sparse, ginger beard and swept upwards over puffy, florid cheeks. His small mouth twisted in sardonic relief on noting the colour of my hair and eyes—glad, perhaps, that I bore no reminder of one of my dark-featured cousins. With no subtlety, his gaze dropped and he leaned back to appraise openly my neck and bosom.

What he perceived must have pleased him, for he inclined forward, thrusting his face into mine. Eagerness and appreciation further heightened the colour of his face and widened his eyes—I saw now they were a faded blue, the whites dull and tinged with yellow. Rather than sway away from him as my instinct urged, I summoned control and dropped my gaze. Even in my disconcerted state, I was able to note the rich gold chain around the King's neck, from which was suspended a medallion embedded with rubies; and across his shoulders, the Collar of the Garter—made up of exquisite goldsmith's work and brilliant emeralds. The sight grounded me and soothed my jangled nerves.

"You are Lord Edmund Howard's daughter, then," the King said to me in a low and intimate tone, breaking another taut silence that had descended on our group.

"Yes, Your Grace."

"I was sorry to hear of his demise . . . he was a fine man and a noble soldier. England is grateful to him."

I looked up at once. The sincerity of the King's kindness struck me with tearful gratitude. Not only had I received little sympathy over the death of my father, but I knew "fine" and "noble" were not words commonly used to describe him. I suspected his memory would forever be bounded by much less flattering adjectives.

"I thank you, Your Grace," I said. "Your words bring consolation in my unhappiness."

To my astonishment, the King's big hand went to my face and his clammy palm rested against my cheek. I sensed a ripple of surprise through the three men watching.

"Tis a sad occurrence when a lass loses her father," the King said. More tears accumulated against my will: his touch reminded me of the soothing hand my father had laid on my cheek after the Dowager had smote it so long ago, on one last occasion that I had seen him. The King straightened and clicked his fingers in Lord Cromwell's direction. "Thomas, bring Lady Catherine a footstool to sit on! She is in some distress."

The eminent Privy Seal gaped before carefully assuming an impassive expression. "Your Grace," he demurred, "we really must make haste to Rochester—."

I watched the King's eyes turn dagger-like and the florid colour heighten until I feared his head would explode. A lesser man would have quailed at the frightening sight, but Lord Cromwell stood his ground and met the onslaught of abrupt fury with an impassive countenance.

"At once!" the King roared. Bishop Gardiner flinched, and even my uncle shifted his weight from one leg to the other in apparent discomfort. Lord Cromwell flicked a glance at my direction, and for the first time I looked into the face of the King's most trusted advisor. A startled expression passed across his pale, heavy features before he bowed and hastened to do the King's bidding. I noticed the Duke watching proceedings with immense and, it seemed to me, gleeful interest.

When I had taken a seat on a padded footstool, the King leaned closer to me. I issued an embarrassed, tremulous smile before again dropping my gaze. My chest rose and fell with rapid breathing. I tried to hold my breath, but only issued a strained gasp after several taut seconds. The sound seemed to enchant the King further, for once again he turned my face to his with his spongy, hot fingers and I looked into his ardent expression. I sensed the tension and incredulity of the watching men.

The King cleared his throat. "Tell me, my dear, do you like music?"

In truth, music was only useful to me as an accompaniment to dancing, but I provided the suitable answer to the music-loving King: "Yes, Your Grace. I have been tutored since a child in the spinet and virginals and music provides me with much pleasure."

"Good, good!" The King nodded in satisfaction. "And how is your scholarship?"

At once, I floundered. My education had been rudimentary—skimming over literature and philosophy, never touching languages, and concentrating on the skills needed to keep a large house. I would not be able to hold my own in the intellectual debates I knew the King enjoyed.

The Duke came to the rescue. "Catherine's education has been suitable for her upbringing and station in life, Your Grace."

I had to admire the slippery way in which the question was dealt with; the King nodded, showing no sign of disappointment or suspicion. "Excellent," he said. "What about dancing? Do you like to dance, Lady Catherine?"

"Oh, yes!" This time, I could not restrain my enthusiasm, and I beamed at the King. He blinked and his thin lips parted in surprise. I attempted to assume some dignity and maturity, but I had done little but imagine twirling in the Palace's Great Hall for many months, and my longing could not be suppressed. I clasped my hands. "I love to dance!"

"Then I shall look forward to your gracing our halls," the King said. He shifted his position, a wince of pain and annoyance passed over his countenance. At once, pity consumed me.

"Perhaps, Your Grace, you would do me the honour of dancing with me," I said before I could stop myself. Once the words escaped my lips, I froze in horror at my forwardness, and the three watching men stiffened in shock.

However, I had paid the King the ultimate compliment, overlooking the invalidity and age that he wore with such reluctance.

He smiled at me and reached down to grasp my hands, bringing them up between us. "It would be my honour to partner such a rose," he said, adding with embittered emphasis to Lord Cromwell, who had urged him to marry a foreigner, "an *English* rose."

In silence, the King turned back to me. He lifted my hands to his mouth and kissed them.

Summoning every particle of my composure, I batted my lashes and smiled. Delighted, the King's eyes flickered over my face, and dropped to my neck and bosom once more.

"Pretty," he murmured. "However, such skin should be decorated with jewels . . . do you not possess any?"

Again, I faltered. If I owned to not having any jewellery, it would cast a poor reflection on my family.

Once again, the Duke intervened.

"Catherine has led a simple, quiet life in the country, Your Grace," he said. "She has had no need for baubles and gems."

"I see, yes, quite right," concurred the King. The Duke's answer had pleased him. He squeezed my hands. "However, now you are at my court and must have some jewels. I will see to it. Meanwhile," he released my hands and again shifted his position with a grimace. "I can see my good men here bristling with impatience, so I must depart for Rochester to surprise my foreign wife."

I rose and stepped to the Duke's side as the King struggled to stand, and I curtseyed with lowered eyes as he stepped off the dais with a pained grunt. He lumbered down the chamber, the Bishop and Lord Cromwell in his wake, the Duke and I watching the procession with a growing realisation that I had passed my trial by fire.

When the door of the chamber slammed shut after them, my knees gave way and I sank to the dais with a sigh of relief.

My uncle came to stand before me. I saw only his legs and shoes; I craned my neck to look up at him, a small smile of triumph forming on my face.

Delight had flushed his own face.

"You did well, Catherine," he said. "I am proud of you." He held out his hand. "Come, we cannot stay here, I'll take you back to your chambers."

Thrilled that I had pleased him, I reached up and slipped my hand into his grasp. Unlike the King's, it was cool and lean, and when I stood before him, my fingers grasped it tighter, relishing the difference.

The Duke did not disengage his hand, but returned the squeeze. I wondered if I imagined a subtle pull in his direction.

"Cromwell looked at you as if he had seen his nemesis," the Duke murmured with the same glee I had perceived earlier. As I did not know the meaning of the word, I only smiled, eager for his continued approbation.

However, the Duke shook himself from his thoughts, as gratifying as they were, and released my hand, stepping back from me; disappointment at once marred my good humour.

"Come," the Duke said, turning and walking from me. "I must also go to Rochester and I have much to prepare . . . make haste."

II

FOR A LONG TIME after my uncle had returned me to my chamber, and after the excitement of my meeting with the King had subsided, I sat on the edge of my bed, wrestling with introspection for the second time that day. The meeting had gone according to the Duke's plan, which disturbed me with its portent for my future, and I could think of no way out of the situation. It seemed again I was being subjected to a will far stronger than mine.

Longing for a distraction, I went to a window and gazed out over the vast gardens. By now, most of the King's immediate household would have left for Rochester. I craved the company of those who remained to divert me from my troubled thoughts. As the impulse came to me to seek it out, the door to the chamber burst open. I spun around in surprise.

A tall, fair young woman with a long, thin face and dancing eyes stood in the open doorway. She was dressed as a lady and, although not conventionally beautiful or handsome, her vivacity compelled me to overlook the plain cast of her features. With the alertness and delight that consumes one in the presence of a kindred spirit or mirror image, I smiled at her in welcome.

"Greetings!" she announced with a grin. "The old rascal told me you would be here . . . you must be Catherine."

"Old rascal . . .?"

"Rogue, scoundrel, handsome devil . . . whatever you want to call him. Of course, I could always do the proper thing and call him Uncle Norfolk . . . but then I never do the proper thing." The chamber rang with her merry laugh and she crossed the chamber to throw her arms around me. "How do you do, Cousin? I am Mary Norris."

III

"I MUST SAY, I am glad you're here, Cousin," said Mary Norris with heart-warming familiarity. "I was so lonely last night, I shared a bed with the scullery maid." She gave a loud hoot of laughter, infecting me with wild giggles.

Bundled in cloaks against the cold, we had seated ourselves on a fallen oak tree in the gardens. To get there, we had traversed many hibernating gardens and stretches of slushy lawn, and walked through ancient groves of elm, oak and birch. However, in Mary's company I did not notice the lapse of time or my wet feet, conscious only of happiness and ease. Mary's ceaseless bright chatter had silenced me; yet it was a relaxed muteness, and I was glad not to have to fill uncomfortable voids in conversation, or talk about myself.

"Of course, it is not so lonely during the day," Mary continued. "I have never seen so many people in one place in all my life! And, my goodness, Cousin, the men! So handsome!" She fanned herself with her hand and blew out a long gust of air. "Mind you, many of the really handsome ones have gone to Rochester now with the King, so you will have to wait three days to see them for yourself. But I warrant, Cousin, they will set your heart racing. Even though I am betrothed, my heart has taken a battering over these last few days." We shared a laugh again. "Tell me, are you betrothed, Cousin? No? Well, that will not last long," Mary raced on with confidence. "You are very beautiful. And what man can resist the Howard name, eh? I am sure our Uncle Norfolk is even now considering a suitable husband for you. Indeed, there are many men at court who need a woman to take them in hand."

The phrase, spoken with sublime innocence, conjured up a vivid picture in my disordered imagination. Perhaps I reacted to it, for Mary examined me enquiringly before realisation dawned. With a raucous laugh, she threw one arm around my shoulders.

"My, you are quite the earthy one! I can see we are going to have fun with these men!"

Giggling I shook my head, mindful of my earlier vow, which I rather suspected was going to be difficult to keep with Mary Norris around. I seized upon a safe topic. "Who is your betrothed?"

"Oh, my dear, he is a simply delicious man by the name of Sir William Norris, a very distant cousin. Alas, he is not at court, but tucked away on his estate in Yorkshire. I said to our Uncle Norfolk when he visited my family last summer that I simply *must* sample court life before being dragged away to Yorkshire to breed more Norrises for England. Our uncle exercised his considerable influence, and here I am! I cannot say Sir William was pleased about my being maid of honour to the new Queen—I am sure he thinks I shall fornicate with every man who takes my fancy, such is the reputation of the court. Of course, I had to reassure him in that regard, but my dear Cousin, there are just too many handsome men here for me to ignore, and what Sir William does not know will not hurt him! As it is quite easy to pretend virginity on one's wedding night, he shall live in blissful ignorance of my waywardness evermore." Observing my fascination at this tattle, Mary regaled me with stratagems and subterfuges for the marriage bed. When I dissolved into giggles again, she rocked back with laughter.

"Have I set your mind at rest now, my dear Cousin? Will you do more now than take a man in hand?"

I shook my head again and wiped tears of laughter from my eyes, deciding not to disabuse Mary of her opinion of my experience. "I have made a vow of chastity until I marry," I said. Mary patted my shoulder.

"That is very honourable, and I admire your strength," she said. "Would that I had the same fine qualities! Why, I confess to having lustful thoughts about the Duke himself, and if he should beckon me with his little finger, I dare say I would leap into bed with him willingly, as many others have done. However, he shows no interest in me, more's the pity. Not young and pretty enough, I expect." Another joyful, loud laugh softened the self-deprecation.

"Indeed you are very pretty," I said hotly.

"Ah no, my dear. I know my shortcomings." Another laugh. "Mind you, I am grateful for my plainness at the King's court. Forsooth, if being plain means the King will not look at me, then I am glad for it. Who ever would have thought that being ill-favoured would be an asset, eh? I am consoled in my unrequited lust for the Duke, I assure you!"

"The Duke does not appear to like Lord Cromwell," I interjected in a desperate attempt to change another sensitive subject—lust for the Duke of Norfolk was most definitely not something I wished to think about!

"Oh, my dear, you are quite right. There is no love lost between those two. Of course, our uncle is a conservative old churl, and Lord Cromwell champions the new faith. Even this business of Anne of Cleves comes from Lord Cromwell's desire to find a Protestant ally for England. It remains to be seen how the King enjoys that, for the King is also a conservative old—"

"Mary!" I interjected on a choking laugh before she could utter aloud such criticism of the King. "There are eyes and ears everywhere," I urged.

"Ah, I can see you are going to be good for me, Cousin Catherine," said Mary with a grin. "You know, though—" her voice dropped to an undertone and her eyes sparkled with mischief, "much of what I say signifies nothing. I am really quite careful and virtuous. Just like you!"

Our self-mocking laughter rang out across the wintry landscape.

IV

WITH MY COUSIN Mary Norris at my side, my transition to court life proved effortless and enjoyable. She had made the acquaintance of everyone from the loftiest courtier to the lowliest scullery maid, and was universally popular. As her new "favourite dear cousin" I was welcomed at once into social circles and cliques.

The sophisticated and fashionable people I met enthralled me. At first, I felt gauche and plain but my gregarious nature was soon to the fore, and I no longer required Mary's presence to ensure attention. Like a butterfly emerging from a chrysalis, I blossomed in my element, and court life appeared to be everything I had dreamed it would be.

Over three days, Anne of Cleves' household gathered at Greenwich. Although a smaller household than her predecessor's, it was a great court of nobles, gentlemen and gentlewomen as ever had been seen in the King's day: the Earl of Rutland, who had been Lord Chamberlain to Jane Seymour, was to serve Anne of Cleves in the same office, while Sir Edward Baynton was again to be vice-Chamberlain and Sir John Dudley Master of Horse. Six ladies-in-waiting headed the list of female attendants. Three of them—Lady Margaret Douglas, my cousin the Duchess of Richmond, and the Duchess of Suffolk—had gone to Rochester; however, on my second day at Greenwich I met Lady Rutland, wife of the Chamberlain, Lady Edgecombe, and also Lady Rochford, widow of my cousin Thomas Boleyn—she who by her evidence had been instrumental in the downfall of both her husband and Queen Anne. Apart from Mary and me, fourteen other noblewomen occupied positions as maids of honour—ladies of the Bedchamber and Privy Chamber. Anne of Cleves would retain some of her Flemish household, but most of them would be sent back to Cleves soon after her arrival.

On the third day of January, the bustle and excitement heightened. The Lord Chamberlain advised us that the Queen would sup in her apartments that evening, to become better acquainted with her household in its more intimate atmosphere; afterwards there would be entertainment in the Great Hall, in the form of music, dancing and masques.

At dusk, the Lord and vice-Chamberlain and the ladies-in-waiting travelled to Shooters Hill to meet the Queen, and those of us left behind prepared for the auspicious moment, when we, too, would be introduced to her. The one suitable garment I possessed for such a regal occasion was a low-cut gown of green velvet, lined with white silk, and with white silk sleeves embroidered with gold and silver; never a slave of fashion, and cognisant of the long night ahead, I shunned a French hood, choosing instead headgear in the Spanish style—a coif of twisted cloth of gold adorned with gold butterflies, within which could be seen my hair hanging behind me as far as my waist. I wore the coif with a small bonnet of green velvet embellished with gold beads and a white curling feather.

On learning of the Queen's arrival at Greenwich, we adjourned to the receiving chamber and aligned ourselves on either side of the carpeted central aisle. I jumped when I heard the three thumps of the halberd and, as one, our heads turned to see the doors pulled open.

A tall, fair-haired woman with a plain, pale oval face, long nose and chestnut eyes was the first to enter. She wore a wide-sleeved gown composed of rich brown velvet, decorated with bands of gold brocade, and an odd circular flat bonnet of yellow velvet. She was an unprepossessing sight, and my gaze at once moved beyond her. Three other ladies in similar garb followed; behind these came the bright and glittering figures of the English ladies-in-waiting.

I followed the lead of the ladies on either side of me and lowered my eyes as the fair-haired woman proceeded down the aisle, stopping to exchange stilted words with each person. Shocked, I realised she was the subject of the portrait that had so smitten our King—our new Queen!

I heard her talking in a deep, heavily accented voice to the ladies as she stopped before them. Out of the corner of my eye, I saw her brown skirts halt in front of Mary.

"Greetings, what is your name?" I heard her say, as if by rote.

Mary bobbed a curtsey. "I am Mary Norris, Your Grace." As usual, her voice held genuine cheer and friendliness and I sensed a lightening of tension in the tall woman. She paused for a long moment as if struggling for something to say. Mary took the initiative and spoke again: "I am happy to be in your service, Your Grace."

"And I—I too is happy—I thank you."

The brown skirts moved on and stopped before me. I curtseyed low and straightened, keeping my eyes lowered although in truth I longed to examine this woman more closely.

"Please." A thin, white hand waved with an upward gesture of the fingers. I looked up into placid chestnut eyes. "Greetings, what is your name?"

"I am Catherine Howard, Your Grace." Anne of Cleves bore a kind expression, and I detected in her a subtle cleverness and sense of humour. My sudden smile at her was broad and instinctive.

She returned my smile and nodded without speaking. Her hand moved as if to touch mine, but then she allowed it to drop. She nodded again, and moved on, her attention now on Lady Rochford, next in line.

Although I—along with everyone else—had been expecting someone different, Anne of Cleves impressed me. She possessed no beauty, but for certain she would be a strong and respected Queen of England for a long time. It was only when I perceived the grim and anxious expressions of the English ladies-in-waiting as they passed, that I realised my opinion might not be shared by all.

V

GREENWICH PALACE possessed two halls, connected by a gallery overlooking the tiltyard. One was for banquets, the other was used for entertainment. After a quiet and dignified supper in the Queen's presence-chamber, we proceeded to the latter.

The magnificence of the cavernous hall struck me with awe every time I entered it. Carved gold pennants, royal arms and badges decorated its high hammer beam ceiling, and priceless Flemish tapestries adorned the dark, gleaming wooden walls. Tall, arched windows of stained glass set in deep embrasures marched along one wall and flashed with hundreds of blazing torches. Many dancers weaved to the tuneful sounds of lute, pipe and tabor, and the horn, and professional actors conducted plays and parodies in any available space. It seemed that every one of the near one thousand people in residence at the Palace must have gathered in the hall to celebrate the arrival of Anne of Cleves, and—except on the two platforms at the head of the hall—the noise was deafening.

On one dais, the King sat in his velvet-backed throne, silent, morose and glowering, surrounded by the hovering figures of his Lord Great Chamberlain, the Garter King of Arms, and other members of his Greater Household. On the dais to his right sat Anne of Cleves—plain, impassive and placid—attended by her ladies-in-waiting. The King's ill-humour was an uncomfortable sight. I was glad to be soon swept up in a pavane, and forgot all but the magic of the dance.

After a long period during which I indulged in every dancing fantasy ever held, the pace slowed with the introduction of the candlestick bransle: with men and women spread out across the floor, the men, bearing lighted candles, chose and circled a partner; the couple danced alone for several bars, then the men handed the candles to the women who would dance alone, before finding another partner, and the routine was repeated. Feeling weary and hot, I did one turn, and retreated to a window embrasure to cool down and catch my breath.

Actors had taken their places before the King and Queen and were performing a mime of, it seemed, the King's choosing of his new foreign bride. In the circumstances, it was a poor choice of theatre, and it roused no humour in its audience of two. I looked away from the awkward scene and, as a gap opened up through the shifting dancers before me, my idle gaze fell on the far side of the cavernous hall.

Then I saw him.

A dark-haired man of medium height in a green doublet and surcoat watched me unwaveringly. I recognised hair as black and as gleaming as a crow's wing framing a face with a trim beard and moustache. Then the dancers crossed before my line of vision, hiding him from my view.

Giddy with excitement, I stood on tiptoe and craned to peer around thronging revellers to catch sight of him, the noise of the hall becoming a dull roar in my ears. The dancers parted again . . . and he was still there.

He flashed me a familiar illuminating grin, and I gasped aloud with amazement.

Thomas Culpeper.

Tom!

The subject of my long-held fantasies and erotic dreams began to walk towards me with a languid, cat-like grace, down the path through the dancers that had somehow opened between us. As the scales fell from my eyes, my every other lover—real or imagined—faded into insignificance. I knew I wanted him, and was determined to have him.

My vow of chastity had lasted all of three days.

Chapter 13

"The art of life lies in taking pleasures as they pass, and the keenest pleasures are not intellectual, nor are they always moral."

Aristippus
Greek philosopher,
(435—366 BC)

I

"CONTAIN YOURSELF, my Kate," Tom said in an undertone, and dealt me another of his knee-weakening grins.

He stood before me in the window embrasure, watching with avid interest how I trembled and bounced on my toes, as I struggled to stop myself from jumping at him.

"Oh!" I stopped bouncing but had to grip my skirts to prevent my arms springing out to grasp him. "I missed you, Tom!"

"Did you now? So you did not find solace with that fop—what was his name? Horatio?"

"Henry," I said suppressing a smile. "And, no, I did not."

He watched me with narrowed, sharp eyes. "But perhaps with someone else?"

I shifted my shoulders in some discomfort. "There was someone," I admitted, adding, with deplorable disloyalty to Francis' memory, "but there would not have been if you had been there."

"My, I am flattered!" Tom crossed his arms and rocked back on his heels. "Here I was, thinking I was none other than an annoying cousin to you, and now you are bestowing all manner of compliments on me, and behaving as if thrilled to see me! To what is owed this change of feeling?"

I shrugged. "I assume I grew up, you will be pleased to know. And I have always been fond of you," I said crossly. "Do we have to talk about this, Tom?"

"I am enjoying the compliments! I am quite starved of compliments, you know. Do you have any more for me?"

I had no intention of saying that the sight of him had evoked such lust in me that reason was almost lost. I frowned in my pretence of thinking hard, and swept a cool glance over his form.

"You look—nice," I said at last. "Far different from when I last saw you."

A vivid memory of him in a revealing wet undershirt assailed me, which did nothing for what little composure I still possessed.

Evidently, Tom recalled the occasion.

"You did not find me appealing in my undershirt?" he asked in mock hurt.

I declined to answer as heat crept into my cheeks and my memory became fixed on the image.

Tom leaned closer.

"The evidence says otherwise, my Kate," he murmured, "both now and back then." He stared at my mouth, which felt fuller, hot and soft, and surreptitiously he ran a knuckle down one hot cheek.

"Let us go somewhere," I whispered.

He seemed to take a step back, in his mind, from the brink of the fiery morass we had evoked. Tom had always been clever and calculating, even in the throes of the most daring, mind-numbing excitement. I relinquished what little restraint I possessed, knowing he had the situation under control as always, and stepped closer. My hand nearest to the window passed beneath his surcoat and doublet and slid up his silk-clad thigh. I thought I would collapse.

The touch lasted no longer than a second before Tom stepped back and my hand fell. His control evidently now splintering, he again inclined his head towards me.

"Later," he said in a low promising voice, which raised the hair on my nape. "This is not the time or the place, trust me."

He was right, of course. "Then, let us go somewhere," I repeated, mesmerised by the shape of his mouth.

"You have picked a most inconvenient time and place to grow up," he grumbled. "When I think of all the occasions when we were alone at Oxenheath—!"

When I nodded in rueful agreement he laughed so loudly he drew the amused attention of others around us. He indicated with a jerk of his head that we should move closer into the shadows of the window embrasure. "There is not much that is private around here, if it's privacy you want," he said, and I wondered in my tumult if I should dare to kiss him. He then said: "Do you know the fallen oak tree in the gardens?"

"Aye!" I roused myself from my distraction and gave a small skip of delight.

"When you can slip away, meet me there."

I nodded and turned to leave.

"Oh, and Kate?"

I turned back. His wicked gaze roamed over my form, disrobing me.

"Yes?" I asked on a gasp.

He dragged his eyes away from where they had again settled on my cleavage. "Wear a cloak," he said with supreme nonchalance. "'Tis cold out there."

II

I FETCHED MY CLOAK, although the speed with which my blood raced through my veins had elevated my temperature to boiling point. I slipped out into the gardens, grateful for the moonlight that showed the way.

As I sped through gardens and across the lawns, I noted that I was not alone in seeking privacy outside the Palace. Couples strolled along the pathways or huddled in dark corners, the cold no hindrance to affection and passion. Consoled to find myself amongst others of like mind, I quickened my pace, eagerness lending wings to my feet.

I plunged without hesitation into a shadowy grove of birch trees. Beyond the grove, a small knoll rose gently from an expanse of lawn on which the fallen oak tree sprawled. As its trunk came into sight through the trees, glowing silver in the moonlight, my steps faltered. Tom was not there.

Now I was aware of the whispering of the trees and the deep shadows around me, and trepidation tripped my heartbeat. I gripped my skirts and ran to the safety of the lawn.

A firm grip clutched my arm as I made to burst from the grove. I squealed with shock and fright. At once, I was pulled back into the shelter of the trees and a shadowy form spun me around until I my back thudded against the wide, smooth trunk of a tall birch.

A hot familiar mouth clamped on my throat. I relaxed and pulled Tom closer, sighing with delight.

"Why did you leap on me like that?" I murmured. "Why didn't you wait for me at the log?"

Tom lifted his head.

"I needed to feel your blood racing against my mouth," he remarked, "and I decided this was more private than out there."

I glanced over his shoulder as a giggling woman scampered past the log, a man in laughing pursuit. They disappeared down the knoll.

Now that we were alone and I could give in to any urge I pleased, perversely, I felt nervous. I had never been afraid of rejection, but now the fear of it crippled my impulses. Within me, it waged a fierce battle with raging lust and emerged the victor.

"So you made it to court after all," I said with admirable calm and aloofness.

Tom narrowed his eyes in a concentrated study of my manner and words. When he spoke again it was with the same detachment I had assumed. "Aye," he said. "I am one of many who serve the King in his Privy Chamber, no less." He grimaced slightly before assuming a carefully impassive expression. As a Gentleman of the Privy Chamber, he would be entrusted with some of the more intimate duties involving the King's person; however, it also meant that he was would be held in high regard by the King and much trusted.

As if reading my mind, he remarked with a self-mocking smirk: "I am much favoured by the King. He has been generous to me."

"No doubt he is enraptured by your considerable charm," I said dryly. The nearness of his body nudged aside my fear of rejection. I continued with the casual conversation as desire stirred again, and my heart recommenced its irregular pounding, causing a tremor in my voice. "You can be quite charming when you choose. In what way has he been generous?"

"By granting me lands, mainly. Guess who owns the property formerly known as the Abbey of Saint Bede in Kent?"

Impressed, I asked, "What are you going to do with it?"

"I am rebuilding now . . . I plan to move there in the spring if the King will release me. It is good land."

The shock sobered me.

"Move there? Why? You do not like it here?"

"Ah, I have had enough of serving the King. It is exciting at first and is still an interesting experience, but the novelty is wearing off. My time here has served me well, I can have no complaints . . . especially now, when my favourite cousin is here! You must be in the Queen's household then?"

I nodded, now doubly distracted. "Favourite cousin? Is that all I am?"

"Do not flirt, my Kate, you could get yourself into serious trouble."

Deliberately provocative, I tilted my head back against the tree and allowed my gaze to settle on his mouth.

"Such as?"

He placed his elbow on the trunk above my head and he leaned towards me. His closeness and his mouth were so alluring I thought I would faint. I rested my head back against the tree, closed my eyes and waited in an agony of anticipation.

Then I sensed his abrupt withdrawal. When I opened my eyes, I saw his palm pressed once more against the trunk, and with an impassive countenance, he had resumed his former distance.

I realised, as my initial confusion passed, there could be another reason for his retreat. Tom could be betrothed or even married. Worse, he might no longer have an interest in me.

I swallowed against a surge of despondency.

"So, how do you find the Queen?" Tom asked with forced lightness.

I shook away my unhappy distraction.

"I like her . . . she seems kind and shrewd."

"Oh, she is that, all right. Unfortunately, the King was not seeking kindness and shrewdness in a wife. He's quite unhappy with the turn of events."

"That was obvious in the hall," I admitted. "But there is nothing he can do about it now, is there? They are already married in the eyes of God, tomorrow's nuptials are a mere formality."

"True enough. Even if there was something he could do, it is doubtful he would do it, and risk the wrath of the Duke of Cleves and the damaging of his reputation across all Europe. Aye, it seems this marriage will proceed, but I can assure you, Lord Cromwell is not in favour at the present!"

I sighed in impatience. Lord Cromwell and the King's marriage had lost their interest for me. My distraction over Tom's own marital status urged me to seek enlightenment. I pretended an avid interest in his cloak as I spoke: "Who will accompany you to Kent when you move there?"

A deep silence ensued, but for the far off sounds of revelry. I wondered if he could hear the swift thudding of my pulse.

"I do not have anyone in mind," he said. I looked up, searching his expression. He winked and grinned. "Unless of course you are keen to revisit old haunts, in which case I would be happy to take you along."

A wide smile of concord spread across my face. In response, he again lowered himself to his elbow. He regarded me with a curious mixture of eagerness and wariness.

An icy gust of wind swept through the grove, setting dead leaves swirling and branches of trees scraping against each other. We shivered.

"Ah, my Kate, I am cold, "Tom said. "Let us warm each other in the time-honoured fashion, what do you say?"

I smiled in delight.

"I am willing," I said. My eager hands once again found their way beneath the voluminous clothing over Tom's upper body and splayed over lean, silk-covered thighs.

He gave a start and a grunt "Actually, I had in mind hugs and kisses."

"Yes, I am sure you did, Tom Culpeper," I said witheringly. I allowed my hands to slide around to taut buttocks. My world spun in reaction.

"I am not certain I wish to expose myself in this temperature," Tom went on, undeterred, although his voice held some breathlessness. "No doubt it would have a shrinking effect—which would defeat the purpose you had in mind."

I found the flap of his codpiece and exposed him. I glided one hand inside and my breath came in a sharp hiss. "I feel no sign of shrinking. Oh!"

116 ⬥ Anne Cato

His face loomed very close now, and his breathing was as swift as mine. He touched the corner of my mouth with an index finger. "You are salivating," he murmured. "What is it you desire to taste?"

My hand against his body left him in no doubt of my answer. Tom's hungry mouth found mine in response. Being the first time he had kissed my mouth, what little composure I had left was annihilated. I opened to him like a flower as with desperate hands, he groped futilely at the barrier of my bodice, and then rummaged beneath my skirts and farthingale.

"Ahoy, Culpeper! Is that you? Ahoy!"

The hail came from the knoll just as Tom's intimate touch drew a deep moan from me. He glanced over his shoulder. Two shadows moved in the gloom. A man guffawed and a woman giggled.

"What is it, Paston?" Tom barked. "Why do you interrupt?"

Paston remarked jovially, "I thought I had better tell you—the King was asking of your whereabouts. I think his leg wants dressing."

"Cannot a man have a private moment any more?" grumbled Tom, as the couple moved off. He faltered in indecision while I continued my wanton exploration of his body.

"You know," I murmured, "I have lived to rue the day you told me about cauldrons and broomsticks. Now when I think or dream of you, or when I am with you, as now, I am quite invaded by such images! Not to mention wicked impulses. Surely I must be a witch! It has all made me quite fearful of being with you."

Tom chuckled. "You are no witch, Kate. Your body simply brooks no rules, and it knows I shall not enforce any. And you ought to know you are safe with me—you can say what you want and do what you want!"

His mouth found mine again while his own delving touch fuelled heightened ardour. As if on cue, fireworks whined and burst through the night sky.

III

WITHIN MINUTES, the knoll thronged with spectators, gazing upwards with exclamations of awe. With reluctance, we arranged our clothing and stepped out from the shelter of the trees to watch the celestial celebration of Anne of Cleves' arrival on England's shores. Crackers blazed a brilliant, humming trail into the sky and burst into fiery waterfalls of white and green and red, the dark sky flashing as bright as day with every explosion. Tom stood close behind me. He paid no attention to the show, preferring to caress my body through my clothes while whispering coarse things into my ear. He seemed to have forgotten the King's needs, or did not care. I found his recklessness both exciting and troubling.

When the fireworks display drew to an end, the gathering throng dispersed. Eventually, only Tom and I remained by the log.

"Did you know your cousin Anne Boleyn and the King used to meet here?" Tom murmured in my ear.

I shivered. "That is not such a good portent."

"It depends on which way you look at it. Theirs was one of the greatest, most significant love affairs while it lasted."

I was not convinced the meeting place was steeped in good omens. I moved out of Tom's embrace and took his hand, leading him from the scene. "Come," I said. "Perhaps we should get back. I would not like the King's wrath to be directed at you."

"What do you know of the King's wrath?" said Tom as we started the journey back.

"I met him. On the day of my arrival, just before he left for Rochester. He lost his temper with Lord Cromwell."

"Is that so?" Tom's tone was thoughtful. My hand was still in his and I delighted in the feel of his skin and the light grip of his fingers. In the inner courtyard we paused. There were many people lingering about so we no longer touched, only stared at each other.

"If you still want—privacy—I can arrange it," said Tom in a low voice. "It may be a few days, for we both will be busy with the nuptials, I expect. But after that—?"

"Yes," I said at once. "I want privacy. A lot of it."

"Does it matter if we indulge in wickedness?"

"The more the better." We both laughed. "But, please, do not let there be too much of a delay, or I am apt to go up like one of those fireworks."

"I am sure you'll be able to find a field in which you can lie and pleasure yourself," Tom said, reminding me of how he had come across me once at Oxenheath. I give him a withering look. "You have very adept hands in bringing satisfaction, I suspect," he insisted, and I knew he was not thinking of touches on my own body. "However, on second thoughts—" Tom pursed his lips. "No, do not find your own relief. I would rather deal with the fireworks myself."

"Are you sure you can?"

"Oh, I am sure of it." He dealt me one of his grins and a small gasp of desire escaped my lips in response.

"Sweet Jesus, I think the firecracker has been lit already," Tom murmured. He hesitated. Knowing there was little he could do for me now and with the memory of the King's rage foremost in my mind, I jerked my head in the direction of the stairs.

"Go," I whispered. "I'll wait for your word."

"I'll come for you in a few days . . . be prepared."

With a jaunty stride, he left me staring after him. He took the steps three at a time, while I sighed with mixed longing and contentment.

Chapter 14

"Being asked whether it was better to marry or not, he (Socrates) replied, "Whichever you do you will repent it."

Diogenes
Greek Philosopher
(412—323 BC)

I

Greenwich Palace
January, 1540

THE KING DELAYED THE WEDDING for two days.

Having found Anne of Cleves to his distaste, he clutched at any straw that would enable him to annul the union. To extricate himself from the situation with his dignity and the friendship with the Duke of Cleves intact, he seized upon Anne's pre-contract with the son of the Duke of Lorraine. However, the delegation from Cleves satisfied the Privy Council that the pre-contract had been nullified. The King had no choice but to proceed with the wedding, although he was heard to shout to Lord Cromwell on the morning of the ceremony: "If it were not to satisfy the world and my realm, I would not do that I must do this day for none earthly thing!"

The Queen herself, whether because of language difficulties or simple indifference, did not appear perturbed by the delay. She amused herself by learning the English terms for all the objects in her apartments, and the names of all the trees and shrubs in the gardens. She played long into the night at cards and dice, and when she lost—as she frequently did—she graciously paid over to us substantial amounts of money. She earned the respect of all of her household for her dignity in the face of the King's blatant and humiliating distaste for her person. This enforced my initial instinctive conviction that—if permitted to do so—she would make a formidable Queen of England.

I had two grievances in my new position—one was Anne of Cleves' plain apparel, the other her pet parrot. As the Queen's maid of honour, I must care for and repair her clothing when required. Although I hated sewing, I had looked forward to tending bright, beautiful fabrics and to absorbing and encouraging new styles. However, Anne of Cleves preferred gowns that were unilaterally dark in colour and devoid of intricacy or glamour. Fortunately, she did insist upon adorning herself with beautiful and rich jewels—large necklaces of gold embedded with diamonds, long emerald or ruby earrings, pearl chokers. I had to admit the plain clothing set off the jewellery to perfection.

The one pet she possessed was a large, garishly-coloured parrot that screeched from a gilded cage when it was not terrorizing her household from its perch on her shoulder. My task was to make sure this creature was fed, watered and cosseted. Unfortunately, the bird developed a fondness for the colour of my hair. Immediately on my coming into its detestable presence, it would swoop on to my shoulder and angle its beak straightaway at the part of my hair on my forehead revealed by my French hood. I like all animals and they had never frightened me, but I admit the sight of that open, axe-like beak aiming for my face evoked a terror that smote me to the core. Instinctively, I would throw up my right hand as a shield against the advancing beak, with the result that one or other of my fingers would be dealt a vicious nip. On the second day of this torture, Anne of Cleves noticed the propensity of the bird to attack me, and one thickly bandaged finger. It is a measure of her kindness that she at once absolved me from bird-care duties and took special care to ensure it was caged whenever I was present.

Apart from my seething dreams and fantasies, I saw Tom only at the sombre meal times. He would shoot me hot looks across the hall or flash me one of his grins, and my loins would immediately ache with yearning. I discussed Tom with no one, not even Mary Norris: the emotions newly induced were too fantastic and treasured to share. Reliving my tumultuous reunion with him, and fantasizing about its consummation, disturbed my sleep so much that I found it a relief to rise from my bed in the mornings and start the day. Sometimes while I worked, images of Tom or a recollection of how he felt or tasted would cause my heart to skip a beat and I would gasp aloud at the consuming surge of lust. Not knowing when I would be with him added to my turbulent state, and I hoped he was not planning a mere quick coupling in some dark corner, for I knew it would not satisfy me.

On the morning of the wedding, being so obsessed over what—if anything—Tom planned, I sent an obscure message via a dim-witted chambermaid to say that Thomas Culpeper was required in the Queen's apartments. I then hovered in the hallway for what seemed an eternity, trying to appear casual to passers-by while desperately watching for Tom to round the bend.

I gaped in disappointment and amazement at the man who did appear in response to my summons. Thomas Culpeper approached me with a leering grin, but he was not the Tom I desired. It was Thomas Culpeper senior—Tom's older brother.

"Well, well!" Thomas said, stopping before me with a smirk. "Cousin Kate! To what do I owe the pleasure of this summons?"

My old childhood enemy bore some resemblance to Tom in that he was black-haired and blue-eyed. However, he was taller, significantly heavier and quite without the charm or sense of merriment that Tom possessed.

His appearance so perplexed me that I continued to stare at him with open-mouthed amazement.

"What are you doing here?" I spluttered at last.

"You sent me a note," Thomas answered witheringly.

"No . . . I mean, not here . . . I mean . . . are you at court too?"

"Of course! I am in Lord Cromwell's service!" He frowned at my idiocy until comprehension dawned. "Ah, I see! It was my beloved brother you required! A common confusion here at court, I must say. Still consorting with him then?"

"That is none of your affair," I snapped. Desperate to see Tom, I was nevertheless unwilling to attempt further communication via notes or chambermaids. Nibbling my lip, I assessed Thomas's willingness to assist me.

He perused my form again, making my skin crawl.

"I must say all that fat has gone into the right places," he remarked.

I turned from him, but felt a surprisingly gentle grip on my arm, detaining me.

"I am sorry, Cousin," said he as I reluctantly faced him. The leer had gone from his expression, so too the lasciviousness. Nevertheless, I did not think the apology had arisen from anything other than either a respect for our kinship or—the one saving grace of his personality—total loyalty to his brother. "Do you wish me to fetch Tom?"

I swallowed my hurt pride. "Aye," I mumbled. "I—er—wish to discuss something with him."

"Of course," he said with a smirk. "May I suggest, though, for this discussion that you meet him somewhere more private than this hallway? Shall I tell him to meet you in the oratory?"

Despite his coarseness, I was grateful to him for his help. I nodded and attempted a feeble smile. Thomas sighed and rolled his eyes.

"That brother of mine has all the good fortune," he muttered without rancour.

II

THE ORATORY is an antechamber to the chapel set aside for quiet devotions. Fortunately I found it empty.

When Tom burst in a few minutes later, he immediately closed the door and leaned against it, his mouth forming a wolfish grin.

"Fireworks about to explode, my Kate?" he asked.

I rose from the pew and approached him. I spoke only when I had pressed my body against him and my mouth hovered over his.

"Aye, and I thought you would like to be there when it happens." Our lips met.

I had hardly tasted my fill when I heard the outer door open and soft approaching footsteps. Tom lifted his head, also alert to the sound. At once, I slipped into the nearest pew and, as nimble as a goat, Tom bounded over other pews to settle several rows away. We both sank to our knees and lowered our chins to our pressed hands.

We must have made a devout picture. Whoever entered paused for a second before walking to a prie-dieu. As he came into my line of vision and knelt in front of a painting of Our Lady of Perpetual Succour, I recognised him as a chaplain from the King's household— Father Timothy, a congenial, middle-aged man in long black robes. He also lowered his head to his hands and was soon lost in his devotions.

Tom watched me while pretending to be deep in prayer. When I sneaked a glance at him, he mimed a kiss with his lips. Suppressing giggles, I rose with dignity and moved to the door. As I opened it, I looked back. He nodded.

I hovered inside the empty chapel, near the confessional. When Tom approached me with his wanton, lazy stride and intent gaze, my little remaining decorum abandoned me.

I pulled him into the penitent's compartment and shut the door. As we were plunged into thick, musty darkness, I felt my way down his body, falling to my knees.

"Marry," he swore reverently, as I put my head under his doublet and leaned my face against the large, hard bulge in his codpiece, feeling for the garment's opening. He grasped my shoulders. "Kate!" he breathed in deep surprise as I freed him, took him in my hand and tasted him.

With a loud squeak, the hatch in the wall behind Tom slid open. Tom at once fell to his knees before it, his shoulders shaking with barely suppressed laughter. As mirth surged in my chest, I pressed one fist to my mouth; my other hand I allowed to snake up Tom's thigh. He jerked at my touch, sending me into a paroxysm of stifled giggles.

"Commence when you are ready, Father Timothy," murmured a voice on the other side.

While I rocked with silent laughter, Tom recovered.

"Er—Father Herbert, Father Timothy is still in the oratory," Tom said at last. "Should I come back later?"

Evidently, Father Timothy and Father Herbert secretly practised confession. The sacrament had not been banned but it was certainly criticised as Popery, and the King now never gave his confession to a priest, tainting the practice with royal disapproval.

"Aye, my son, perhaps that would be best . . . ," said the voice behind the window, dashing my hopes that Tom would have to make his confession, ". . . to avoid confusion . . . I am reluctant to turn you away, but—"

"Do not trouble yourself, Father," said Tom quickly, nudging me with his foot. I scrabbled on my hands and knees to the door. "Thank you, Father . . . God bless you."

The little window slid closed. Tom opened the door and peered out. We burst into the chapel and scampered to the exit, just as the door to the oratory squeaked opened. Once out into the empty hallway we burst into laughter.

Sagging against the wall and passing his hand across his forehead, Tom said, "You will be the death of me, my Kate." He reached out and grasped my hand. I gladly curled my fingers around his.

"I was looking forward to hearing your sins," I said. "What would you have confessed?"

"Oh, let us see." Tom's hot gaze dropped to my lips then my bosom. "I probably would have described my wicked, lustful thoughts about a certain beautiful lady in the Queen's household . . . only I suspect I would then be responsible for poor Father Herbert's heart failure."

I giggled and seized on the moment. "Speaking of lustful thoughts . . . when and where will you be putting those into action? I have some that need expression also."

"Aye, that was apparent," he said. His hand drifted to his groin as if to relieve a discomfort. My gaze followed. Tom pulled me to him in ardent response. As we kissed, our conjoined palms became damp with perspiration. Tom shook his head as if to clear a fog, straightened and blew out a long, tremulous whistle.

"All right—*when* and *where*? *When* is a surprise, I want to keep you in suspense," Tom said. "But it will be very soon, I promise you. I'll come for you, so be prepared. *Where* has also been decided, but that too is a surprise. Rest assured it is private and comfortable and we have access to it all night, and every third night!"

I stared at him in amazement and gave a small jump of excitement. I longed to throw my arms around his neck once more and press grateful, happy kisses over his face.

"Now, be off with you, my Kate, before we become the object of court gossip. This must be between ourselves for the while."

I nodded, and Tom released my hand. I backed away, reluctant to leave the hold of his gaze, loath to depart from the radiating warmth of his body and the promise it held. Three words bubbled to my lips . . . words I had never spoken, even in passion . . . words I had never felt the need to utter. I paused, startled. Tom looked questioning. I laughed with a false lightness, and finger-waved airily as I turned. I grasped my skirts and sped down the hallway as if demons snapped at my heels.

III

THE NIGHTS OF DISTURBED SLEEP had exhausted me. As soon as I returned to the Queen's apartments, I longed to curl up on my bed and plunge into a long refreshing rest. However, there were many tasks to complete before that liberty could be mine. That evening after the nuptials there would be pageantry and feasting, and it was one of my duties to ensure the arrangements were in place for both. It seemed my reputation as an accomplished dancer had preceded me, for I was to participate in main dance of the pageant—an honour I was sensitive to and much humbled by.

In the evening, the King and Queen proceeded into the Queen's Closet where the brief marriage ceremony was conducted. Afterwards, the Queen and her ladies-in-waiting continued to the great hall where they awaited the commencement of the pageant.

Dressed in crimson satin and plunket embroidered with gold and pearl, I took my place with five other ladies inside a huge device called the Riche Mount, an artificial mountain on hidden wheels. Decorated with silk flowers and trees of green satin and gold damask, the Mount bore a lit beacon at its summit, and around the beacon sat the King and others, including the Dukes of Norfolk and Suffolk. The gentlemen wore cloaks and caps of crimson velvet, the cloaks set with spangles of gold and the caps embroidered with flat gold of damask.

Four wooden horses operated by artisans drew the Mount into the Great Hall until it came before the Queen. In its dark, hot bowels, I was unable to see what occurred next, but I knew the King and his lords would have descended and would be dancing around the Mount. After an allotted number of muffled bars of music, we lined up one behind the other, and the hidden door in the Mount opened.

To thunderous applause, we emerged from the stifling interior of the mount. The musicians launched into the music for the new La Volta dance and we took our places before the King and the Lords of the Mount. The Duchess of Suffolk was to dance with the King. Whether through good or ill luck, I partnered my uncle, the Duke of Norfolk. I could ask for no better dancer in all the realm to accompany me, but La Volta necessitated daring physical contact between the partners—which of course made it a perfect spectacle for onlookers—and I did not trust myself to such contact, particularly when it was to be combined with seductive music and dancing. I faced my uncle with dread as one of his arms passed around me to hold my back, and his other rested on the front of my bodice, in the required hold. Our hips melded, I slipped one arm around his back and grasped his shoulder, my other steadying my skirts, in preparation for the opening steps and the subsequent leaps.

I kept my concentration on a point of embroidery in the Duke's cloak. However, while we took the steps, I felt his black eyes boring into me. Nauseating excitement churned in my stomach when he lifted his right knee so that I sat upon his thigh. He pivoted on his left leg in the required turn, before I conducted the required leap from that position. Using his arm, leg and shoulders with practiced aplomb, the Duke lifted and spun me.

When he set me back down at the commencement of the next steps, he lowered his head and whispered in my ear.

"You are amazingly beautiful . . . and I am not the only one who thinks so. See the King!"

Shocked, my gaze sought the King and his partner. Despite his physical ailments, the King was managing the dance with reasonable skill; however, his attention was not on his partner. Nor was it on the Queen, who sat plain and placid in her throne on the dais. He watched me with such ardour that I blushed in furious embarrassment, my gaze skittering away at once and seeking comfort in the Duke's face. As we moved through another leap and spin, he met my pleading and frightened stare with a softening expression that both startled and comforted me.

"Do not trouble yourself with thoughts on this," he murmured close to my ear again. "Rest assured that you are in my care. I shall protect you, Catherine, I promise."

He had chosen the right words. I sighed. Entranced, I closed my eyes, enveloping myself in the dance, the music, the nearness of the Duke's warm, controlling form, and his soothing utterance. His mouth, with those sensual Howard lips, hovered so close to mine. I moved my head slightly . . .

The Duke swung his head away, as a curious wave of heat, nausea and perspiration swept over me. Just in time, his thigh came up beneath me again and I sank onto it. Somehow I managed the leap and spin, while shivering with a bone-gnawing chill. When the dance ended to more applause, I filed away with the other ladies, back into the Mount. The door closed behind us, and we were conveyed out of the hall.

IV

"YOU LOOK UNWELL," said the Duchess of Suffolk in the inner courtyard. While the other ladies chattered with excitement, I sank onto the parapet of the fountain to catch my breath and to give the nausea a chance to abate. I liked both the Duke and the Duchess of Suffolk. Kindly, bluff Charles Brandon was the King's greatest friend, and had been married to the King's late sister, the Princess Mary. The current Duchess, Catherine Willoughby, I liked for her good humour and maternal manner. I smiled now in gratitude as she placed a soft hand on my forehead.

"I am very tired," I said with a forced laugh. "I am not sleeping well, and it was very hot in the Mount."

"Aye, 'twas indeed" said the Duchess. "You are quite warm, perhaps with a fever. I believe you should make for your bed and rest!"

For once, I had no desire to go on dancing. I nodded.

"Aye, I think I shall. If the Queen should ask of my whereabouts—"

"I'll explain your absence to the Queen—or the King," added the Duchess with a dry tone. So my Uncle Norfolk had not been the only one to notice the King's rapt attentions. Seeing my discomfort, her refined features formed into a kind smile. "I will," she promised. "Go and rest, Catherine Howard."

In the quiet cool of the bedchamber, I felt better at once, although still deeply tired. The heat and airlessness of the Mount's interior, the shock of dancing so closely with the Duke, and then observing the King's interest in me, had upset my inner workings, I concluded.

I stripped to my shift and collapsed onto my bed. At once, blessed deep sleep took me and I surrendered to it with relief.

I dreamed I was at the fallen log in the garden. In my dream, I had arranged to meet Tom there, just as many years ago the King had arranged to meet my cousin . . . Tom is sitting on the log and I am kneeling between his splayed thighs, fumbling desperately with his codpiece, longing to touch and taste the allurement beneath.

"No, that's wicked." The voice echoing in my mind is familiar, but not Tom's. "You must stop or you will burn . . . *burn . . . burn as a witch!*"

I look up at the owner of the voice. I perceive a glittering and bulky silhouette . . . I glance down and see a bandaged thigh . . .

"The Duke smote me there with his lance." Another recognisable voice resonated in my head. "He is proper-false . . ."

I see the bandaged ribs, not a leg . . . there is a hard brown belly below . . . a broad solid chest above . . . I look up, eager to bring my first lover's features into focus . . . they waver before me . . . handsome, gentle, noble . . . *Francis!* I stand, reaching for his face, happiness eliminating a deep-seated grief . . .

However, the face I grasp is not Francis' . . . handsome and familiar, yes. He is blood of my blood, flesh of my flesh. However, his expression possesses no gentleness, just ambition and ruthlessness . . . this man is proper-false indeed! I look away to seek my liberator, my champion, my ally, *my love . . . Tom, where are you?* My cry is silent, although I can feel my mouth trying to open and my chest heaving with the effort to speak. My face is grasped, and I am looking back into black, hypnotic Howard eyes. As I drown in their darkness, I am struggling for air and deliverance. I try to extract myself from his suffocating hold, as I feel his caressing, tormenting hand on my body . . .

I manage to pull away from him and run. I am running down long dark hallways, with many closed doors on either of me. I am searching in desperation for *something* . . . in breathless fear and dread I open every door but see only some dark peril beyond each one.

The door ahead is different though . . . there is a crack of brilliant light beneath it. I fall against it and struggle with the door handle. The handle is stiff! I cannot breathe and am weakening from lack of air. I make a last-ditch effort at liberation . . . I must open this door . . . must . . . beyond it is my destiny . . .

"Kate!" I hear a far-off whispered entreaty. "Wake up!"

The dream faded. My eyelids sprang open. Tom loomed over me, his hand on my mouth. Beside me, Mary Norris was in a deep sleep. My erratic heartbeat began to steady.

When I nodded, Tom removed his hand. I sucked back refreshing air, realising I must have slept long past the conclusion of the marriage celebrations if Mary's deep sleep was anything to go by.

"Are you ready?" Tom whispered. As I struggled to sit, and swung my legs over the side of the bed, I nodded again,.

It was time . . . Tom had come for me.

Chapter 15

"The sexual embrace can only be compared with music and with prayer."

Marcus Aurelius
Roman Emperor
(AD 121—180)

I

TOM LED ME FROM THE BEDCHAMBER and down the narrow flight of stairs beyond.

He plunged on past the closed doors of the Queen's apartments, holding my hand tight. When the stairs levelled out into a small landing, I saw by the flickering torches that we could either continue the descent into inky darkness, or proceed along a narrow dark passage. Without hesitation, Tom took one of the torches and led me into the passage. In his black cloak he looked dishevelled and dangerous.

"Where are we going?" I whispered. Tom only glanced behind at me and put a finger to his lips

Several passageways branched off from the one we traversed, which itself steered a straight course in the direction of the King's apartments. Were we going to Tom's own quarters? I wondered. Unlikely, as I knew he shared a dormitory with other Gentlemen of the Privy Chamber.

We negotiated many dark stairs and narrow hallways before Tom finally stopped on a large landing outside a closed door.

"Here we are," he whispered. He winked at me and my heart skipped a beat in eager response.

He opened the door and pulled me inside. I looked around.

"Whose bedchamber is this?" I asked, as Tom, suddenly agitated, moved to the table to pour himself wine from the flagon. He tossed it back and poured another.

"My brother's—Thomas's," he said. "The apartments one flight down are Lord Cromwell's. I know my brother can be a knave, Kate," he said, "but he was good enough to give us the use of this room every third night, and I can trust him not to tattle."

"Hmmph . . . what else does he want? Your brother isn't usually so generous."

Tom shrugged. "He's asked for nothing . . . although I grant you, he may call in the favour. However, we have better things to do than talk of him, have we not?"

By way of answer, I undid the fastenings of my cloak and let it fall to the ground. He gulped back the wine in his mug, straightened from his lounging position, and turned to pour himself another.

"Want one?" he asked. The tension in his shoulders belied his casual tone.

I stepped up behind him as he drank yet another serving of wine. When he thumped the mug down on the table, I reached around him and pushed it away. My other hand I allowed to pass beneath his shirt, moving upwards over skin as smooth as silk, over sinewy, warm flesh.

"Do not drink any more," I murmured. "Let not wine affect our pleasure this night." He bore an unusually sombre and wary expression. I frowned, leaving my exploration of his body, and linking my hands around his waist. "What ails you?" I said. "Tell me!"

"Ah, my Kate." He did not flash his smile or make some clever quip. He stroked my hair off my face and grasped its thick heavy mass into a long tail; fresh air swept across my nape as the weight of hair was lifted from it.

After a long minute of silence he spoke.

"I was watching you tonight," he said. "You had every man in the hall under your spell, including that scoundrel your uncle, and the worst rogue of all, the King of England! I was aware of it the other night in the gardens, but tonight it was driven home to me just how much I have to lose here—and how easy it would be to lose it."

I gaped at him. He seemed uncomfortable with his own frankness.

"Tom," I pleaded at last. "You know the King, he is nothing but an old lecher. It means nothing that he would, as you say, fall under my spell. . . and I really wish you would not use such witchcraft terms around me, you know they upset me." I had attempted a weak jest, but Tom did not smile and did not meet my eyes.

I continued on with effort. "And it is no matter, in any event. He's now married, he and the Queen will have a long, happy marriage, despite the inauspicious beginning . . . you will see! As for the Duke—." I stopped, at a loss for words.

I had Tom's full attention now.

"Aye, the Duke," he repeated. "I know well your uncle's reputation at court for taking to his bed whoever pleases him—and you did please him tonight, that was clear!"

"Well, he has not taken me to his bed!" I said with heat. "Nor do I wish him to." I wondered if Tom had perceived my reactions during the dance tonight. He studied me intently. I detected a softening in his expression, and when he touched my sulking mouth his touch was tender.

"Ah, Kate. Beautiful, *flawed* Kate! Such a slave to your body! If there is a mutual attraction between you and that wily old warrior, I blame him entirely. He ought to know better than to take advantage of your nature, or encourage your feelings."

"I do not think he has intended to do so, not entirely," I mumbled, anxious to be fair.

"Such family loyalty!" Tom said dryly. "That could get you into serious trouble. I would moderate that inclination, if I were you."

"Well, you are not me, you are not a Howard," I snapped, unable to help myself. At once I regretted my words. I tightened my arms and rested my cheek on his chest. I listened to his heart beating a steady rhythm, steeling myself to be as frank with him as he deserved. "Oh, Tom, it's not only family loyalty which drives me to defend the Duke in this matter, " I mumbled. "I am not blameless where any of my dealings with men are concerned, and that includes the Duke." I raised my head, summoned some spirit and remarked archly: "In any event, I thought you said you imposed no rules—so I have to wonder why you are reacting as if I have disappointed you!"

"Aye, I impose no rules where the lusts of the body are concerned! And you do not disappoint me, you never have—you may desire what and whom you please, my Kate, for your passion delights me. No, rather I am distressed about a problem I have that is so profound, I am driven not to take what is offered to me tonight!"

"What problem?" I said in a frenzy of despair.

"I thought I made that clear," Tom said. "I am afraid of losing you—to the Duke, to the King, or anyone—or anything!" When I frowned in puzzlement, he sighed. "Let me explain."

He remained silent for a long moment.

"When I was a lad of eight or so," he said at last, "my father promised me he would make me a miniature likeness of the Great Harry—you remember he was good at carpentry and loved ships?" When I nodded, he continued. "I wanted that ship so badly that every other toy I had became meaningless to me. I dreamt about my ship, planned the games I would play with it, I thought about how I would show it to everyone and how everyone would think I was so lucky to have such a splendid toy. There were some dreadful times when I thought I would never get it—my father became ill at one stage, and then he went to war and no one knew whether he would come back. But he got better, and he did come back. I knew he still worked on my ship, and that one day it would be mine."

I shifted in some impatience, but Tom did not notice.

"And then the great day came," he said dreamily. "My father came to me with this bundle rapped in muslin. He grinned at me, laid it in my hands, ruffled my hair and left. I knew from the feel of the structure beneath the muslin that it was my ship. It felt magnificent . . . I could feel every intricate outline—and even smell it. I remember I hugged it, tried not to cry my joy . . ." Tom grimaced, sinking into another lengthy silence.

At length he said, "I was scared . . . too scared to unwrap my ship and start to play with it. I had wanted it for so long that I feared to play with it, lest I should love it . . . which meant that if I broke or I lost it, it would devastate me. So, I did not unwrap my ship. I stood on a stool and placed it high on top of the armoury, where no one would find it and it would be safe. Every now and then I would get it down and tentatively stroke its outlines through the muslin. It was mine, and that made me happy, but I would not unwrap it to see its beauty, I would not play with it. It was safe—and *I was safe*."

He looked at me, seeing me for the first time since beginning his narrative. He lifted a thumb to wipe away a tear that trickled down my cheek. "You're like that ship to me, my Kate," he murmured.

I allowed him to wipe my tears, to stroke my hair. I recalled my dream . . . that dark hallway down which I ran . . . all the closed doors with nothing behind them but dark peril. Then the other door, with the brilliant light showing beneath. Now I closed my eyes and pictured my hands on the handle of that door. When I looked at Tom again, I grasped his face in earnest.

"I am not going to break and you shall not lose me, Tom—not to the Duke, not to anyone, not to any *thing*!" I said, as I opened the door. "I love you." With my proclamation, I stepped out into blazing light and a fertile, colourful garden.

He drew a sharp breath. With every second that passed as he studied my face, the selfishness and immaturity of my girlhood shrivelled a bit more, until at last it died, and in its place blossomed something that was strong and true and womanlike.

He grinned. My heart leapt. The old Tom was back with me, devastating me with his allure, filling my heart with adoration. As the intensity of our previous exchange faded away, he hoisted me high and spun around. I laughed, the sound cut off with a gasp when he set me back down and his hands slid up my bosom, tracing its outline through my shift.

"I do believe I can unwrap my gift now, and play with it," he said.

His hands grasped the top of my shift. With a sharp tug and a loud *rip*, he tore the garment from neckline to hem.

When he pushed it from my body and it slid to the ground, I shuddered and closed my eyes. I had often being naked before Francis and Henry, and had been comfortable. In my youth and innocence, it had not troubled me. Now, though, nervousness and shyness sickened me. I wanted Tom to approve of what he saw and to obtain fulfilment from it. And if he didn't, I knew the pain would be indescribable. I squeezed my eyes shut, afraid to see his expression.

I heard a swish and rustle of clothing and knew that he had disrobed. Still I kept my eyes clamped shut. Prickles of my skin told me that he circled and examined me.

He came up behind me. I felt every nuance of his naked body pressed against my back. Whimpers escaped my lips when his hands closed over my breasts and his mouth clamped on the racing pulse in my neck.

While his hands roamed my body with voracious desire, his mouth slid to my ear and the coarse words he whispered left me in no doubt of how much he approved of me.

II

WE DID SLEEP EVENTUALLY. Although my own unconsciousness was deep, it was so turbulent I emerged from it with relief, more exhausted than when I had closed my eyes.

When I dragged my lids opened, it was to see the torch had burned low, and Tom propped on his elbow beside me, examining my right hand with a deep frown. Starlight still showed through the small window above our heads.

"How did this happen?" he asked, noticing I was awake. Uncomfortably hot and perspiring, I kicked the bed covers from my body and closed my eyes again against a pain in my head. "Kate?" Tom urged.

"The Queen's parrot bit me," I mumbled. "It's of no import."

"I disagree! Look at it. You need to get this examined, Kate," he said. I dragged open my eyes, glanced at my finger and recoiled with surprise. Tom had removed the bandage from what was an ugly, oozing and swollen welt. Angry red veins snaked from the wound down my finger. My finger and hand were swollen and coloured a deep purple hue. I realised my arm throbbed and every movement jarred.

Tom looked anxious. "Promise me you will get this looked at," he urged. "Ask the Queen to have one of her doctors attend you . . . promise!"

I turned my attention away from the ugly sight and reached up to kiss him. "I promise . . . but do not worry, it doesn't hurt," I lied.

He seemed satisfied and kissed me back. Our desire spent, we only embraced for a long period.

"Come," said Tom at last, "we must be getting back or we shall be missed."

Forsaking my ruined shift, I wrapped my cloak tight around me . We slipped from the chamber and Tom led me back through the chilly early morning to my bedchamber. I was so tired and now feeling quite poorly, that I stumbled several times, drawing Tom's anxious attention. At the door of my bedchamber, I made a supreme effort to show I felt well, wrapping my arms around his waist and leaning into him.

"I love you," I said.

"I know," Tom murmured, stroking my back beneath my cloak, and kissing the top of my head.

"On Friday night then?" I asked.

"Aye. You'll be able to make your own way there when it is safe to do so?"

I nodded and with my good hand drew his head down to me for a last kiss.

I stumbled to my bed, dropping my cloak and noticing only that Mary still slept soundly. I collapsed onto the mattress, devoid even of sufficient energy to pull the covers over me, and plunged at once into oblivion.

It was to be many days before I awoke.

Chapter 16

"Amor tussisque non celantur"
(Love, like a cough, cannot be concealed)

Ovid
Roman classical poet
(43 BC—17 AD)

I

DAY FOLLOWED NIGHT, ONCE, AND TWICE MORE. Alternately burning and freezing, I struggled with belly-clenching nausea and a feverish, dream-like state. Faces appeared before me—Mary, sobbing in distress, the Queen, pale and anxious, and unrecognisable male faces, and fingers that prodded at my agonised hand, and voices that murmured . . . .

Often I sank into hallucinations, dreaming of my mother—pretty, aloof and fatigued from endless childbearing—and my happy childhood. In one dream, I came across my mother resting in an arbour in the gardens at Oxenheath. She looked at me with no change of expression, as if she did not recognise me; then she smiled, and held out her arms to me, and I ran to her to be enveloped in a bony embrace, especially for me.

My ten brothers and sisters, and my numerous half-siblings, passed through my dreams, followed by my cousins . . . and Tom . . . always Tom was there. Tom, who always made time for me, his Kate, above all his family . . . Tom, who involved me in his schemes and games . . . Tom, my champion, my ally . . .

"My love . . . Tom . . ." As I tried to utter the words aloud, I struggled to surface to the present day. I recalled the cycles of the days that I had observed from a pained, foggy distance, aware of their importance to Tom. Was it Friday yet? A terrible sickness swept over me and I turned my head to retch, clutching my burning, agonised belly. Mary's face wavered before me and I felt her wiping my cheek, dark circles beneath her tear-filled eyes. Observing that I watched her, her lips moved and she attempted a smile; but I could not hear her through the roaring in my ears.

I tried to clutch at her, tried to shake away the deafness. Mary leaned closer. When she spoke again, I could hear her as if from a distance.

"What is it, my dearest? You tried to say something just now."

My lips felt dry and stiff, yet I tried to speak again.

"Tom . . ."

Mary frowned. "Tom?"

She had my hand in hers now—my good hand—and I attempted to squeeze it in affirmation, but I could not summon the energy and felt my mind slipping. Desperately, I forced myself to speak again.

"Culpeper . . . cousin . . . the King."

Mary shook her head in pained confusion. Tears of despair sprang to my eyes. As one hot droplet coursed down my cheek, realisation dawned on Mary.

"Tom Culpeper? Your cousin? He that is in the King's service?"

With a furious effort, I jerked my head in a nod.

"You wish to see him?"

"Tell him . . . Friday . . . cannot . . . sorry."

Mary's face distorted in puzzlement again; no wonder, for my whisper had been hoarse and inaudible. Her lips pressed together in determination.

"I shall fetch him for you . . . rest easy, dearest!" She leaned forward to kiss my cheek and as the fog closed once more over my eyes, she hastily left my side.

II

THE EFFORT TO COMMUNICATE with Mary had exhausted what little reserves I had; I could not summon the energy to rise from the enveloping fog, even when I became aware of Tom's face—white with fear—before mine. Soothing relief, however, eased the agony of my soul; at least Tom knew now I would not be meeting him tonight; he would not be in an agony of fear, believing his ship was lost or broken. I slipped back to oblivion.

Tom's face loomed closer, although his voice came from far away.

"Kate, my Kate!" he whispered. "You said you would not break and that I would not lose you! It was a promise! Do not leave me!"

Leave him? At once I realised the seriousness of my predicament. *Was I going to die?*

I struggled to hold on to wakefulness, fearing now that if I relinquished it, it would never be mine again. I saw Tom's face in a blur. His desperation struck fear into my heart.

"Stay with me, please! Try!" he begged, as my eyelids fell.

Now I am eight years old again, and floundering far beneath the surface of the river at Oxenheath. I am choking and drowning, reaching out for the golden disc of the sun far above. The shape of a hand appears across the glowing orb, fingers spread like talons; it plunges towards me, clamps around my wrist and hauls me upwards . . . *up* . . . *up*. I can feel the grip on my wrist—strong and fierce, fingers biting into tender flesh, a welcome pain . . . I surrender to its power . . .

I burst through the fog of fever, pain, and nausea, in response to the will of my saviour. Now at last I saw him clearly, and tried to smile. He drew a deep breath of relief. Fear, fury, determination passed in turn across his countenance.

"I shall take care of this . . ." he said to me with gritted teeth. "I shall take care of *you!*"

His image swam out of my vision. Relief swept through me. I could trust Tom to make sure I survived . . . Tom, my champion, my ally, *my love.*

I gladly surrendered to darkness again.

III

OTHER PEOPLE CAME . . . more strange male faces, more fingers to prod my hand. One echoing voice said, "Twill have to come off . . . 'tis placing poison in her blood."

I froze in horror, wanting to scream "No!" but I could not make a sound. Terrifying visions of axes and swords passed across my mind. Suddenly, it was not my hand these unknown men were discussing, but my head. "Twill have to come off . . . 'tis placing poison in her blood . . . wicked, poisonous thoughts! . . . she is a slave to them . . . she does their urging . . . she is a witch . . . she must burn . . . *burn.*"

I was burning, my entire body enveloped in tongues of flame. Soon it will be over, I thought. I will be consumed by the flames; perhaps if I surrender to them and do not fight, my agony will be short-lived. However, before I could admit defeat, I felt my offending hand being taken in a firm grasp.

No! Let me die first! Oh, God, be merciful!

"See the trails of poison, Your Grace?" said a voice. "Her hand must be removed or she shall surely die."

"No," rumbled a vaguely familiar baritone. "Where is Ruydale? Fetch him at once!"

I struggled to open my eyes to see who had delivered me from peril. His image filled my vision—a great, glittering colossus, a large, heavy-featured face, small, faded blue eyes, an almost feminine mouth, sparse ginger beard.

The King saw I recognised him and inclined closer.

"I am fetching another doctor, Lady Catherine. You shall be well and whole, I promise you!"

I nodded. Nothing could withstand the power and influence of the King, not even death. I turned my head and yielded once more to sleep.

IV

MORE FACES, more prodding, more ministrations . . . my uncle the Duke had come; Mary and the Queen and some of her ladies hovered nearby; and Tom—always Tom with me, gaunt, pale, and dull-eyed with exhaustion. More cycles of day and night ensued.

At last, miraculously, a blessed coolness and comfort seeped through my body. The faces before me appeared less anxious. I heard once a short, gay laugh from the irrepressible Mary.

I opened my eyes, and I everything I saw was sharp. The fog, the pain and the giddiness had given up the fight and had left me. Mary sat beside the bed, sewing and humming softly. Apart from the two of us, the bedchamber lay empty.

I cleared my dry throat as a precursor to trying out my voice. Mary looked up at once and dropped her sewing to the floor.

"Oh, my dearest! You're awake!" She grasped my good hand and beamed at me. Overcome, she pressed my hand to her lips. "Oh, I am so pleased!"

The refreshing comfort after my long illness was intoxicating. I sighed with relief, while Mary placed my palm against her cheek. I remembered my injured hand, and lifted it to examine it. My index finger was bound in a small, clean bandage, but apart from that, my hand appeared—and felt—normal.

"It appears that parrot poisoned you when it bit you," said Mary with bitterness. "The doctors said it carried a foreign germ with it which passed into your blood . . . it nearly killed you! If it had not been for the King's doctors . . ." She shuddered.

I cleared my throat again. When I spoke, my voice was hoarse from disuse.

"The Queen told the King of my illness?"

"I believe she mentioned it to him . . . but it was Tom Culpeper who told him you needed urgent attention. He saved your life," Mary said. "Tom—er—was much troubled. He'll be wanting to see you, I am sure. Shall I fetch him for you?"

"Aye, please," I murmured. "But first—Mary, thank you. I know you were nearby during this time and cared for me. I am grateful."

"Tis nothing," Mary said and kissed my hand again. She rose to leave, then sank back into her seat, looking troubled. "There's something I must tell you before you see Tom . . . it's about the parrot."

I nodded enquiringly. Mary glanced behind her before she spoke.

"When Tom was first here and found you so ill, he was furious!" she said in an undertone "So furious at *that parrot*! He stormed downstairs, and grabbed the bird from its cage." Mary's bottom lip trembled in some distress. "My dearest, Tom wrung that bird's neck, threw the creature to the floor . . . then stamped on it!"

I recoiled in shock and abhorrence. Mary nodded. "Fortunately no one saw him do it but me—I had followed him downstairs for I suspected he was going to do something terrible. I know the bird nearly killed you, and clearly he did it for you . . . but it was awful, Catherine, to see his rage." She shuddered.

Willing myself to be calm, I sucked back a gulp of air. While I tried to steady myself, Mary rushed on with her account.

"I put it out that Tom was afeared for the King's safety, and that is why he killed the bird," she said. "The King has red hair similar to yours, as you know, which clearly attracted that creature. Of course, news of Tom's gallantry went down very well at court, the King was pleased, and the Queen could not object. Tom is more in the King's favour than ever now" Mary said dryly. "Not that he cares for that, of course . . . he does love you, doesn't he?"

I felt myself flushing. "Does he?" I asked, forgetting for the moment the abhorrent destruction of the parrot.

Mary laughed and patted my hand. "I shall fetch him for you and he can tell you himself!" She kissed me again, before rising from her stool.

"Mary, how long have been ill?" I called after her.

"Two weeks!" she exclaimed, disappearing out the door.

V

ONCE ALONE, I became aware of a blazing thirst. A pitcher stood on the table across the chamber. I hesitated only a second before struggling to sit.

My world spun. I closed my eyes, waiting for it to settle. When I peeped at my surroundings again, all seemed in its right place. Cautiously, I slipped my legs over the side of the bed and wriggled until my bare feet touched the ground.

The pitcher drawing me like a charm, I placed my weight on my feet and pushed off from the bed. I had taken several steps forward when my legs gave way, my world revolved again and I crumpled to the ground, just as the door to the bedchamber swung opened.

"Kate!"

Tom was by my side, scooping me into his arms.

"What did you think you were doing, getting out of bed?" he exclaimed. He laid me on the bed as weak tears filled my eyes and began to trickle down my cheeks. "Oh, Kate, I am sorry. Forgive me for being harsh!" His arms went around me and his strong warmth enveloped me.

"I am so thirsty," I wept.

He left me at once and strode to the pitcher. I heard the heavenly sounds of water being poured into a mug. When he returned to my side, he lifted me to sitting position and placed the mug to my lips. "Drink slowly," he urged.

I finished the water in several huge gulps. At once I became aware of another need and my vulnerability struck me anew. I began to weep again.

"What is it? Do you feel ill? In pain?" Tom twisted his hands in agitation. "Shall I fetch the doctor?"

"I need to use the privy, you little fool!" I sobbed, frailty making me horrid.

Tom blinked. "Oh. Do you want a chamber pot?"

Despite our intimacies I could not imagine using a chamber pot in Tom's presence.

"No! I said the privy!" I glared at him challengingly, swiping tears from my face. "Will you take me downstairs to the Queen's apartments or shall I go myself?"

I thought I saw something fleeting pass across Tom's face, quickly suppressed, but I knew from the glint in his eyes that it had been a smile.

"I will take you . . . Sweet Jesus, Kate, you are skin and bones," he remarked as he passed one arm beneath my knees, the other around my back, and lifted me against him.

"Maybe when I am on the close stool you can make yourself useful by getting me something to eat," I remarked crossly.

"Heartless wench," said Tom as we passed down the stairs into the Queen's bedchamber. When his eyes, close to mine, invited me to share the amusement of the moment, I looked away, although inside I laughed with joy.

Tom settled me on the Queen's velvet-covered close stool and left me to my ministrations while he called for some food. I had pulled my shift down and was waiting for him primly when he re-entered. He said nothing, although he did not meet my eyes and seemed flushed with suppressed amusement as he scooped me up and we passed into the Queen's bedchamber. Several ladies had entered in the interim and stared as we emerged. I smiled weakly and Tom nodded, as we left them to their wonderment.

Back in the maidens' bedchamber, Tom returned me to my bed and fussed with bedclothes and pillows until my patience snapped.

"Godbodkins, Tom, will you stop that and just kiss me?"

He sank onto the bed with a sigh and drew me into his arms. "I thought you would never ask," he said.

The kiss was chaste. I still felt weak and Tom was obviously curtailing his usual vigour. However, deep down the monster of my lust awoke and stirred sluggishly.

When Tom at last moved away from me, my tumultuous emotions and impatience had been put to rest. I sighed and stroked his face. He was less gaunt and exhausted than in my memories of my nightmare.

"I am so relieved you're better," he said, as if reading my mind. "These have been the worst two weeks of my life."

"I remember you were here often," I said. "I did not know you cared for me so much."

"How could you not know?" Tom asked, surprised. "I thought I had explained how I felt, on that first night."

"Sometimes a woman wants to be told in plain words how her lover feels about her, than being described as a toy ship," I said dryly.

Tom regarded me in brief silence.

"There is only one man I know who fears not to be blunt where matters of the heart are concerned—and that is the King," he said. "He will say 'I love you' as easily as he says 'fetch me some wine'!"

"And what can be wrong with that?" I asked, glaring at him. The memory of how the King saved my hand remained raw in my mind.

Tom held up his hands defensively. "Nothing wrong with it, especially as he usually means it! I was merely attempting to explain that lesser men cannot express love so freely."

"Oh, bah!" I said, exasperated. "Tom, I heard you when I lay here in a fever, I saw your grief." I stopped. I would not think of his distress and the slaughter of the parrot, it was too unpleasant to bear. "You can show your love. Why do not you just admit it?"

"Admit what?" Tom said in discomfiture.

"Admit you love me, you sweet, little fool. Just say it—three little words, Tom!"

In aggravated amusement I watched him while he battled with demons. I knew the demons myself. They had pursued me when I realised my own love that day outside the chapel. However, I also knew the one way to banish the demons was to admit to love. Admitting to love made it a reality, and even though love made one vulnerable, which we feared, the reality of it made one strong in the face of this, its greatest adversary. It is one of life's greatest competitions.

As he was still silent, I took pity on him.

"I shall make it easy for you," I said, stroking his face. "Repeat after me, Tom Culpeper. 'I—'."

He put his finger on my lips, and then replaced it with his mouth. I sensed the relinquishing of the fight in him. When he drew away to study my face anew, to stroke my hair and my skin, I watched as a lifetime of training in determined detachment drained from his countenance, and a new strength took its place.

His arms went around me. He nuzzled my neck and breathed into my ear, he stroked my shoulder blades and spine through my shift. When at last he kissed me again, I knew there was no need for words.

VI

I WAS RECLINING ON THE BED, ineffectually darning one of the Queen's underskirts and chatting idly with Mary Norris, when the door opened and my uncle Norfolk entered. Mary rose to her feet and hastened across the room to sidle past him, but he detained her with a touch of his hand on her arm.

"You may stay, Mary."

She hovered beside the door while my uncle strode across the chamber. As if standing to attention, he stopped a short distance from the bed and examined me with an expressionless countenance. Only a recollection of his obvious concern as I had lain dying ensured I met his gaze with equanimity.

"You feel in good health, niece?" he asked.

"Yes, thank you," I murmured. "I am a little weak, but grow stronger by the hour."

"That is good news." He paused. "I am leaving on the morrow to visit the embassy in France for a period—it seems Lord Cromwell has had his wish to remove me from Court.

May I suggest, if you require any advice in my absence, that you consult with the Bishop of Winchester?"

I frowned. "Why should I need to consult with Bishop Gardiner?"

He looked at me as if I was a senseless fool. "In matters concerning the King," he said.

My frown grew deeper, although a niggling awareness of what lay behind his words stirred giddiness in my stomach.

"Thank you for the advice," I said coolly.

The Duke nodded. "I am only sorry that I must leave you at this time," he said, "especially as I promised you I would take care of you. These must be nervous times for you."

I dismissed his words with an airy wave of my hand and a casual smile. "I shall be fine, uncle," I said. "I am sure there will be no need for me to seek advice from the Bishop or anyone else. Have a safe journey and I will look forward to your return."

His lips compressed into a hard line, he appeared irritated, and then shook his head in resignation.

"So be it," he muttered. "Good day to you, Catherine."

"Good day," I said. Mary scuttled to my side and together we watched as our uncle strode from the room.

"What was that all about?" she asked. "I couldn't hear all of what he said."

"Oh, he is just indulging in some long-held ambition for me which he believes is being realised," I said, picking up my sewing. "Quite absurd and improbable . . . not worth speaking about."

Mary laughed, lifting her own sewing. "You ought to know by now that the Duke's ambitions usually come to pass," she said.

"Not this one, I assure you," I said with conviction.

Chapter 17

"O tempora! O mores!"
(Oh, the times! Oh, the morals!)

Marcus Tullius Cicero
Roman lawyer, writer, scholar, orator and statesman
(106-43 BC)

I

TOM CULPEPER VISITED ME EACH DAY of my long recuperation period, and usually several times a day. During the busy daylight hours, his visits would be fleeting: he came only to check on my wellness and to banter with the other ladies, who would simper and flutter helplessly around him like moths drawn to a flame.

With the passing of my illness, the other maids of honour had returned to their quarters, making intimacy impossible. Tom took to missing supper to visit me. It was quieter then in the bedchamber and, although it was still too risky to indulge in our preferred activity, it was possible, with discretion, to obtain some minor satisfaction. Even that had to be abandoned after one of the ladies burst in on us at a crucial moment. In truth, we both found the subterfuge and danger exciting, and though we exercised some caution, we continued to engage in some swift, daring antics.

After two weeks of recuperation, I was fretting with boredom. I felt strong and perfectly well. I also longed for intimacy with Tom with a smouldering lust that disturbed my sleep and left me distracted during waking hours.

He came to the chamber the evening before I was due to resume my normal duties. After giving me a long kiss, he took his place beside me on the bed. We clasped hands chastely.

"I am not liking this very much," I said, wriggling against the tender yearning between my thighs that he always provoked. "I think I shall die if we cannot be alone soon. Can you not just come over here and very quickly—?" I slid my hand up his thigh to his hip while beneath the bedcovers my legs parted.

Tom swallowed.

"If I join you in bed, and someone discovers us, all pretence of my being just a childhood companion and cousin to you will be shown as the farce it is—I suspect your uncle already knows there is more between us than that."

That gave me pause. I could never shake the vague impression that Francis' removal from my life had not been simple misfortune. I did not want Tom to experience a similar banishment . . . or death.

However, the heat of his flesh beneath my palm proved too enticing for such troublesome ideas to dominate me for long.

"It is of no consequence now if others know we love each other, is it?" I asked rashly, as I ran my knuckles over his codpiece. I no longer cared if there was tattle about me and Tom—from wanting only to hug our secret love close to my heart, I now desired to shout it to the world.

"Mmm, I think you're right," he said, as we beheld hard, hot flesh revealed by my next wanton impulse to open his clothing. A quiver swept through my body and my hand slipped around it. Tom whistled, shifted, and lifted the bedcovers to slide beneath them.

We both jumped as the door swung open and Lady Lisle entered. She cast us a cursory glance as she hastened to rummage in a coffer. His back to her, Tom grimaced briefly, inclined away from me so my hand fell from his body, and surreptitiously closed his codpiece over his nakedness. He smiled in merry innocence at Lady Lisle when she looked at us again. She blushed and simpered at him as she left the room.

"You are incorrigible," I grumbled. I reached for his clothing again.

"Nay, Kate, I realise I must draw the line at putting on a show that I sense would not meet with your uncle's approval. Under any other circumstance, now—." He winked, assuming control, like the drawing on of a mantle.

I sighed. "Are you ever foolish and unpractical?" I asked. "And just once I would like you to abandon all restraint!"

"I am all those things aplenty when I am with you, as you know too well," he said. "However, I repeat, there are some places where even I must be circumspect. Speaking of practicalities—would you like to resume our trysts in Thomas's bedchamber? I could arrange for it tomorrow night if you feel quite well."

"I am perfectly strong!" I insisted. "Oh, how wonderful!"

He nodded in a matter-of-fact way, his lips pursed in further thought. "Another thing—we both have duties that can keep us preoccupied at odd hours. How long do we wait for each other in Thomas's chamber before returning to our own apartments?"

I was desperate enough to insist on the dawn hour. Tom laughed and placed his mouth on mine in a deep, exploratory kiss. As we heard the sounds of many light footsteps ascending the staircase, we parted.

"I challenge you to have me abandon all restraint tomorrow night, then," he murmured.

II

IT WAS CLOSE TO MIDNIGHT the next night when at last I managed to make my way through the cold passageways to Lord Cromwell's quarters and to my tryst with Tom. I wore only a cloak over a gown and shoes, and carried a torch. With my hair hanging loose and my frantic expression, I would have startled anyone who chanced upon me. Fortune favoured me, however, and I made it to Thomas Culpeper's bedchamber without incident or encounter.

When the handle gave under my shaking hand, I pushed the door open. To my disappointment, I found the room dark and empty. Presuming that Tom had been delayed with some task pertaining to the King, I placed the torch in the sconce and wandered aimlessly about the chamber before helping myself to some wine. Bored and frustrated I fiddled with my nails, braided my hair and drank more. When at last tiredness and the wine fuddled my perception, I stripped naked and crawled beneath the bedcovers.

I fell at once into a deep sleep, to be woken by the sound of voices outside the door. The voices were rough and clearly agitated. I recognised one as Tom's, although I could not discern the nature of the heated conversation. I heard one set of retreating footsteps and the door to the chamber yawned open.

Tom paused, framed in the doorway, ashen-faced, with clenched jaw and fists. His doublet was stained dark with . . . I gasped in horror and bounded out of bed, naked, as Tom shut the door and leaned against it. I stumbled to him, my hands reaching for his doublet . . . *blood*!

He clutched my hands. His grip was like ice.

"I am well," he muttered. "'Tis not my blood." He released me and tugged at the doublet, removing it and throwing it into the far corner of the chamber. All his other clothes went the same way, his agitation growing with every second. At last, naked, he pulled me into his arms. His body was rigid and freezing, his embrace suffocating.

I pushed at his shoulders and craned away from him.

"What happened?" I cried. "My God, Tom!"

"There was just a—an affray. All's well now. No need to talk about it . . . all's well ." He pulled me back against him and kissed my mouth.

The fierceness of his embrace told me all was not well. With an immense effort, I pushed away from him and staggered backwards.

A raw gasp rent my throat when he examined my body with a ferocious desire. I retreated as he approached me, until the back of my thighs came up against the table. I turned my back on him in a feeble effort to waylay his attentions.

"No, something terrible has disturbed you! I need to know, Tom!"

His arms swung around me again and I was hauled back against his body.

"Shush, dear heart!" he whispered against my neck. "I need something beautiful and sweet and simple right now! Let me—!" Lost, I sagged back against him, my head lolling on his shoulder.

One of his hands went between my legs and roughly stroked my inner thigh. I moaned, immune to all but the delight of his intimate touch. When he nudged my legs apart, I fell forward to clutch the edge of the table.

He plunged into my body with an intensity and a wildness such as I had never known, and I cried out in ecstasy. He grasped my hips and met every powerful involuntary contraction of my deepest muscles with strong thrusts of his loins until at last, with a loud growl, he too was spent.

I was whimpering when he scooped me into his arms and carried me to the bed.

"Forgive me," he whispered lying down beside me. "Did I hurt you? I am so sorry. It has been too long."

"No, no, you didn't hurt me." I sniffed, dashing the tears from my face. "It was so—so—. That surely must satisfy me for the rest of my life."

When he did not laugh or jest I knew he was still overwrought. I decided not to press him on what had happened to cause his agitation and the blood on his doublet. In truth, I was not certain that I wished to know. What was important was that he was with me now—and uninjured. I snuggled against him with a sigh.

At times over the rest of the night I would wake to see him lying alert and wide-eyed beside me, staring at the ceiling. On the third occasion, as instinct told me dawn approached, I raised myself onto my elbow and addressed him.

"Are you sure all's well?" I murmured.

"Aye, do not concern yourself. Come here." He lifted me up and pulled me across him so that I sat across his hips. Draping my hair back over my shoulders, he regarded my form with a catch of his breath, and I realised our earlier coupling had not satisfied me after all.

I raised myself to my knees, moved back and down. A hair-raising shiver swept across my body as I settled myself on him, and I threw my head back with a gasp of delight.

He began to tease me with earthy invocations, and his skilled caresses and touches urged me to the heights of desire and beyond. When my final whimper had faded into the silence, and I suspected he had been exercising that iron will of his until it had done so, I leaned over him. I kissed him deeply and encouraged him with a whispered summons and expressions of desire, matching his own words in earthiness, and with a groan and a shudder he too was lost.

"You have done it," he muttered later.

"Done what?"

"You have made me abandon all restraint."

I giggled, but could see that his smile did not quite reach the corner of his eyes, and my merriment faded. His gaze evaded mine.

"We had better return to our own quarters," he said, lifting me off him and swinging out of bed.

Sighing, I followed suit. When we were both dressed, and he had bundled the bloody doublet into a ball and tucked it under his arm, we made for the door, pausing there.

"On Thursday night then?" he asked, running a knuckle down my cheek.

I nodded and turned my face into his hand to kiss his palm.

"I love you," I said.

I knew he was not himself when he clearly struggled for his usual composure. "That's good to know," he said gruffly after a long pause, and ruffled my hair.

III

I LAUNCHED MYSELF into vigorous activity, relieved to be free from the stifling recuperation period set by the King's doctors. In the afternoon I noted many of the ladies huddling together in whispered consultation, and even intercepted a few curious, sidelong glances in my direction. However, only Mary's pale countenance when she exploded into the Queen's bedchamber and sought me out, caused my first feeling of trepidation. I laid down my darning as she rushed over.

"Dearest, I must talk with you," she whispered, grabbing my arm. I followed nervously as she led me up the stairs to our bedchamber and to our bed by the far window.

"What perturbs you, Mary?" I asked as we sat on our bed.

Mary glanced behind her, although the room was empty.

"It's about Tom."

My heart gave a sickening lurch. I gripped Mary's hand.

"What about him? What's happened?" My last question ended on a wail.

"Shush! He is physically well! But I have heard news . . . you must be told!"

"Told what? Godbodkins, Mary! Speak!"

She drew a tremulous breath. She grasped my hands in both hers in an attempt to comfort me. "You know Tom went hawking with some of the lads in the park yesterday aftermeal?"

I shook my head but urged her along impatiently.

"Afterwards, there was some drinking and carousing in the woods. The park-keeper's wife was passing through at the time. . . . Catherine, it appears that—."

Her voice trailed off. She swallowed and shook her head. I heard her mutter "I cannot . . ."

"Mary!" I urged, my voice breaking. "You must tell me!"

"Catherine, while the other lads held her down, Tom violated the park-keeper's wife!"

I stared speechless at Mary as an icy chill swept through my body. Mary continued in a rush.

"I am sorry, dearest, but there is more. Before the attack, he took a knife to the woman's escort who tried to come to her assistance—and killed him!"

Vile sickness welled in my throat. Just in time, Mary snatched up the nearest chamber-pot and held it beneath my chin. I retched into it, emptying my belly of all its contents.

Mary wept as she cleaned my mouth.

"Dearest, I am so sorry, but you would have learnt of this eventually, and I thought it best that it should come from me." She folded me into her arms. As weak and as pliable as a cloth doll I sank against her. Tom—a violator of women—and a murderer? I thought of his agitated state the night before . . . the blood . . . the wildness of his lovemaking . . . his appeal that he needed something "beautiful and sweet and simple"—to drive out the ugliness and violence of his crimes?

Another thought struck me, more horrible to me than any other.

I pushed away from Mary with a sob. "He will be arrested! He will hang for this surely!"

Mary shook her head and gripped my upper arms in emphasis. "No. That's something else I must tell you. He was arrested and charged, but at once received the King's pardon. It seems the King's high regard for Tom has saved him from the gallows!"

I sagged with relief, until the horror of the crimes struck me anew. Not Tom! He surely would not commit such heinous deeds!

"Mary, how do you know this?" I asked, clutching at straws "It could all be vicious rumour."

Mary shook her head. "I am sorry, dearest, but it is true. None of the lads who were with him will talk—such loyalty he inspires!—so for your sake I decided to seek further. I have just come from the King's quarters. I spoke with the King's secretary and he told me he saw with his own eyes the charge document and the pardon signed by the King. I am so sorry."

With all hope dashed, I lowered my head to my hands and Mary placed her arms around me, holding me tight.

IV

ON THURSDAY MORNING, the Queen was summoned to the King's presence-chamber to aid him in hearing petitions. forepart from Mary Norris, who was abed with illness, the Queen's entire household accompanied her.

The cavernous chamber was thronged with courtiers and petitioners. I glimpsed the Duke of Suffolk, Bishop Gardiner, Lord Cromwell and other men whom I vaguely recognised as members of the Privy Council. The King sat down heavily in his chair on the dais and the Queen took her place beside him. Uncharacteristically lost in morose reflection and melancholy that had beset me since learning of Tom's crimes, I began to drift among the gathering.

"Lady Catherine Howard!"

I jumped at the King's bellow and at once I swung around to face the dais, the embarrassment warming my cheeks. When the echo of his call subsided, silence fell and all heads turned to me. Through the throng a path to the dais opened magically before me.

The King had his hands braced on his knees and was leaning forward, staring at me. At once I dropped to a low curtsey.

Another bellow: "Come hither, child!"

On shaking legs, I straightened and somehow managed to walk towards him without tripping. Profiting by past experience, Lord Cromwell now drew forward a footstool and placed it beside the King's chair, earning himself a royal smile. Out of the corner of one eye I could see Tom Culpeper watching the proceedings with ill-concealed astonishment. The Queen appeared indulgent and interested. She smiled at me gently.

When I knelt before the King, he patted the footstool beside him. "Sit," he ordered. I obeyed, smoothing my skirts over my legs and then clenching my hands against their shaking. The gesture drew my attention to my finger injury, now well-healed, and I remembered how the King had saved my hand. I looked up at him and could not prevent a grateful, tremulous smile.

A splotch of colour suffused the King's broad face. His small mouth stretched into an eager smile.

"You are recovered from your illness, Lady Catherine?" he asked in a low, intimate tone. I could sense our audience craning forward to hear the words.

I spoke loudly and clearly. "Yes, I am fully recovered, Your Grace. I sincerely thank you for your kindness whilst I was ailing."

"You had us all very concerned—did she not, Thomas?"

I gave a start, thinking that his question had been directed at Tom, but the King dragged his gaze away from me and fixed it on Lord Cromwell. The King knew of the enmity and opposing factions at court—the religious conservatives, led by my uncle and Bishop Gardiner, and the advocates of the new faith, led by Lord Cromwell himself. I cared not for politics or religion but, by virtue of kinship, I was a conservative, and hence Lord Cromwell's adversary. Whether it was from wiliness or idle amusement, the King had issued a challenge to Lord Cromwell to side with his enemies in this instance.

Lord Cromwell did not look at me. He inclined his head at the King's query.

"Your Grace, you care greatly for all your subjects, it is what has made you England's finest and most noble King!"

It seemed the Privy Seal could be as slippery as my uncle in dealing with awkward questions. I glanced back at the King. Although he appeared gratified at the compliment, his mouth thinned into a brutal line as if he also recognised Lord Cromwell's cunning.

However, he closed his eyes briefly and grunted in dismissal, before turning his attention back to me. His gaze dropped to my neck and bosom. I felt more comfortable under his perusal than I had at our first meeting, for my green velvet gown had a high neck and voluminous overskirts. A black velvet hood almost covered my hair. I declined to colour my cheeks and daub my eyes, so I must have appeared pale and uninteresting, something that did not perturb me at all—rather, here I was grateful for it.

However, when I lifted my gaze to the King's, I saw not dissatisfaction, but admiration and ardour in his expression! In preparing me for my first meeting with the King, my Uncle Norfolk had deliberately provoked the King's baser instincts. Now, through no effort, by my decorous clothing and manner, I had incited nobler feelings. On the first meeting, I had walked in the shadow of my cousin, Anne Boleyn. Now, I suspect, the decorous Jane Seymour hovered at my shoulder. I repressed a squirm of discomfort. Of the two spirits, I knew which I found to be kindred.

The King reached down and lifted my hand. At once, a ripple of astonishment swept through the spectators.

"I have not forgotten my first promise to you, Lady Catherine," the King said, clasping my hand tight.

"Promise, Your Grace?"

"Indeed." He clicked his fingers at one of the hovering gentlemen, who scuttled to his side and leaned to listen. On the whispered command, the courtier bowed and rushed from the chamber through a side door. The King turned back to me. "Do you not remember my saying you ought to have some jewels and that I would attend to it?"

Flustered, I opened and shut my mouth several times. "I remember you saying it, Your Grace," I stuttered, "but—such generosity, it is not necessary."

"Nonsense," said the King. "It pleases me to give you jewels, and you wish me to be pleased, do you not, Lady Catherine?"

"Indeed, Your Grace," I murmured. "I am Your Grace's most devoted servant."

The King grunted in satisfaction as the courtier returned, who bowed and placed in the King's hands a flat satchel of black velvet, tied with a leather thong.

"Here," said the King, handing me the satchel. "I hope it is to your liking."

The satchel felt heavy in my hands. I hesitated. I didn't know the protocol when presented with such a royal gift. Did I open the satchel to examine the contents, and then display it to all by donning it? Or did I merely make my thanks and my hasty retreat with the satchel unopened? What would those experienced women of the court, Anne Boleyn and Jane Seymour, have done?

I remembered my uncle's advice. Through my lowered eyelashes, I glanced in Bishop Gardiner's direction. He seemed gleefully enthralled by the proceedings. With small, subtle nods and movements of his eyes he indicated what I should do.

With fingers that shook a little, I unfastened the leather thong and opened the satchel. It took all my strength not issue a childish gasp of amazement.

A necklace of heavy goldwork lay before me, the intricate weaving embedded with emeralds and diamonds. In the centre of the weaving, the letters C and H were entwined in pearl-encrusted gold. The initials of my name, or something else? I closed my eyes for a second against the blinding vision and my fearful thoughts.

I looked up. "It's beautiful, Your Grace," I whispered. "Thank you."

He waved his hand. "Put it on! I wish to see what it looks like against you!"

I lifted the ornament reverently and fumbled with the clasp before placing it around my neck. It lay heavy against my chest, evoking in me a deep sadness and apprehension. With the placing of that necklace around my neck, my life had changed irrevocably.

Feeling as if the jewellery was a yoke, I faced the King. Wearing a satisfied expression, he nodded.

"A beautiful adornment for a beautiful woman," he declared. "I hope to see you wear it often, Lady Catherine! Now—," he clapped his hands on his knees and regarded the throng before us. "I see I have more petitions to hear. A King has duties to his subjects just as the subjects have duties to their King," he said, clearly in high humour.

At once, I rose to my feet and backed away from the dais, curtseying as I went. Aware that I was the subject of intense speculation, I weaved my way through the murmuring gathering, seeking Mary's comfort and support, until I remembered she was not there. I steeled myself against looking for Tom: to do so would arouse further unpleasant rumour.

I found myself at the back of the chamber, surrounded by people, yet alone, with that heavy, beautiful yoke about my neck.

Chapter 18

"Suppressed grief suffocates.
It rages within the breast, and is forced to multiply its strength."

Ovid
Roman classical poet
(43 BC-17 AD)

I

BEFORE DEPARTING THE BEDCHAMBER for my tryst with Tom, and without understanding why, I snatched the necklace from its pouch and hung it around my neck. I tucked it beneath my gown where it lay cold and heavy against my skin, and stole through the dim passageways to Lord Cromwell's quarters.

When I slipped into Thomas's bedchamber, I stopped short. Tom awaited me, taut with impatience. He spun around to face me and a grin lit his face. I gave a start—he was half-naked, dressed only in slops. No matter that I knew his body as well as I knew my own, and despite my confused state, his nakedness jolted me from my uneasy humour. When his arms went around me, I sighed, my hands sliding eagerly over his back.

However, when he drew away from me and his mouth sought mine, I turned my head. It was a measure of my disordered mind that he could arouse me, yet at the same time repel.

His fingers lifted my chin and turned my face. "What's the matter" he asked with disturbing quietness.

I swallowed and shrugged. I dared not speak for I knew my voice would reveal my nervousness and antagonism.

After a second's reflection, his face cleared.

"Ah. I think I know. You fret about what happened in the presence-chamber?"

"I do fear what this gift from the King portends," I admitted. "I do not think it a simple generous gesture, signifying nothing."

Tom nodded. "Aye," he said. "The King was cock-a-hoop afterwards—I think it had more to do with you than any of the petitions he heard."

I felt myself grow cold. "He said as much?"

Tom shrugged. "I know him well. I have seen him in love before."

I felt ill. "In love? Surely not, Tom!"

"Do not be perturbed, Kate," he said, his arms closing around me tighter. "If anyone should be perturbed it is I, but I am not. You will never have to share his bed!"

"Because his marriage is unbreakable?" I said in desperate hope.

"No marriage is unbreakable for the King," Tom answered with a rueful smile. "And even if it were, he can have a mistress. No, I am at ease because the King has long desired in his bed a replica of Jane Seymour in all else but her looks—or at least, what his image of Jane was—and he will never find her, either at court or beyond it."

"What is that image?"

"Oh, a beautiful and simple young English maid, of rank, chaste and unsullied. You are all but the last two, methinks!"

His teasing smile took any sting out of his words, though I knew I could feel no affront, for he had spoken the truth. I gave a short laugh. "I must say that does reduce the field somewhat."

"Of course it does." He draped my hair over my shoulders, as he was wont to do, until it lay across my chest, uncovering the back of my gown. I felt his fingers fiddle with the laces there. "And even if the King's marriage is dissolved, and he abandons his hopes of the perfect woman, and decides he wants you after all—why, just tell him what Christina of Milan told him when he was looking for a foreign wife."

"What did she tell him?" I said, as my gown gaped open and coolness tickled the bare skin of my back.

"That she would consider marrying him if she had two heads, but as she only had one, it was out of the question."

I laughed. My gown tumbled to the floor and in a swift movement, Tom removed his slops. He drew my body against his and our naked hips locked together as if made for it.

"Failing that," Tom said, "do what Marie of Guise did when the King turned his attentions to her."

"What was that?" I said.

He looked into my eyes.

"She quickly married someone else."

My heart skipped a beat, but I shook my head.

"Marie of Guise doubtless has freedoms that I do not," I whispered. In a moment of stark reality, the truth stared at me: I was and always would be a pawn to be played as my family saw fit. I sighed as I realised all my efforts to forestall the King's intimate attentions had come to naught. "It seems this is what fate intends," I muttered miserably, unaware I had spoken aloud.

Tom frowned.

"Fate intends that you shall be with me," he said. "To do otherwise is to go against what is written in the stars and to mock God!"

He swept my hair away from my breasts and his hands closed over them. And then he froze. "What are you wearing that for?" he said, staring at the necklace. A shiver of apprehension snaked up my spine. I had no answer.

Now his voice was like frost. "Can it be you relish the King's attentions—that you want to share his bed? *That you want to marry him?*"

As sickening dread overpowered me with his manner, and along with it a vivid recollection of the parrot's fate, and of the rape and the murder. Fear brought tears to my eyes, but the tears did not move Tom to pity or tenderness.

He thrust his face close to mine. I cringed. "Am I not good enough for you now?" he hissed.

"Tom! Stop this!" I burst out at last on an anguished sob.

My entreaty had no effect. Tom grabbed hold of the necklace, his nails scraping my skin. With a yank, he tugged at it until I heard the fastening snap, then with a wild movement he hurled it away from him. The necklace pinched and choked me before it broke free, and I sobbed in distress as the bauble skidded across the floor and came to rest in the far corner of the chamber.

I staggered after it, and tripped, falling to the ground. On hands and knees I scrabbled across the floor towards the heap of twisted gold and gems.

A vice curled around my ankle. I was dragged away and over onto my back.

"No!" I cried, in desperation and fear.

Tom loomed over me. Unable to move as he gripped my thigh with his other hand and leaned on me, I closed my eyes and turned my head with a cry, not wanting to see this terrifying stranger.

Our ragged breathing rent the silence. I clenched my fists, ready to strike at him if he should dare assault me.

I felt something touch my breast. I gave a raw, frightened gasp; but my fearful shaking became tremors of delight as I recognised the tender touch of his mouth and tongue. My insides coiled, my loins melted, and my breathing became a long, shaky hiss. He was back! My childhood companion, my champion, my love . . .

My fingers curled into his crisp hair as his mouth burned a path across to the other breast, then down my torso. He drew my compliant legs apart and I felt his beard tickle my inner thighs. When his tongue flickered at the growing fire there, I cried aloud, and was lost.

However, my shattering climax incited a surge of tears. Played against my closed lids were visions of a stranger, angry and brutal. My body had betrayed me. Sickened, I rolled onto my side, away from him. He did not detain me. On his knees, he watched me as I retrieved the necklace and reeled to my gown, pulling it over my head. Not bothering to attempt to lace it, I staggered to the door.

I looked back at him. He had sunk to sitting position, and he watched me with impartiality.

"Good-bye, Tom," I whispered. "We shall not meet here again."

He did not respond. I pulled open the door and slipped into the dark.

II

I LAY AWAKE UNTIL DAWN, sobbing silent sobs of deep loss.

When first light began to creep across the sky, I knew the falsity of Father Vyncent's favourite Psalm: *Vesperum commorabitur fletus et in matutino laus*: "weeping may endure for a night, but joy cometh in the morning." For me, when my tears were exhausted, no joy consumed me, only heavy apathy. I cared for nothing—not for my glorious position at court, nor for what my uncle or the Dowager wanted from me, nor for the King's attentions.

As I lay staring at the ceiling in the cold dawn, Mary stirred beside me. She gave a groan and pushed herself to sitting position. The veil of my detachment lifting a little, I watched as she reached down for the chamber pot beside the bed, and frowned when I heard the sounds of retching.

I raised myself to my elbow. When she straightened and saw me watching her, Mary's expression became rueful.

"You look as bad as I feel," she said in a low voice so as to not awaken the other maids.

I sat up. "You're ill. Should I fetch a doctor?"

Mary shook her head. "I am not ill, Cousin Catherine. I know well what ails me and it is not illness. It will pass in time.

"What ails you?"

Mary regarded me bleakly. She dropped her voice further. "I suspect I am with child," she said.

I gasped. "Mary! Surely not!"

"Aye." Mary sighed. "I have committed the cardinal sin for a woman at court. Fornicate with whom you will, but if you should fall with child, then woe betide you!"

Speechless, I grasped her hand in sympathy.

"Do not worry about me, Cousin," she said with a heartiness that grated in its falseness. "I shall go home, and then in time I shall be bundled off to Yorkshire as Sir William's wife. It was always going to happen—this just brings it forward somewhat." She examined me sadly. "I am only unhappy that I must leave you. I fear you will need a friend soon."

Although Mary had not been present at the giving of the necklace, she had quickly learned of it before I had an opportunity to tell her myself. I dropped my gaze to our clasped hands as yet another loss smote me. I began to wonder how much more heartache I could stand.

"But do not be sad," she said with more forced cheer. "You have Tom, do you not? He shall look after you."

I shook my head. "Not any more," I mumbled, my voice breaking.

Mary placed her fingers under my chin and raised my face to examine it. "Oh, my dearest," she whispered. "I am so sorry. I had such hopes for that union. The perfect alliance in every way from your heart's stance and that of your family! However, I do understand why it has to be so."

I did not mention that my family—my uncle and the Dowager at least—aimed higher than Tom Culpeper. Tears choked my throat again.

Mary put her arms around me and held me close. "Well, you do have someone else here who will advise you well and take care of you."

I drew away, dashing hot moisture from my eyes. "Who?"

"Why our Uncle Norfolk of course! Oh, I know he is in France at the moment, but he will return and I expect he will return soon, once he learns of yesterday's happenings."

I grimaced.

"I agree," she said, "he is a rogue of the highest order, Catherine, but he takes care of his own—if they do well by him."

She was right. "Aye," I whispered. "But now, let us stop talking about me! Tell me, do you love the father of your child? Cannot you marry him instead?"

Mary threw back her head and laughed. As some of the maids stirred in their beds at the sound, Mary and I pulled the bedcovers over our heads.

"My dearest," whispered she, "I have no idea who the father is—and love never entered into my couplings."

"Perhaps that is the way it should be," I whispered back, mindful that my love for Tom, in heightening my enjoyment of our intimacies, had also redoubled the pain of his loss.

In the darkness, I saw Mary's eyes gleam. "Ah, no dearest," she said. "I do not think that is the way it should be at all. I envy those men and women who enjoy intimate love, no matter the cost. Surely there can be no more wonderful love!"

"Perhaps when the torment of my heart subsides, I shall agree with you, Mary," I said. "But now it is as if Tom has died, and all I can do is lament, and regret that I ever loved him."

Mary stroked my hair at my temple. "I understand. Oh, but it does grieve me to know that you are unhappy and will be alone!"

"You must not fear for me," I insisted at once. "You now have far more important things to think of. Rest assured, Mary, my unhappiness will pass . . . and as you have pointed out, I will not be alone—I have my uncle!"

Mary heaved a sigh. I was glad of the darkness—that she could not see how my face belied the confidence of my words.

III

I HAD KNOWN LOSS BEFORE: the deaths of my mother, my father, Francis and my sister Mary. I knew the pain of loneliness and want of love. Yet nothing could have prepared me for Mary's departure from my life, and for the bereavement that was Tom's absence from it.

I suppressed it with wine, for there was no other way to turn my mind from it, try as I did to wield my old skill at ignoring unpleasant realities. From the time I awoke each morning, to when I retired at night, I drank surreptitiously. It was a mixed blessing that the effects of wine never showed in my person or in my manner: on the one hand, my reputation remained unsullied—fortunately so, for intoxication was looked on with disapproval at the King's court; on the other hand, it meant I drank far too much and, it seemed, the more I drank, the more I needed to.

While it relieved my torment, it also prodded to the fore the vibrant, giddy side of my personality. The wine handed me the mask of the frivolous courtier and I acted the role with enthusiasm.

Of course, I often saw Tom. However, in my stupor, I managed to ignore him. Just as mindlessly, I openly flirted with another Gentleman of the Privy Chamber, Thomas Paston. That was until I turned my attentions on the King . . .

With fulsome charm, and because I knew it to be what my Uncle Norfolk wanted, I encouraged what all the court now understood to be the King's obsession with me. Thrice more the King called me to his side in his presence-chamber and on each occasion his ardour for me became more apparent. In his happiness the King called more often for music and dancing. I partnered him frequently at post-supper festivities, the seduction of the dance contributing to my insensible state.

I did not find the King's attentions objectionable; perhaps it is difficult to loathe someone who is prepared to be so open and lavish with his adoration. I found him tender and charming, in possession of a quick sense of humour, sharp wit and excessive generosity. He incited my sympathy with his apparent distaste for his age, his physical ailments and the discomforts associated with them, and I wished I could relieve him of some of his pain. When I declared as much to him, to my embarrassment he took my hand and, with tears in his eyes, pressed numerous hot kisses over it. Although I could not imagine in my wildest dreams ever yearning to couple with him as I had with Tom, and even Francis and Henry, I did grow fond of the King and was not averse to his company.

If I was able to feel despair, it would certainly have smitten me on learning that the

King had appointed himself my suitor, as he actively sought for a way out of his marriage. The Queen had remained a virgin—so said the gossips—and this paved the way for an easy annulment. This did not appear to trouble the Queen. However, I am sure it passed through her mind—as it did through ours—that, failing all else, the block could end any marriage the King found unpalatable. I prayed I would not be the cause of her death.

My elevated position at court meant that I received favoured treatment and much grovelling attention. Eager ladies relieved me of all my sewing duties, and I was often astonished to find people inclining their heads as I walked past.

One evening in late March, I retreated from the dining hall in a thicker than usual fog of intoxication and tripped upstairs to the maid's bedchamber, where I swooned on my bed. Vigorous shaking from Lady Rochford woke me some hours later.

"Lady Catherine! Wake up!"

I dragged open my eyes and peered into her thin, sallow face.

"What is it?" I mumbled

"Are you ill? I hope not, as I have news. You must arise at once!"

I sat up, rubbing my eyes. "I am only weary," I lied. "What news?"

"The Duke of Norfolk has returned! He would see you in his apartments immediately. Make haste!"

Chapter 19

"Nothing is more noble, nothing more venerable than fidelity.
Faithfulness and truth are the most sacred excellences
and endowments of the human mind."

Marcus Tullius Cicero
Roman lawyer, writer, scholar, orator and statesman
(106 BC-43 BC)

I

A SMALL AUDIENCE OF LADIES gathered while Lady Rochford assisted me into a fresh gown and hood. Lady Lisle made to stroke cosmetics in my cheeks before I waved them away, although I allowed her to dab perfume on my temples and smooth my hair. The Duchess of Richmond offered me sustenance from a silver platter; I shook my head and pointed imperiously to the flagon. After I had taken a large swallow of wine, Lady Rochford and the Duchess escorted me from the chamber and we made our way in a regal fashion to the quarters that the Duke claimed as his own when he resided at Greenwich Palace.

The Duke's steward opened the door at the Duchess's knocking and nodded his dismissal to the ladies, before ushering me inside. He led me at a fast pace across to another door, opened it and stepped aside so I could enter. The door closed behind me with a bang, and I found myself alone with the two occupants of the small, intimate antechamber, which appeared as if it had been set aside for music and casual meetings. Virginals rested on a large mahogany table and several large chairs were positioned around it. Pictures and tapestries depicting jousting scenes relieved the dark panelling of the walls. A large fire in the grate burned a warm welcome.

Beside the fireplace stood my uncle Norfolk and Bishop Gardiner, my uncle leaning casually against the mantelpiece, the Bishop standing near by, his hands clasped behind his back. A thrill of relief and pleasure coursed through me to behold my uncle. I no longer was alone and without counsel in my frightening dealings with the King. Always happy to view a fine masculine spectacle, I also noted that he had regrown his beard and was resplendent in a surcoat of black velvet. Although they would have been aware of my entrance, neither one looked around. I heard Bishop Gardiner say "The devil is not yet gone, for men who no longer wear the friar's habit offer heaven without works!" The Duke murmured his fervent agreement and at last glanced in my direction.

"Ah, Catherine!" His face creased into a wide, rarely-seen smile, which startled me. "Come hither and have some wine! My Lord of Winchester and I have been discussing the heretical views of Dr Robert Barnes . . ."

I am sure my eyes glazed over as I approached. I had little comprehension of the bewildering theological arguments raging throughout the realm and only a vague recollection that Dr Robert Barnes had recently preached the divine service entirely in the vernacular. Martin Luther himself regarded the doctor as a close friend, but I never bothered my head with reflections on the man and his views. As the Bishop pressed a mug of wine into my hand,

I truly hoped that I would not be expected to participate in any religious debate.

I fidgeted, drank some wine and idly studied the Bishop as he continued with his musings: ". . . yea, according to Doctor Barnes and his ilk, a man might live in his pleasure and yet have heaven at the last!" He possessed a long nose, smooth, pale skin that a woman would have been proud to possess, a prim mouth and large, limpid brown eyes. The softness of his features belied his nature, which rumour had it was quick-tempered, sharp-witted and fanatical.

"Outrageous," agreed the Duke, drawing my attention. He looked at me and I hastily swallowed some more wine to forestall his involving me in the discussion. At once, the haze in my mind intensified, and the wine must have been more potent than I was used to, or—more likely—I had reached my satiation level, for I swayed on my feet. The Duke took a quick step towards me, steadying me with a firm arm.

"My apologies," I murmured. "I am—I have been a little indisposed."

The Duke at once led me to the seat in the window embrasure and urged me to drink more wine. The Bishop followed with some uncertainty.

"I shall leave you with your ailing niece," he said, bowing his head at me. "Perhaps we can finish our discussion at another time?"

"Indeed!" The Duke left my side and walked with the Bishop to the door. I heard him murmur: "Remember, my friend, the King leans neither to the right nor the left hand," and the Bishop respond, "But he holds most firmly to the Catholic doctrines!", before they disappeared through the door. By the time the Duke returned, I felt steadier and had no compunction about accepting another serving of wine from him.

"You feel better?" he asked, taking a seat beside me. Somewhat surprised at his solicitude, I nodded, watching him warily. He seemed brighter of eye than I had ever seen him, exuding excitement as he placed the wine flagon on a table near by.

"Good. The King has stated his intention to call on your step-grandmother on the morrow, and has requested that we both be in attendance, so it is important that you be well," he announced to my further surprise. "May I suggest that we travel by barge to Norfolk House in the morning?"

Now that I was in my uncle's care, I took the startling news with equanimity. "Aye, of course!"

The Duke gave a grunt of satisfaction. He watched with a slight beetling of his brows as I threw back the wine in my mug and looked longingly at the flagon. He hesitated, then poured me another, also filling his own mug. He raised his to me in salute. "I also wanted to see you," he said, "to express my pleasure at how well you seem to be conducting yourself at court. I have heard many good reports. Well done, niece!"

I beamed at him, and his mouth twitched in response. "Thank you," I said. "I wanted nothing more than to please you."

"And you have pleased me, very much!"

Our eyes locked and held for many seconds, before he looked away. He set down his mug, strode to the door and disappeared through it. Several minutes later he returned, followed by a brightly-garbed minstrel bearing a lute. When the Duke resumed his seat beside me, the young lad took a stool and began to play and sing softly.

As light-hearted, simple songs of love and loss filled the silence, the wine level in the flagon sank lower and our forms on the window seat relaxed and inclined towards each other.

What may have been an hour or two later, the minstrel warbled the words:

> Wheretofore should I express
> My inward heaviness?
> No mirth could make me fain
> Till that we meet again

When I sniffled audibly, my uncle leaned forward, rested his elbows on his knees and bowed his head. The wind rattled the window panes and blew needling sheets of rain against them. Despite some shared heaviness of soul, I felt then more than at any other time the comfortable alliance between my uncle and me, and found in it a haven amidst the turmoil of my life. The minstrel sang on in a sweet, mournful tone.

> Greensleeves was my delight,
> Greensleeves my heart of gold
> Greensleeves was my heart of joy
> And who but my Lady Greensleeves . . .

"That's enough!" snapped the Duke, making me jump. He dismissed the minstrel, who sprang to his feet and backed from the room in a low bow.

When we were alone, I attempted to straighten from my half-slumped position on the window bench. Swaying a little, I smoothed my hair and cleared my throat.

"Perhaps I should—," I began.

My uncle interrupted with an abruptness that startled me.

"What is your view of fidelity, Catherine?"

Astonished, I laid down my mug and regarded him, blinking owlishly.

"Do you mean in marriage?" I asked as my thoughts started to move sluggishly.

"Not necessarily." I giggled at my absurd question before pressing my fingertips to my lips to stifle my humour. It was clear what the Duke thought of fidelity in his own marriage. While his wife—Elizabeth, the Duchess of Norfolk—languished in some obscure county, the Duke shared his bed and his home at Kenninghall with Bess Holland, the former laundress in his children's nursery. The Duke slanted me a look, arching an eyebrow, and I was relieved to see his mouth soften. "And I mean not just sexual fidelity. I mean loyalty or devotion to a loved one."

It must have been a measure of his own intoxication that he could muse on such a matter, I decided. However, I was so flattered to be asked my opinion that I considered the question carefully.

"Well, where there is love there is fidelity, is there not?" I said. "And where there is fidelity there is love. There cannot be one without the other."

"A romantic notion perhaps," the Duke said, without derision, and he shifted in his seat so that I could see his full face.

"Why do you ask such things?" I asked, studying him. He glanced over the rim of his mug. When he lowered it, his eyes did not leave my face and his tongue slowly tasted the wine on his lips. I stifled a gasp.

"There was a time I would have scoffed at the idea of fidelity and love going together," he said. "Why, I would have argued that without compunction I have not been true to people I loved."

Sufficiently diverted, I said, "Then you never loved at all."

The Duke shrugged. "Perhaps—in some cases."

"You said you once would have disagreed with my notion. Does that mean you agree with me now?"

"Mmm." His expression became distant. "I have found myself of late, despite the greatest of temptations, wanting to remain faithful to—"

He stopped. With a grimace of annoyance, he muttered "Bah! Why do I talk such nonsense?" He rose as if to leave but I placed my hand on his forearm and he slowly sank down.

"To Mistress Holland?" I asked. He looked back into my face. He did not need to answer—or to explain the nature of his "greatest of temptations."

Many would have relished with glee my discovery that the Duke of Norfolk possessed sexual fidelity, a quality regarded as a poetic weakness. To me, however, it denoted strength and dignity. I envied the mysterious Bess Holland.

He detected my admiration, and smiled sardonically.

"Do not be naïve about me, niece," he said. "I am still not convinced about the veracity of your notion. How do you explain that I would not hesitate to be untrue, if someone I loved—even my mistress—did wrong by me?"

"My philosophy is still valid," I said. "Love and fidelity still exist together in such a scenario. It just so happens in that case that there are two loves within you, competing for the prize of the fidelity, and one emerges the victor."

He tilted his head to the side. "Interesting idea," he mused. "And who do I love so, that makes me betray someone else I love? Tell me that, niece!"

"A warrior such as you, who has fought all his life for survival, loves one person more than anyone else," I said. "Why, it is that very love which makes him a survivor!"

"I do believe you have been drinking too much, Catherine," the Duke rumbled with a frown. "You're talking in riddles. Who is it that I love so?"

"Why, uncle," I murmured. "'Tis yourself."

II

"THAT MAKES ME VERY SELFISH," he said as we strolled back towards the Queen's apartments. He walked with his hands behind his back, while I had tucked my own in my sleeves against the chill. Despite the late hour, we encountered many bustling courtiers who bowed as we passed

"God put us on this earth to survive, did he not?" I said, defending him. "Then to do otherwise is to mock Him! And why should love of oneself be of lesser value than the love of someone else? God made us all!"

We arrived at the gallery near the Queen's apartments. He touched my elbow and I stopped to face him.

"You make a convincing argument, niece." He leaned closer so that his mouth was near my ear. "Yet I suspect a surfeit of wine has robbed you of some good judgement, but I thank you for your loyalty." His leaned down and kissed my cheek.

"We none of us are perfect," I conceded. "As I know well."

"Aye, indeed," he acknowledged. He pressed his lips together, examining my face, seemingly on the brink of saying something of portent.

"Given that I am self-seeking," he said at last in a low tone, "for me to say I also love you, niece, has little value, I suspect?"

I could only swallow and whisper: "It has value." I smiled and he nodded, turning from me, his countenance impassive.

"I will leave you here," he said tersely, "and will see you at the dock on the morrow." I nodded. He inclined his head in farewell and strode back down the gallery. I watched him leave, happier than I had been since the end of my association with Tom. I knew from that moment that I did not need wine to provide solace in my loneliness and fear. I had the second most powerful man at court as my ally.

III

IMMEDIATELY ON ARRIVING at Norfolk House the next day, we became immersed in frantic activity. Arrangements for the King's surprise visit were well under way. We encountered a fraught Dowager in the Great Hall, her grey hair falling from beneath her gable headdress and straggling around her blushed neck, spraying spittle as she shouted orders at the scurrying servants. She nodded a distracted greeting at the Duke. To my surprise, she then turned a wide smile on me and approached me with outstretched arms.

"Catherine! Child! How wonderful to see you again and how beautiful you are!" Stiff with shock, I did not move as she clapped her hands on my cheeks and pressed a wet kiss to my forehead. "Now, you must go and rest before the King arrives. I have set aside the large bedchamber in the northern wing for your use, and you may have a maid to attend your needs—You!" I jumped as she shouted at a passing maid. My former antagonist, Mary Hall, scuttled to her side. "Pray take Lady Catherine's belongings to her bedchamber and make sure she has everything she needs."

I began to murmur some protest as Mary, with a sulky curve to her mouth, stalked off with my belongings. I had been looking forward to sharing my old communal bedchamber with my girlhood friends, and I certainly didn't want Mary Hall hovering at my shoulder every minute. However, the Dowager had turned away to sample a gravy that a servant had brought from the kitchens for her inspection, and was oblivious to my hesitation. I glanced at my uncle, who nodded and jerked his head in the direction of the staircase.

"Go," he said, not unkindly. "Take advantage of this offer of peace and quiet! It may be in short supply over these next few days."

Sighing, I turned to trudge up the stairs. Wanting to delay the moment when I must deal with Mary Hall, I lingered for a moment near my former chambers, hoping one of my friends would emerge. My hopes dashed, I plodded towards the southern wing.

In the large bedchamber set aside for my use, I found Mary already placing my garments in the armoury and coffers. A large four-poster bed dominated the centre of the chamber and a draw-table, a dresser, chairs and stools were positioned about the floor, now covered in rugs woven with silk thread.

Mary ignored me when I entered. As I hesitated in awkwardness, I recalled my old suspicion that Mary Hall had had romantic feelings towards my former music tutor and lover, Henry Mannox. It accounted for her animosity towards me.

Regardless, I was in no mood to be tolerant of Mary Hall and her ill-manners.

"Pray leave that, Mary," I said. "And leave me, I wish to be alone for a while."

Mary seemed surprised, but stalked to the door, pulled it open and swept through it, slamming it shut behind her. Her animosity smarted. I sank to the bed with a weary groan. Self-pity evoked ready tears, until a happy realisation dashed them away.

Someone else was nearby, who placed fidelity to me on a level only with his fidelity to God. Someone who had always loved and cared for me! I sprang off the bed without hesitation and hurried from the bedchamber.

IV

WHEN I BURST INTO THE CHAPEL VESTRY, Father Vyncent looked up, startled. At once he sprang to his feet, his chair crashing to the ground.

"My lady!" He held out his arms, his round face wreathed in a broad smile, and I sank into his embrace.

When we were seated, he poured the customary mug of wine and pushed it in my direction. I shook my head.

"I should not, but I thank you," I murmured. "I have been imbibing too much of late."

Father Vyncent looked sorrowful. "An unfortunate habit that is my fault," he said. "All those nights when I urged you to drink with me while we talked! I am sorry, my dear." He pushed the mugs and flagon to the far corner of the writing table.

"You could not have made me drink had I not wished to," I remarked, "and I have done so of late, for it helped me forget some unhappiness in my life."

"I have heard much of court happenings," Father Vyncent probed gently. "The King seeks a way out of his marriage, and appears interested in making another—." He paused meaningfully.

"He may be interested," I admitted, "but I pray once he learns I have not been chaste, he will not wish to take me as his wife."

Father Vyncent cleared his throat. "Perhaps," he said, taking care with his words, "he will be so in love with you that he will not care about your . . . past experiences. You must also remember, that in the eyes of the Church, you were married to Master Dereham—in that circumstance, it is not unusual for there to be intimacy, as the King would understand."

I grew cold. Perceiving my shock, Father Vyncent pressed my hand tighter.

"I am sorry, child—I see you had not contemplated that possibility. I am sure that is the excuse your family will give the King when the matter is raised. But I regret being the bearer of such news."

I rubbed my temples in agitation. My relationship with Francis had been my way out of this predicament with the King, for no one but Mary Norris knew I had been similarly unchaste with Tom Culpeper. And something—some vague disturbance connected with Francis' death—made me reluctant to reveal my intimacy with Tom to my family . . .

"Father Vyncent, what can I do?" I asked in despair. "I have grown fond of the King, but I cannot forget how my cousin died, nor the manner of Queen Jane's death. I know I have the support of my Uncle Norfolk at court, but he wishes me to be Queen, so I cannot expect him to take my side in this. Oh, I do not wish to be Queen! Especially now that I love another—."

Father Vyncent started.

"You love another?"

"Tom," I whispered. "And we have loved each other intimately."

He sighed in deep satisfaction.

"At last," he murmured. "Why then, my lady, do you look so troubled? If you and Master Culpeper do love, why, you can marry! That's your solution!"

Marry, just as Mary of Guise had done, to waylay the King's ardour, I thought. Tom had also hinted at such a solution. However, I shook my head.

"I cannot marry him now," I said. "I declare Tom Culpeper frightens me more than does the King!"

"Frightens you?" Father Vyncent blinked in astonishment. "Master Culpeper?"

I burst out with the story of Tom's unruly temper—the slaying of the parrot, the violation of the park-keeper's wife, the murder, and his anger over the necklace. When I had finished, Father Vyncent's was gaping at me in shock and sorrow, his own devotion to Tom betrayed.

After a long silence, he spoke, rubbing his temples in agitation.

"I can only assume Master Culpeper has been influenced by the treachery and evil that abounds in King Henry's court," he muttered, "and perhaps the intensity of his love for you has made him behave irrationally when confronted with the prospect of losing you. Aye," he nodded, his expression clearing. "However, that does not excuse such crimes as you say he has committed. Is there no doubt, Catherine?"

I shook my head. "My cousin Mary Norris spoke to the King's secretary who saw the charge document and the King's pardon."

"Hmm." Father Vyncent passed a hand across his mouth. "It makes little sense. Why would he do such a thing when he knew he was to meet with you that very night? Ah! Perhaps I am not able to comprehend such impulses to violence—but it is strange indeed. My lady—." He leaned forward and grasped my hands. "You must talk with him—that is all I can suggest. And talk with him at once!"

I was more than happy to surrender to his advice.

"But, Father, I am not to return to Greenwich Palace for several days!" I said. "I cannot talk to him straightaway!"

Father Vyncent drew his lips between his teeth in determined contemplation.

"Would Master Culpeper be coming here with the King today?" he asked at last, his face flushing in eagerness.

"It's possible," I said. "He is one of the King's close household!"

"Then let us wait and see. And if he does not come—well, you can leave it to me. You shall talk with Master Culpeper before the day is out, Catherine, I promise you!"

In sudden joy, I leaned forward and threw my arms around the priest's neck. "I am so thankful to you! Oh, I knew I could rely on you to set things right, Father Vyncent!"

"Ah, Catherine!" He patted me on the shoulder. "You really must draw on your own resources and rely on God for salvation, rather than on others. You are bound to be disappointed otherwise."

I heard his counsel, yet in my excitement I paid it no heed. Like a child who has had a wound kissed by her mother, I left the vestry feeling light of heart, not caring that the wound itself remained unhealed and festering.

Chapter 20

"To live is to think."

Marcus Tullius Cicero
Roman lawyer, writer, scholar, orator and statesman
(106-43 BC)

I

THE KING ARRIVED AT NORFOLK HOUSE in mid-afternoon with his extensive entourage.

I had returned to my bedchamber after speaking with Father Vyncent. A fleeting visit from Joan and Agnes broke the boredom of the next few hours, but as they could do little but quiz me on my relationship with the King, the conversation soon became tiresome.

"I am sure that naught will come of the King's interest in me," I said, "and certainly nothing has happened that is worth discussing—the King is, after all, still married to Queen Anne!"

"But he has sought the help of Lord Cromwell to extract him from the marriage, has he not?" asked Joan. "And does not this visit to Norfolk House signify something of import?"

A knock on the door prevented me from answering. Mary stepped into the chamber and bobbed a curtsey that failed to be respectful.

"Ma'am, you are required on the terrace. The King wishes you to acquaint him with the gardens."

While she waited, Joan and Agnes fluttered around me in excitement.

"Perhaps His Grace will reveal his intentions today!" gasped Agnes.

"Catherine, you must change into something more comely!" said Joan, pressing her hands to her flushed cheeks. "That olive green does nothing for your complexion. Let us see—." She rushed to the armoury.

I began to remove my hood, and Agnes scrabbled at the lacings on my gown. Mary reluctantly came to her side to help. Joan hurried to us, her arms laden with garments that she laid on the bed—a bodice, sleeves, skirt and train of gold brocade, the sleeves lined and turned back with ermine, and an underskirt and false sleeves of crimson velvet. She returned to fetch a hood in a style different to the current fashion—its white cap cut back so it sat well behind the temples, and curving forward on the cheeks in front of the ears. To this part a narrow chin strap was attached. The cap was edged around the top with gold braid, and a goffering of double gold gauze underneath it rested on the hair. Gold beads alternately spherical and cylindrical in shape masked the wire edging of the crimson velvet hood. Joan gaped in astonishment when the garment was at last secured to my head, and even Mary Hall deigned to look impressed.

A large crowd milled in the Great Hall when I descended the stairs and countless eyes followed me as I moved through the throng and out onto the terrace.

The King waited for me beside the fountain. About him hovered his close personal bodyguards—the Gentlemen Pensioners. These men of gentle birth but little fortune, who wore armour and carried pole-axes, served in closer attendance on the King than the

Yeomen of the Guard. At first it seemed to me that all fifty of them and every one of their personal attendants—each Gentleman had three attendants: an archer, a demi-lance and an armed servant—had assembled on the terrace, along with the scarlet liveried Yeomen of the Guard. However, as my composure returned with the thrill of being the centre of attention, I acknowledged that for this occasion the King had probably reduced his attendants by at least half. I did not see any of the Gentlemen of the Privy Chamber, though I knew that at least some—even, I hoped, one in particular—would be somewhere close by.

As I approached the King, his attendants stepped back. The King gaped at me, the flush on his sagging cheeks heightening. His admiration gratified and flattered me immensely.

On this occasion, the King wore a coat of dark blue velvet, descending to below the knee, with black silk hose and wide-toed black shoes. The coat was embroidered with gold cord, and the gold bands of the bodice and sleeves were barred with goldsmith's work set with emeralds. His doublet of cloth of gold was decorated with silver embroidery, diamonds, rubies, emeralds and pearls. His black velvet bonnet was likewise bejewelled. A massive, glittering figure, he took my breath away.

I curtseyed low before him, but he urged me up almost straightaway.

"Lady Catherine—how beautiful you are," he said. "Come, walk with me."

He gestured to his attendants to keep back and I fell in by his side as we descended the stairs to the flower gardens. With a respectful distance between us, we spoke of the sweet scent of wet grass and battered petals that hung on the air from the storm the night before. Then—his leg clearly paining him—the King slumped onto a stone bench in the rose garden. I hesitated before he gestured to the space beside him. For several long minutes, while I sat stiffly beside him, the King was sunk in gloomy silence. I knew from experience that this silence meant he experienced regret at his infirm condition and, as usual, I felt pity for him. How dismal, I thought with the arrogance of youth, that a man once young and lusty should come to this: aged, ailing and plain! I dreaded the time when I would be the same.

With the skill that I could wield without effort, I sighed in apparent bliss and clasped my hands together. The King slanted me a dully enquiring glance.

"My Lord," I said, "I confess, I am blinded by your majesty's splendour, and my heart has not known such joy in all its days."

The King's gloominess vanished at once, as I knew it would. "It pleases me that you find such happiness with me! Would that the happiness will endure!"

I flushed at the implied meaning. Although the flush was not deliberate, the King seemed further enchanted. He sighed with apparent pleasure and looked away, his thoughts soon reclaiming him.

I wondered what preoccupied him as the silence endured, and at last summoned sufficient boldness to ask him. In response, he reached out and clasped my hand.

"Ah, I ponder always on the troubles in my realm, Lady Catherine. It pleases me that you make such an enquiry. I shall then share with you my thoughts."

It soon became apparent what fixated him and I groaned inwardly at the first mention of the word 'Church'.

"I search for a doctrinal formula no less diligently than my bishops; yea, for I must as Supreme Head of the Church! I pray to know the rightful destination. The Reformers, like the Vicar General, Lord Cromwell, know precisely the direction in which they want me to go—they wish me to follow Continental Protestantism. Fine men such as my Lord Bishop of

Winchester and your uncle of Norfolk, however, want a Catholic Church without the Pope. But they cannot expect me to throw a man headlong from the top of a high tower and bid him stay where he was halfway down!

"I search my soul and see my own inclinations are far from the Lutheran position. Yea, I regard that 'perfect school of Christ' in Geneva to be the font of abominable heresies! I hold firmly to many Catholic doctrines and delight in the ceremonial and customary observance, which accord such solemn beauty to my Mass in the Chapel Royal. On the other hand, I do not uphold auricular confessions or extreme unction . . .

"You may recall in the spring past talk of the great debate perhaps? On that occasion, my Lord Bishop of Winchester and others including Archbishop Lee of York quite bettered the side led by Archbishop Cranmer. Of course I would not agree to countenance compulsory confession but certainly the Six Articles arising from the debate was damaging to the reformist cause."

He stopped and, aware of my silence, shot me a narrow-eyed glance.

"As I search for pure doctrine to settle the disputes about the Scriptures and ceremonies, the feeling of my people is uppermost in my mind—Lady Catherine, of course I know you support the Duke of Norfolk's stance, but what is your view of the feeling of my people? Do my subjects undoubtedly approve of the Six Articles and may I assume that my people are more inclined to the old religion than the new opinions?"

Of course, I had not the faintest notion and I cared even less. I remembered Father Vyncent once dwelling with fascination on the English prayer book and espousing a careful view that it might be a 'clearer way to Christ' for the lower classes; however, I had no idea whether it would serve me well with the King to repeat such a view. I gaped and struggled to say something that did not betray my stupidity and want of scholarship, and all the while the King's faded blue eyes grew narrower and his lips thinned. He released my hand as if it now repulsed him.

"You have no view, Lady Catherine?"

My cheeks burning and perspiration slaking my palms I stuttered, "I—of course, my Lord, I am your majesty's most loyal subject—and, I support my uncle . . . and . . ."

The King made an annoyed sound. Abruptly, he shifted in his seat and gestured to his guards. "I wish to return to my apartments," he bellowed, pushing himself with enormous effort to his feet. At once, several guards hastened to his side. Showing an agility born of aggravation, the King strode swiftly from the rose garden, leaving me staring after him in shock.

I sat in silence for many minutes after the King and his entourage had gone. Only Joan and Agnes remained with me, hovering uncertainly in the far corner of the rose garden. When I looked at them, wishing they would approach and give me their friendship, I saw them staring in apparent nervousness in the direction of the steps leading down from the terrace. I turned to follow the direction of their regard.

My uncle Norfolk, his black cloak billowing behind him, swiftly descended to the gardens, with long, agitated strides, fists clenched at the ends of swinging arms.

I wished the ground would open up and swallow me. When my uncle stopped before me, I did not look up at him.

"What happened?" he barked. "How did you anger the King so? Did you tell him—." He bit off the final question.

Despite my turmoil, I concluded he was about to ask if I had revealed to the King my unchaste life. Evidently, as it so worried the Duke, it was after all my ace in the hand. I stored the information up for future cogitation and the power it gave me lent me some strength to respond to the interrogation.

"The King asked me my views on a religious matter," I said sulkily. "I had no views. He was not impressed."

The Duke gasped. If he was not wearing a cap, I am sure he would have raked his fingers through his hair in despair; as it was, he only rubbed his mouth in agitation before exclaiming: "Of all the things that can destroy our hopes it is your foolishness which is the undoing! Swounds, Catherine!"

I flared up at once, our alliance forged the previous evening forgotten. "Is it my fault that I have had little training in the theological arguments which abound?" I raged. "Is it my fault that I have no theology?" In high umbrage, I rose and made to brush past him.

He grabbed my arm at once. His jaw was tense with fury and his black eyes seemed to release fiery sparks; yet I met his anger with a like stare and did not quail in my righteous indignation.

A fleeting expression passed across the Duke's face—for a second I thought it was admiration—before impassiveness cast itself on his features and the sparks were reduced to a muted glitter. He dropped my arm.

"You say right," he said at last. "Your untutored condition is not your error."

I smoothed my skirts with hands that trembled and felt my lips purse into a deeper sulk. "You knew how I had been raised before you set me on this damnable course," I said with admirable bravery. At long last righteous anger at being subjected to another's will stirred my tongue. How long this would last, I did not know, but I intended to take full advantage of the inclination. "You have only yourself to blame for this turn of events!"

The Duke folded his arms. The gesture bunched the muscles in his arms and chest, which I noticed all too readily. Again I thought I detected his admiration. "Aye, I agree," he said, and my appreciation of his appeal heightened. "I can only assume that I—like most men—was too taken with your more obvious charms to give much consideration to the King's appreciation of a woman who can think for herself occasionally." His attention went to my lips, and dropped to my bosom. I drew a sharp breath. The sound drew the Duke's attention back to my face and I sensed his withdrawal. His next harshly spoken words confirmed my suspicion that I had lost the advantage in the discussion.

"It is your duty over the next days you make every effort to undo this grave error," he snapped. "See to it." His boot grated on pebbles as he spun around and he crunched away with a swirl of his black cloak.

Joan and Agnes followed him without a backward glance at me. My anger and indignation deserting me as well, I sank onto to the stone bench, and lowered my head to my hands.

II

SUPPER IN THE GREAT HALL that night was a sombre affair. I shared the high table with the King, the Duke and Dowager, my uncle Lord William Howard and his wife Margaret, and my aunt the Countess of Bridgewater; however, everyone followed the King's lead and did not talk to me. The King himself ate well and congratulated the Dowager on the food and wine, yet he seemed sunk most of the time in deep reflection.

Afterwards, dancing brought the hall to life. For the first time in my life I did not participate, and the King merely watched with a gloomy countenance.

Someone who did dance with considerable gaiety was Tom Culpeper. He had accompanied the King to Norfolk House with the other Gentlemen of the Privy Chamber, although I had not seen him until supper. The sight of him set my pulse racing. He always tended to draw attention because he went hatless, and he had a lustiness that made everything he wore seem the epitome of good taste. He wore a doublet of rose silk with four slits on the chest showing his white lawn shirt, and a surcoat with gold damask sleeves, lined and turned back with black fur over black hose, and black shoes—all befitting a man of wealth and prestige.

He chose as his partner for La Volta none other than Katherine Tylney. In my pangs of jealousy I concluded that he had fancied her ever since they had met long ago at Horsham. After the dance, their heads were together in the shadows of an archway. I was staring at them when Tom happened to look up. For a long moment we gazed at each other. He looked away and smiled once more into Katherine's face.

The King retreated early to his apartments. Unwilling to stay a moment longer I also escaped as soon as I could. I walked into a dank and dark bedchamber where Mary Hall dozed in a chair. She roused herself but did not stand. My earlier rage, which I had so effectively wielded at my uncle, again surged to the fore.

"Light more candles and the fire, and then leave me," I snapped. "I do not require your assistance again, and you can be sure that I will report your insolence to the Dowager on the morrow!"

I had the satisfaction of seeing Mary shoot to her feet, blush and look shamed while she bobbed a curtsey. As she hurried about her tasks, I undressed, dismissing her when she approached to help. She slunk away. I wrapped a crimson velvet dressing-gown around my nakedness and pulled on a white night-cap. Feeling quite without the need to sleep, I wandered miserably to the window and slumped to the seat there, staring out into the dark night through the half-open casements.

I could see the glimmer of the river beyond the gardens. To my surprise, a manly silhouette stood on the riverbank, carrying a smoking torch. I detected a movement on the water and thought I heard the slough of a vessel slipping towards the dock. I pushed the window further ajar to better my view.

A barge appeared in the shifting halo thrown by the torch. When the vessel grated alongside, a small cloaked form stepped from it and she and the man on the dock embraced. I held my breath. The vessel receded into the darkness. The man and woman, their arms around each other, walked along the dock and approached the house.

When they came close to the wall below me, I drew away from the window but I was unable to resist taking another peek. The man placed the torch in the sconce in the wall and then turned once more to the woman, drawing her into his arms. Her hood fell back and I saw long, wheaten hair and the arms, which wound sensually around the man's neck, were white and slim.

The ensuing kiss conveyed such ardour and desperation that I almost looked away, ashamed to be witnessing something so intimate. Just as I debated retreating from the window, they parted and the man turned to retrieve the torch, its flame illuminating his face. I pressed my fingers to my lips to quell a gasp of surprise. It was none other than my uncle, the Duke of Norfolk.

I recognised the wheaten hair then—it belonged to the Duke's mistress, the former laundress of his children's nursery, Bess Holland.

The impression of their kiss remained on my mind long after they had disappeared. It heightened my misery. At that moment, it seemed everyone but me had a loving companion. I imagined a long, wretched life ahead of me, enforced chastity, loneliness and obscurity.

Two hard knocks on the door roused me from my unhappy ruminations. The door swung open before I could make a move. Framed in the doorway stood Tom Culpeper. I sprang to my feet, speechless. Tom stared at me coldly with and a stern expression, then moved into the chamber, closing the door behind him.

"You had no maid to announce me," he said.

I crossed my arms before me defensively.

Tom spread his hands. "Well? Father Vyncent sent a message that you wished to talk with me. Make haste, as I have things to do." Deeply hurt, I turned my back on him to stare unseeing out of the window into the black night.

I sensed rather than heard his approach. The prickling of my nape told me he stood close behind me. "I am sorry," he murmured, his tone softer. "I ought not to have been so harsh. Not to you, of all people."

Still I said nothing. I jumped as if struck when I felt his hand on my shoulder, urging me around to face him. When I did so, he dropped his hand and stepped backwards, but the sternness had gone from his features.

"What is it that you wish to talk with me about?" he asked with some gentleness.

I almost wept at his manner. I cleared my throat, tried unsuccessfully to speak, and cleared it again.

"It's about the—attack and murder in the park at Greenwich," I croaked.

Tom stiffened and his eyes narrowed.

"So you did hear about that. I wondered. Well, what do you want to know?"

"What do you think I want to know, you little fool? Why did you do it?" I cried with renewed spirit.

He crossed his arms. "So you believe I did it then?" he asked. "I thank you for your faith in me."

I floundered. "Well, of course I believe it," I spluttered. "What other explanation could there be for the charge and the pardon? Not to mention the blood on your doublet!"

"What indeed?" Tom said coolly. He turned and walked away from me, slumping into a chair and stretching his legs. He regarded me with a bitter expression. "Do you know what your problem is, Kate?" he said. "You are so absorbed in satisfying the needs of your body that you have completely lost touch with what your wits and heart are telling you."

"That's not true!" I flared. "I know I love you!"

He gave me a withering look.

"I do!" I protested.

"You only think you love me because you know I can protect you from some calamity," he said.

"No!" I cried. "That is laughable!"

"Is it? I think not." Tom sighed. "Sometimes, Kate, I think I know you better than you know yourself. Your love for that fop, Mannox, did not last—or likely did not even exist—because he could not offer you the protection you required. I suspect you loved your first lover because he could. This quirk in your nature explains your bizarre dealing with your uncle—you love him because you know he is powerful enough to save you from harm, but you also despise and fear him because he can just as easily destroy you. Perhaps he has said as much? Ah, yes, I thought so!" he said as I blushed. "And then of course I made the error of saying you were safe with me. It cannot be a coincidence that shortly thereafter you told me you loved me."

"Then if I am so abhorrent to you, why are you even taking the time to talk with me?" I cried. "Why not just be off with you? I am sure Katherine Tylney would appreciate your company!"

Tom placed his hands behind his head and stretched out his legs further. The movement raised his skirt above his thighs and my traitorous gaze was drawn at once to his loins. He smiled mockingly.

"I do not think you wish me to go," he remarked. "And to be honest, I would very much like set you an exercise of the mind, in the hope that you will discover the truth of those crimes I was supposed to have committed. I do have my pride."

I rubbed my head. "I am slow of wit, and the King quite exhausted me today with all his religious disputations," I said. "Just explain what happened—in simple language."

Tom, lowered his arms, swung from the chair and approached me. As usual, his alluring way of walking weakened my knees. Flustered, I made to leave the window embrasure and dodge past him by sidling along the wall, but he changed his path and soon had me trapped, one arm on either side of me, palms against the wall. I pressed back into it, wishing it would swallow me.

"I challenge you to think, Kate," he said, his face close to mine. "Let us first consider the charge document, shall we?"

"How do you expect me to think when you have me pent so?" I said pitifully. "I cannot think at all."

Tom threw back his head and laughed. "Ignore your inclination to grab at a certain part of my anatomy and turn your attention to your underworked wits."

"You are very insulting, Tom," I said, affronted, crossing my arms. "All right, I shall prove to you that I am not stupid. The charge document you say? It would have originated from the sergeant at arms, I assume, and it would have had your name on it."

"Aye. My name."

"Aye, Thomas—. Oh!" I stared at him, expelling a long, astonished breath. "You mean—your *brother* did it?"

"Now, let us not cut short the lesson when you are doing so well," Tom said with a trace of sarcasm. "Let us now think about the pardon signed by the King."

I uncrossed my arms and again rubbed my head with one hand. Of its own volition, my free hand moved outwards and passed under Tom's skirt until my immodest fingers encountered his silken thigh. "Uh, uh," Tom said. Flushing I snatched back my hand, pressing it between my breasts as I struggled to gather my thoughts.

"The pardon," I began and stopped with a frown. "The King would not pardon someone in Lord Cromwell's service, surely!"

Tom shrugged. "Perhaps he would, perhaps not. Given that both Thomas and I were at the scene after the—affray, and let us just say we both assumed the King would not pardon

Thomas for his misdeeds. What do you think we would have decided to do?"

I clasped my hands together between my breasts and grimaced with effort. Finally, as the answer knocked on my mind, I said: "Perhaps—you decided to take the blame, for you knew the King would pardon *you?*" When Tom looked approving, I shook my head in astonishment. "But, why would you do such a thing?" I asked aghast. "I know he is your brother, but to take the blame for these crimes!" I shook my head in amazement. "All I can say is that you did him quite a favour—which I trust he will repay!"

Tom lowered his face so that his lips were against my ear and his beard scratched my cheek. "Perhaps," he murmured in the husky tone he used to whisper earthy intimacies, "it was I who owed him the favour."

I shuddered even as I tried to construe this hint. Another piece of the puzzle fell into place. I drew my head back and stared at him. "For the use of his bedchamber at Greenwich!" I whispered. "Tom! You place such a high price on being with me?" My words came out as a squeak.

"You may think of it thus if you wish," he said. His hands went to my head and he removed my cap. "This thinking is quite a game, is it not?" he said, his fingers raking through my hair. "You have done well, Kate, I applaud you."

Although his slights to my wits were becoming tiring, encouraged by his approbation I surged on. "I assume the blood on your doublet meant that you came on the event afterwards . . . perhaps you tried to revive the man!"

"Now, do not go imbuing me with all sorts of chivalric qualities, Kate," Tom said. The rise of my bosom beneath my dressing gown had diverted his attention, and with fascination he inspected how the garment was loosely wrapped around my form. "You are getting carried away with all this thinking. The important thing is that you no longer believe I am a violator of women and a murderer, is that so?"

I clasped his face. "Aye, I no longer believe it," I said. I put my lips to his mouth. After a few heady seconds, I drew my head away to regain my breath. "Oh, Tom, I have been so unhappy these past weeks, believing you were lost to me!" My roaming hands swept beneath his clothing, and slid up his thighs to his buttocks. This time he did not stop me.

"Unhappy? You appeared happy enough most of the time. Flirting merrily with Thomas Paston and the King!"

I winced. "I hardly knew what I was doing," I said. "Most of the time I was intoxicated, I am ashamed to say. And anyway, what about you! You have done your fair share of flirting with Katherine Tylney tonight!"

"Clearly, we all do things we should not when we are in despair," he said. "You forget, you were not the only one to feel abandoned these past weeks."

I nodded. "I am so sorry for it." We shared another open-mouthed kiss. When he slid his mouth down to my neck, I murmured, "Tom, I have to tell you—I have never said 'I love you' to anyone but you. That must count for something surely!"

Distracted now by the fold of my gown, Tom did not heed my words. When he had unwrapped the garment and pushed it from my body, I tried again, even as he began to stroke my bosom.

"Tom, did you hear me? Oh!"

He threw off his surcoat. In one swift movement, he yanked off the doublet and undergarments and pulled down his hosen as he kicked off his shoes.

"I have another challenge for you," he said after another kiss. "I am interested to see how well you can concentrate on things in here—," he touched my temple, "when there is temptation here—," he slid his fingers between my thighs.

I gulped and summoned sufficient wit to grumble: "It seems a thinking woman is quite valued by men these days!"

"It sometimes has its benefits as I hope to show you," he said. "Let us see now, what can I give you to think about while I tempt your baser instincts?"

"I do not think you have to give me anything to think about," I protested. "I can resist you easily enough without a distraction—oh, marry!" I whispered writhing against his intimate touch.

"I think not," Tom said with a grin. "And I have an idea. Why not practice being a good Catholic and recite part of the Mass—in Latin, of course?"

I laughed before it struck me that to do so was probably improper. "That's sacrilegious," I said, trying to suppress my amusement and fascination.

"Who's going to hear? Come on now—how about the Gloria? Let me see how well you have been paying attention in Mass. I will start you off—*Gloria in excelsis Deo . . .*"

" . . . *et in terra pax hominibus bonae voluntatis*," I added at once, on a giggle. Tom grinned, scooped my hair away from my neck and buried his face there. I tingled at the touch of his mouth and teeth against my skin but soldiered on. "*Laudamus te, benedicimus te, adoramus te, glorificamus te,*" I said in a strangled tone as his mouth slid lower. "*Gratias agimus tibi propter magnam gloriam tuam. Domine Deus rex coelestis, Deus Pater omnipotens.*"

"Oh, well done!" said Tom in a muffled voice, dropping to his knees before me, trailing kisses down my belly, and attempting to prise apart my legs.

"*Domine Fili unigenite,*" I gasped, trying to keep my legs clamped together but failing. "Ah, *Jesu Christe,*" I whispered as Tom lifted one of my legs over his shoulder and lowered his head. My gripping hands on his shoulders felt him shake briefly with laughter before his lightning tongue flickered against me. "*Domine Deus, Agnus Dei, Filius Patris.*" I moaned prayerfully. "*Qui tollis peccata mundi, miserere nobis. Qui tollis peccata mundi, suscipe deprecationem nostram. Qui sedes ad dexteram Patris, miserere nobis.*"

I felt perspiration prickling my forehead as I struggled against the inevitable climax, trying all the while to ignore what Tom was doing so skilfully and recall the words of the prayer. I gripped Tom's shoulder with one hand, and the fingers of my other wound through his hair. Yet he persisted and with each passing second it seemed the fulfilment I reached for became more potent and more intense. Why had I never seen the benefit of self-denial, when beyond the denial lay even greater ecstasy? This was clearly the point of Tom's thinking game. But for my ragged breathing, I became silent in my struggle and my pleasure, until Tom shifted onto his haunches and retraced the path of kisses up my body, until his mouth once more was on mine.

"Continue," he muttered, gentle fingers taking the place of his tongue between my legs. "Fun, is it not?"

"*Quoniam tu solus Sanctus,*" I mumbled against his lips. "*Tu solus Dominus, tu solus altissimus . . .* Oh, dear God," I gasped as Tom grasped my buttocks and hoisted me up and back against the wall. I automatically clutched his waist with my legs.

"Wrong," said Tom, sliding into me. Countless shivers began to trill up my spine.

"*Jesu Christe,*" I whispered.

"That's better," he mumbled, his hips beginning their delicious rhythmical plunging.

"And?"

"Cum Sancto Spiritu, in gloria Dei Patris!" I ascended to the pinnacle and soared beyond it, as innumerable rapturous thrills shook my body.

"Amen," whispered Tom reverently.

III

MUCH LATER, I lay entwined limply with Tom on the bed. He stroked my back with his fingertips and I felt his lips touch the top of my head.

"I shall never be able to regard that part of Mass in the same way again," I muttered. "I expect I shall lose control each time I recite it, from the memory of this night."

Tom shook with laughter. "You had better hope saying the Mass in the vernacular catches on, then," he said.

We shared a long, helpless giggle. I began to stroke his lean belly.

After an interval, during which I tickled my nails over the renewed development at his loins, I said: "I hope you do not really abhor me."

"You know I do not," he replied. "I want nothing more than to whisk you away to Kent as soon as possible, make love with you against every wall in my new house several times a day, and make ten Culpeper babes with you in ten years—ah, what bliss that would be!"

I gave a yelp and, grinning, I lifted my head to look into his face. He grinned also, yet his gaze was watchful. I kissed his cheek.

"That sounds wonderful," I said with fervour, closing my tickling hand around the delectable part of his anatomy, ducking and sliding down his body. Indeed, the prospect was far more alluring to me than life at court had ever been.

Part 3: Peril

"This know also, that in the last days perilous times shall come."

The Bible, 2 Timothy 3:1

Chapter 21

"Et tu, Brute?"
(Even you, Brutus?)

Gaius Julius Caesar, Roman general, statesman and historian (100-44 BC),
to Brutus, his friend and one of his assassins

I

TOM COULD NOT TARRY with me for long, so we made the most of what little time we had. After he left, I sank into a deep and contented sleep.

In the morning, without assistance, I put on a new gown in the old Italian fashion, a style I had heard was much favoured by the King's beloved late sister, the Princess Mary. Of pale blue tissue, it had a low-cut panelled bodice covered in a network of pearls and jewels; the sleeves were cut in the Italian style in two parts, the upper cylinder laced to the shoulders; the lower part laced to the upper, the sides unseamed and tied together. The untrained skirts, worn with a farthingale, had narrow panels of silver tissue bordered with gold braid and laced together with gold cords, the ends finished off with fine pearls. By the time I had struggled into the gown, I was puffing, and so decided not to go with the Italian coif that would have completed the outfit, instead donning a more fashionable French hood.

In the late morning, I ran down the stairs to the Great Hall to attend dinner. It seemed the entire household had already gathered there and I made my way through the clamour to the empty space at the high table.

"Good morrow, step-grandmother!" I greeted the old woman gaily as I passed her; to the astonishment of all, I bent and kissed the parchment of her cheek. My uncle Lord William, his wife Margaret and the Countess, I greeted all in like manner. By the time I reached the Duke of Norfolk, I was enjoying the attention. I rested my hands tenderly on his shoulders and placed a soft kiss on his bearded cheek. He murmured something polite but I did not miss the sharpness in his expression when he looked at me.

When I reached the King I curtseyed low, breathing a rapt "Your Grace!" The King stared at me, his knife half raised to his mouth. Before he had regained his composure, I had taken my seat at his left.

"To what is owed your fine cheer, niece?" boomed Lord William heartily, breaking the awkward silence. "You slept well perhaps?"

"Indeed, I had the perfect sleep," I rejoined. "However, that does not account for all my happiness."

I cast a fleeting glance around the tables closest to the dais, glimpsing Tom at once. He stared at me in a passionate and possessive fashion, which he quickly quashed before anyone else noticed. Joy filled me at the very sight of him, not to mention that I also found exceptionally exciting to behold in public a fully clothed and refined gentleman who just hours before had been naked in my bed. I was bursting to reveal the paradox to all. It was only with an extreme effort of will that I dragged my attention away from Tom and returned to my plate.

"Well, do not keep us hanging!" called the Countess, joining in with her brother's awkward heartiness. She issued a braying laugh. "We must know what has caused such brilliance in you so that we can order some for ourselves!"

By this time, the attention of all at the table, including the King, was pinned on me in intense curiosity. I laughed, taking a sip of spiced ale.

"Why, I am in love," I declared.

Then I deliberately and provocatively cast a sidelong glance at the King.

I dropped my gaze as an incredulous silence vibrated around the table. The King's knife clattered to his pewter plate. With a calm I didn't feel, I began to eat.

"Lady Catherine," said the King in an adoring tone audible to all. "Perhaps you would like to take another walk with me in the garden this morning?"

I dabbed at my mouth with a cloth before answering. "Of course, my Lord," I murmured. I flicked him a shy glance.

The food stuck in my throat for the rest of the meal, as I inwardly railed at myself for what I had done. The King, however, was possessed of a newly vigorous appetite and his loud laughter and exclamations echoed around the hall. His good humour infected all. By the time he departed to his chambers with his entourage, the cavernous chamber resounded with merriment.

I made my way to the terrace to await him, accompanied once more by Joan and Agnes, who had fetched my cloak. I hugged it around me against the chill as the King and his followers emerged. The retainers dropped back at a wave of the King's hand, and he smiled at me, before we descended the stairs once more to the garden.

Seated on the stone bench again, I could not suppress a shiver, though whether it was nervousness or chill I did not know. To my shock, the King sidled closer to me and placed his arm around my shoulders.

"You are cold," he proclaimed. "Such light dress you wear, Lady Catherine, but it has a beauty I delight in beholding for it is a reflection of your own."

Gratified, I smiled at him. "Your Grace, I live only to please my lord and majesty so your words gladden my heart."

He grasped me closer. My heart began to beat a rapid tempo as the portent of the gesture grew clear to me—as no doubt it was growing clear to our watchers. My uncle would have been doubly pleased if he had heard the King's next words, spoken close to my ear.

"Sweetheart, there's no need to call me by such titles when we are alone. We know each other well by now, do we not? If it please you—you must call me 'Henry' henceforth."

Speechless, I could only nod my concurrence. The King edged closer.

"I must tell you, Catherine," he said. "After dinner, I arranged for the bestowing on you of a property in Wiltshire formerly belonging to Queen Jane. "It's a token of my true love for you!"

"My lord!" I gasped. "I mean—Henry!" I struggled in my wonder for the appropriate speech while the King looked on indulgently. "I thank you, but fear I am not worthy of such a generous gift!" Inside, my soul thrilled at the recognition that I was now a landowner of repute!

"Indeed, Catherine, you are worthy of so much more," the King insisted. "And I intend to give you more gifts. Yet I am sad, for I am as yet unable to bestow on you the ultimate gift which will raise you above all ladies on the land—do you know of what I speak?"

I stared into his fervent countenance. The breath frozen in my lungs, I could only nod.

"But I hope to soon be free to take a new Queen," the King said. "I fear I will never have more children if I continue in my marriage for, before God, I believe Anne of Cleves is not my lawful wife. Knowing that she has a pre-contract with Francis, the Marquis de Pont a`Mousson, has been a great burden on my conscience, and for that reason this will be a fruitless marriage. For my subjects and my realm—yea, for my heart, Catherine!—I must take another wife!"

As I tried to swallow a lump of trepidation in my throat, the King frowned into the distance, one hand clenched into a fist and resting on his parted knees, the other gripping my shoulder. "I shall call a meeting of my council," he said at last. "This marriage must be brought to an end!" He looked back at me, withdrew his arm from around me and grasped my hands, bringing them to his heart. "Catherine—my love—before I depart from you, may I have your consent to join with me in holy wedlock and be my Queen?"

"My lord—Henry," I whispered. "I am so humbled and quite overwhelmed! If it please you . . . if I may be allowed to speak—."

"Indeed, it does please me," the King said firmly and with a touch of impatience, drowning out my last words. He smiled in childlike excitement and kissed my hands. "I shall talk with your fine family before I depart and avow them of my intentions."

I gaped at him as he vibrated with exuberance and impatience.

"Ah, Catherine, you have made me a happy man!" he declared. "As I leave you today, you must know that I will be true to you and that I will be working hard to ensure that some day very soon you will be my Queen! Come, let us return at once to the house!"

II

I TROD THE FLOORS OF MY BEDCHAMBER in impatience, waiting for the news of the King's meeting with my family. Either he would be disappointed to learn of my relationship with Francis Dereham and would return in sadness to Greenwich Palace, knowing I could never be his wife and Queen, or it would not perturb him, as Father Vyncent had suggested. In the latter case, of course, Tom would marry me to deliver me from the fate I dreaded. Whatever the King's reaction to the news of my unchaste life, I was desperate to know it, and have this matter put to rest for once and for all.

I was summoned to the Dowager's apartments before supper. Joan, with an air of expectation, restored my hair and clothing to order, and accompanied me with commendable deference to the door of the Dowager's receiving-chamber.

The Dowager, Lord William and his wife, and the Countess of Bridgewater waited for me. The Dowager, sitting upright on a large chair, bore a hectic flush on her cheeks and her beady eyes gleamed when I entered. My mild-mannered Aunt Margaret sat at the far window. I knew she possessed poor eyesight, which accounted for a silent and vapid manner in social gatherings, so I expected to hear little from her on this occasion. The Countess—plump, assertive and handsome—hovered beside her brother Lord William, near the fireplace; for his part, he stood with a haughty angle to his double chin, stout legs slightly astride and hands clasped behind his back. As the Duke of Norfolk was absent from the gathering, I assumed from Lord William's authoritative air that he was the nominated leader of the discussion that would ensue.

"Welcome, Catherine," he said, not unkindly, and gestured towards a nearby stool. "We have been in talks with the King," he said as I sat down before him. "We are pleased to inform you that he has expressed his intentions to make you his Queen!"

The Dowager made an odd strangled sound. She appeared fit to burst with pride, her entire face bathed in a rosy glow.

Uncle William and the Countess also beamed, the Countess's chest rising and falling with sudden excited breathing.

"The King still wishes to marry me after talking with you?" I asked in desperation.

"Why, of course he does!" said Lord William. "Among many other of your virtues, we extolled your pure and chaste condition. He is more enraptured with you than ever!"

I swayed with shock. Pure and chaste condition? Struggling for control, I looked back at the Dowager. She dropped her gaze at once.

"But, step-grandmother knows I—," I gasped.

"That is enough!" Lord William interrupted with force. The smile had vanished from his features and he looked thunderous. "We will not talk more of this!" I flinched at his vehemence. "Suffice to say your step-grandmother has informed us of all she knows of your past, and we made a considered judgement. Which is the lesser misdeed? Inform the King of all the details of your past, have him lose his interest in you, and risk the rise of Lord Cromwell and the reformers? Or not tell him, open the way for your Uncle Norfolk to take control of the Council, and thus save the Church from abominable heresies? It was an easy choice!"

I rubbed my head with trembling fingers. "And my Uncle Norfolk?" I asked in a husky voice. "He supported this lie?"

"He was not present," snapped the Countess. "We all determined that your step-grandmother and ourselves were in a better position to vouch for you than the Duke." The Countess ignored my amazement. "The Duke is closeted with the King now, discussing other details. He will be with us anon, and the King will be departing for Westminster."

Even as she spoke, the door to the chamber yawned opened and my Uncle Norfolk strode in. Like the others of my family he bristled with excitement until he sensed the tension amongst us and came to a halt, frowning. He glanced at me and considered the others.

"Pray leave us," he said to the others, coming nearer with a slow, soft tread. "I need to speak with Catherine."

As my family filed out of the chamber, my head teemed with agitated thoughts. Evidently, my family had judged my dealings with Francis Dereham as not beyond reproach, despite our promise to be wed; perhaps they even had other suspicions, which could not be so easily explained away . . . and so they had lied! And, worse, they likely expected me to support the deception! Deceive the King? My soul quailed in fear at the notion.

My uncle William hesitated just inside the door.

"Catherine must support her family's stand in all things, must she not, brother?" he asked pointedly

"Indeed, yes," the Duke said coolly, as if knowing to what Lord William referred. "Catherine knows her duty."

Lord William grunted in satisfaction. He swept through the door and slammed it behind him, leaving me alone with the Duke.

At once I sprang to my feet. "Uncle, my family has sworn to the King that I am of pure and chaste condition!" I burst out. "That's a lie! Why, a lie you made sure you did not need to utter to the King!" But his gaze was on his silver staff, grasped tight in his white-knuckled hand. Seizing the advantage, I ran to him, put my hand on his and squeezed it in desperation until he lifted his eyes to mine. They were black and fathomless, his mouth pressed into a grim line, creases in the skin around it etched deeper. The old rapport flashed between us. I forged on. "A lie, uncle! You know it . . . certainly the Dowager knows—."

"Silence!" barked the Duke. "I am aware of no lie!"

I flinched and stared at him. For a long moment, he stared back at me. My gaze was the first to fall. I lowered my head to my hands, staggered back and slumped into my chair.

The Duke approached. Kneeling at my feet, he pulled my hands from my face and held them.

"Catherine, you are distressed. Do not think I do not know the reason. You are afraid, I know it. There is no need to be afraid. Have you forgotten last night? I love you, I will take care of you! This is a truly wondrous development for our family and I will support and nurture you—while you continue to do well by me in the manner that you have done already!"

I did not appreciate the threat behind his final words, even though I understood it. However, my uncle's tone was kind and his grasp so warm and reassuring that I felt comforted. I sniffed, and pulled one hand away to swipe my sleeve beneath my nose. I returned my hand to his.

"Your words at dinner this morning, Catherine," said the Duke squeezing my hands. "were wondrous wise. My compliments to you."

"I meant it," I mumbled, not caring now what I said. "I am in love." As I remembered why, I sighed with relief. All was not lost. The action I had to take was laid out before me. I would marry Tom . . . he would save me, as he had always done.

The Duke hesitated, but seemed to think better of questioning me. I examined him with uncharacteristic shrewdness. Ever the survivor, he had taken the stance that what he did not know could not condemn him. Or did he know of Tom? Was it a case of what others did not know of him could not condemn him? I recalled Tom's mentioning my uncle's suspicions in the aftermath of my illness. I searched the Duke's expression for an answer. To my confusion, I indeed detected a flicker of knowing . . . and sympathy . . . and a strange sense of conspiracy, before he became unreadable again.

"I see—well, being in love with the King will serve you well in your marriage," he remarked glibly. "Now, I must talk with you about some details the King and I agreed upon." He rose to his feet and pulled me up. "The King has decreed that you shall remain here at Norfolk House rather than return to Greenwich. He will visit you here as often as he is able. He considers it preferable to conduct a dignified courtship, rather than woo you in the presence of the Queen. I will arrange for the remainder of your belongings to be brought here. Do you find this satisfactory?"

Indeed I did not. Events were whirling out of my control. I longed to speak with Tom. My tears started to flow again.

"Oh, Catherine." Exasperated, the Duke drew me closer and enfolded me in his arms. I sank into his warmth, winding my arms around his waist. At once comforted, I sighed and pressed my cheek to the Duke's doublet.

"So it is done," he said above my head. "All our hopes of the last few years have at last been realised. Catherine, I am grateful to you, yea, the whole family is grateful! You've done us a great service."

To add to my day of marvels, he drew away from me, bowed over my hand and kissed it.

III

CLAIMING WEARINESS, I missed supper and remained in my chambers. No doubt word of the day's development would be sweeping through the household. I had no desire to witness it or be subjected to stares and whispers.

I suspected Tom would not take the risk of visiting me until much later, if at all. I longed to speak with him, to receive his reassurance that he would save me from my royal doom.

In desperation, I decided to ask Father Vyncent to deliver another message to Tom. Close to midnight, I slipped from my bedchamber, having dismissed my new maid, and made my way once more to the chapel.

Father Vyncent knelt in the front pew, deep in his solitary devotions. I waited impatiently in the candlelit dimness until he made the sign of the cross and pushed himself to his feet. I cleared my throat to announce my presence and advanced down the centre aisle.

"Catherine! Child!" Father Vyncent greeted. "I have been praying for you. Come, talk to me."

We took a seat at the pew.

"You've heard no doubt of the day's events?" I said.

"Of course," he said with gentleness. "There's talk of nothing else."

"Doubtless you do not know all the diabolical details," I murmured.

"Diabolical? Why such a choice of word, my dear?"

"Father, my family have lied to the King. Well, except for the Duke," I added bitterly. "He made sure he did not have to. My Uncle William, my aunt and the Dowager have vouched to the King for my pure and chaste condition. They expect me to uphold this claim, and of course it is my duty to do so."

Father Vyncent passed his hand across his mouth in agitation. "This is not good!" he murmured.

"They consider that it is better for the Church and the realm if I should marry the King even if it means deceiving him in the process. If my past was to be revealed, and the King did not marry me, the heretical Reformers would take over the Council and all would be lost!"

Father Vyncent grunted and looked doubtful. "The King is conservative in his own views," he said. "I doubt that such a calamity would occur while he lives. If the Prince Edward came to the throne, however, the Protestant Seymours would certainly exert their influence. Nevertheless," he sighed, "I rather expect there may be more selfish motives behind this deception . . . . Do they not know danger such a deception entails? Aye, 'tis diabolical indeed!"

"The matter must not advance, Father! For me, for my family." He nodded, pressing his palms together. I rushed on. "Father, last night Tom said he wished to take me away to Kent—yes, we resolved our differences." I babbled the explanation for the crimes at Greenwich while Father Vyncent listened with avid interest. "Father, listen! Tom will take me away! Why, perhaps you could even marry us this evening!"

Father Vyncent clasped his big hands in tense reflection then nodded. "Aye, that's a solution to the crisis," he agreed. "I will send a message to him. Catherine, make haste into the vestry and wait for him there."

IV

TOM BURST INTO THE VESTRY almost an hour later.

"I shall stand guard outside the door," said Father Vyncent as Tom swept me into his arms. "I have spoken briefly with Master Culpeper, Catherine—he will tell you his thoughts on this matter." He was steeped in gloom.

"You know what has occurred today?" I said to Tom as the door closed behind Father Vyncent.

"But of course!" said Tom with an excited gleam. "Kate! Queen of England!"

My heart plummeted.

"I have no wish to marry the King," I wailed. "I want to marry you!"

He lifted me onto Father Vyncent's writing table and insinuated himself between my parted legs. He caressed my face and neck with hot hands.

"And I want to marry you," he said. "And we shall marry—but not yet."

I swallowed the sickness in my throat.

"Tom, why cannot we marry now? It would deliver me from this calamity!"

He sighed. "Kate, listen to me." He grasped my face. "The wrath of your family and the King, should we marry now, would make our lives not worth living! Why, perhaps we would even be imprisoned!"

I quailed.

"Aye, I believe that," said Tom, driving home the advantage. "The King is so in love with you that already he is behaving with wildness—why, this afternoon he made Lord Cromwell Earl of Essex and Lord Great Chamberlain, in the belief that Lord Cromwell will soon find a way to end the King's present marriage. Kate, if we fled together, we would be hunted down like foxes, I know it."

"Then there is no hope," I said. "I must surrender to this. I once vowed 'No other will but mine', but it was a foolish vow to make for a Howard woman! I am not my own person, I am just a pawn!"

I dropped my forehead to Tom's shoulder, cold and tearless with the deepest despair.

"Yet, there is one last alternative," I muttered. "I must fail in my duty to my family, and reveal to the King myself that I am not of pure and chaste living. I can do it in such a way that my family has not appeared to lie, although I know they will be incensed with me even so—."

"Catherine." Tom's unaccustomed use of my full name had me pulling away from him in surprise. He grasped my face again and his fingers bit into my skin. "You must not do that. Listen to me! I have been thinking, your becoming Queen of England could benefit us both enormously!"

He took of my hands and brought it to his codpiece. His excitement was evident and his chest began to heave with passion at my touch. I felt my body responding.

"How could it benefit us?" I whispered.

He pressed closer. I could smell his clean, warm, male scent, and the intense blue of his eyes hypnotised me. He unfastened his codpiece and guided my hand inside before pulling up my skirts.

"Think of this," he said against my ear, as he stroked my thighs, finding their juncture, gentle touch provoking my lust. "The King is old and ailing, easily struck down with all manner of illnesses—this I know better than most. In three, maybe five years at the most—he will be dead." Despite his expert ministrations and my own reactions thereto, I stiffened at his treasonous utterance, and cast a concerned glance over his shoulder. However, he had spoken in a low voice and the door remained fast closed. "Aye," Tom said, pulling me closer to his body. "He will be dead—and you—you will be Dowager Queen, yea, perhaps mother to a future King! The richest and most powerful woman in all of England! Think of the riches, Kate! Think of the power, the influence! And me there with you to share it!"

I felt dizzy with contradictory sensations. My legs wound around his waist and I guided him towards me. He plunged into me at once, filling and stretching.

"Why settle for a former monastery in Kent," Tom whispered, "when we can have Hampton Court or Whitehall! Think of it, Kate!"

I did think of it. As Tom stifled my whimpers with his mouth, I embraced my destiny, while inside my chest my heart seemed to break.

Chapter 22

"And the King said unto Esther the queen, The Jews have slain and destroyed five hundred
men in Shushan the palace, and the ten sons of Haman; what have they done in the rest of
the King's provinces? now what is thy petition? and it shall be granted you: or what is thy
request further? and it shall be done."

The Bible, Book of Esther, 9:12

I

IN THE MONTH OF JULY 1540, the King divorced Anne of Cleves. He ordered the
executions of Lord Cromwell, Dr Barnes and other heretics. And my uncle the Duke of Norfolk,
Bishop Winchester, and the conservative faction, seized control of the Privy Council.

Without demur Queen Anne consented to the divorce. The King presented her with
a generous divorce settlement—not only did he offer her precedence over every other woman
in England save myself and his daughters, but he tempted her with an income of five hundred
pounds, as well as Richmond and the manor of Bletchingly as her residences. When she made
no protest and insisted to her brother of Cleves that Henry had treated her well, the King
was pleased and gratified. Thereafter, she made her home in England, basked in the King's
fondness for his new "dear sister", and overnight abandoned her plainness and dowdiness. To
the surprise of all, she became pretty and vibrant, and each day appeared garbed in some new
bright fashion.

For reasons no one could fully understand, Dr Barnes and two of his supporters—
Masters Thomas Gerrard and William Jerome—were burnt at the stake in Smithfield. It was
rumoured afterwards that Martin Luther had dubbed his friend Dr Barnes "Saint Robert."

On Saturday the tenth day of June, during an afternoon session of the Privy Council,
the captain of the guard seized Lord Cromwell, now Earl of Essex and Lord Great Chamberlain
of England. My Uncle Norfolk took immense delight in stripping Lord Cromwell of his
decorations. The King's most trusted adviser was then charged with selling export licenses
illegally, granting passports and commissions without royal knowledge, freeing people suspected
of treason, and usurping and misusing royal power. Most significantly, he was charged with
heresy. This charge, which swayed the King decisively, had arisen through the cunning of my
Uncle Norfolk. The charge stipulated that Cromwell had encouraged and spread heretical
literature, allowed heretics to preach, released them from prison, and allied himself against
their enemies. It was reported that in March 1539 he had said that, even if the King turned
from Protestantism, "yet I would not turn, and if the King did turn, and all his people, I would
fight in this field in mine own person, with my sword in my hand against him and all other."
Therein lay his high treason. He was beheaded on 28 July 1540.

On the day of his death, I became the fifth wife of King Henry VIII.

Rule and benefaction now belonged to the Howards. The Bishop of Winchester
regained his seat on the Council and he and my uncle set the course of conservative action. My
uncle's ally and relation, Robert Ratcliffe, Earl of Sussex, became Lord Great Chamberlain; and

another conservative by blood if not inclination, William Fitzwilliam, Earl of Southampton, became Lord Privy Seal. Thomas Audley, Lord Chancellor, Anthony Browne and Sir Thomas Wriothesley all thought it prudent to make their peace with the conservative faction. However, my Uncle Norfolk, with Sussex and Bishops Gardiner and Tunstall, ruled the roost and controlled all approaches to the royal presence. It was my uncle's finest hour.

And what of me, the impetus to this revolution?

The spring preceding my marriage passed in a blur. The King made many secret visits to Norfolk House and, when he thought it prudent to forestall further gossip, we often met at Bishop Winchester's residence in Southwark. Because the visits were informal, only a small legion of his guards and two servants accompanied him—but never Tom Culpeper. I saw Tom just once, when he managed to sneak into Norfolk House in the early hours of one May morning. However, in our fear of discovery, our coupling was rushed and dissatisfying. As we clutched each other afterwards on the back stairs, we consoled ourselves with imagined scenes of our future life as husband and wife, living in Hampton Court Palace, amidst enormous riches, and receiving the deference and respect of all.

In May I travelled to York Palace to sit alongside the King at the international joust. Queen Anne had been sent to Richmond, ostensibly for her health, and this constituted the first public acknowledgement of the King's intentions towards me. While we looked on from the new gatehouse, Sir Richard Cromwell defeated Tom in the individual joust. However, in one of those paradoxes where the victor was less popular than the loser, Tom was much lauded afterwards. To my seething jealousy, my former bedchamber mate in the Queen's household, Lady Lisle, showed me a coy and touching note that she intended to give to Tom. It enclosed two bracelets of her colours and she boasted that they were "the first that ever I sent to any man." Afterwards, I had to live with the torment of watching them dance, and seeing Tom bestow on her the bright grin and admiring gaze that I had thought reserved for me.

In a fit of pique, that evening I indicated to the King that I was ready for our own relationship to proceed to intimacy. I had been maidenly up to that point, which the King interpreted as being virginal nervousness, although I had been keen only to delay my coupling with him for as long as possible. Fired with fervent passion, he summoned me to his chambers that night.

I do not wish to cast into disrepute the King's virtues as a lover. I daresay he was not as skilled as rumour had his counterpart in France, and certainly he did not measure up to Tom, Francis or even Henry in that respect either. One assumes that developing skill at sexual relations is not at the forefront of the mind for a man desperate to produce a healthy line of Princes to secure the succession. Nevertheless, he was a tender and affectionate lover—for the blessedly short time it was required. So intensely excited had he been when he first joined me in bed, and on many occasions afterwards, that our coupling lasted only several beats. On that first night, while he snored beside me, I extracted a needle that I had earlier inserted into my corset and pricked my thumbs until the blood flowed. I then blotted the blood on the undersheet. The King would notice the blood in the morning, as would his attendants. Mary Norris's advice had been opportune, although I resented my need for the subterfuge. The tangled web of my family's deception tightened around me.

Once intimacy with the King had commenced, I knew it had to cease with Tom. As soon as I went to the King's bed, I planned to abandon the tincture I had used for many years, and I could not risk giving birth to a child that might resemble Tom. I was glad to discard the remedy, for—by placing stones in my womb—it had upset my monthly courses and often they afflicted me with extreme discomfort. Now perhaps my courses would resume a normal pattern—at least until I fell with the King's child, which I hoped would be sooner rather than later.

The risk of bearing Tom's child aside, we also neither of us intended that the King should be cuckolded.

II

THE KING CHOSE AS MY DEVICE: "No other will but his." I bore the irony with outward stoicism, while inside I wept over yet another broken, foolish vow that the device had replaced.

I received as the marriage jointure the castles, lordships and manors that once belonged to Jane Seymour, as well as the lands of Thomas Cromwell, of Walter, Lord Hungerford and of Hugh, late Abbot of Reading. The King also bestowed on me numerous jewels and rich apparel. When I had cause to travel between Chelsea and Baynard's Castle that summer, I had my own private barge with twenty-six bargemen and twenty other gentlemen to serve the train, and fresh rosemary and rushes were always spread on the deck. In honour of my first state entrance into London, the Lord Mayor and aldermen with all the guilds of the city rowed out in barges decorated with banners to meet us as we passed down the river. Reminding me starkly of my cousin Anne Boleyn's coronation, the great cannons of the Tower and the guns of the fleet fired into the air as we passed by.

However, I had no coronation. When I enquired of the King when my crowning would be he said in a cool voice, "When you carry my child, I shall bestow on you the crown, and not before." When I sulked and railed, in a fit of remorse he arranged for me to be proclaimed Queen of England on 8 August. It satisfied me, but I had had a timely reminder of how important it was to bear the King a child as soon as possible. Unfortunately, as summer slipped into autumn there came no interruption in my monthly courses, despite the King's regular attempts to impregnate me.

I did have many diversions to distract me from thoughts of fulfilling this most important of Queenly duties. I put together a large household, comprising a lord chamberlain, a chancellor, a master of horse, a secretary, a solicitor, an auditor, four gentlemen ushers, two gentlemen waiters, a cup-bearer, a clerk, two chaplains, six great ladies, four ladies of the privy chamber, nine attendants of exalted rank, five maids, twelve yeomen of the chamber, four footmen, seven sumptermen, two littermen and seventeen grooms. It thrilled me bring my old friend Father Vyncent to court as one of my chaplains. Unfortunately, however, as she was heavy with child, I could not have Mary Norris join me—but I wrote asking her to attend me when she was able. My legion of siblings and other relations descended upon me to remind me of my obligations; accordingly, three out of the six great ladies were my relations, one of whom was my half-sister Lady Isabel Baynton, who had been a childhood companion; another sister-in-law Lady Anne Howard; and a third the widow of my cousin George Boleyn, Lady Rochford, who had also been in service with me to Anne of Cleves. My aunt Lady Margaret Arundel and my cousin Lady Dennys I made gentlewoman attendants. The King needed little persuasion to make my brother George a Gentleman of the Privy Chamber, and George also received lands formerly belonging to the monastery of Wilton. My brother Charles was appointed to the exclusive and coveted position of one of the King's spears, and he and George were also accorded a license to import 1000 tons of Gascon wine and Toulouse timber into England, a lucrative monopoly. The Duke of Norfolk requested that I ask the King to send my uncle Lord William as ambassador to France, and the King, in his never-ending generosity and desperation to please me, was swift in granting the request.

I had other less gratifying appointments. Soon after my marriage, I received a letter from Joan Bulmer in which she begged me to remember the "unfeigned love that my heart hath always borne towards you" and demanded that I save room for her at court. Although she sweetened the request with a pronouncement that the nearer she was to me, the happier she would be, I saw in her request the unmistakable sign of blackmail. Joan of course knew all about my previous life at Horsham and Lambeth and my associations with Henry Mannox and Francis Dereham. Sick with fear, I gave her the position of chamberer. In the same way, I felt compelled to bring my other friends, Katherine Tylney, Alice Restwold, and Margaret Morton, into my household. Agnes Ap Rhys, however, had recently become betrothed to Sir Edward Baynton and was now living in Wiltshire.

My duties as Queen should have kept me busy—daily I had to hear petitions, listen to requests to influence the King, and administer my household and my estates, while at all times conducting myself in a meek, patient and sober fashion. After a mere few months, I found these duties tiresome and the required manner foreign to my nature, so I more often than not delegated these duties to the honourable and able men of my household. I preferred to indulge myself in dancing and pageantry, and wished only to embrace the heady pleasures of the moment.

Of course, I tried to turn my mind from Tom Culpeper, with the instinct gained in years of ignoring things unpleasant. However, the necessity of depriving myself of Tom's companionship and loving was something that touched the deepest parts of my soul and heart. The pain of it infested my nature, squeezing it of all that was good and selfless and dignified.

As if I was some animal, obeying instinct, I became obsessed with him. I watched for him constantly, and when I did see him, which was often, my heart leaped and my face would grow hot. When he smiled at me, my spirit sang. When he ignored me, despair clutched my soul. When my mind teased me with his remembered touch, wave after wave of heat engulfed me before I collapsed under the subsequent frustration. Sudden recollections of our shared childhood, our time at Oxenheath, and many of our times before I married, brought hot tears of desolation. In those moments there was nothing I would not have given just to be alone with him, speak with him, laugh with him . . .

Except being Queen of England. And I would not relinquish that—could not. I relished the riches and glamour; I basked in the attention and in having my every need met; the elevation of my family and their gratitude to me—especially that of my uncle Norfolk—elated me. I was proud of myself for my accomplishment for, no matter the machinations of my family to bring me to this point, I, Catherine Howard, had been crucial to their success. Being Queen of England was my one worthy achievement. No, I would not—could not—surrender that.

No doubt I appeared gay and vibrant, embracing my new life. It was only at night that my inner torment rose biliously to the surface. Many mornings I would wake burdened with doubt over Tom's explanation for the crimes supposedly committed by his brother, as if in sleep my mind had been grappling with the matter. In those first waking moments I would suffer such anguish that I would writhe with the pain of it. The doubt would be accompanied by the memory of his betrayal when he pushed me towards my marriage, and I could only curl into a ball until I managed to summon my defences against the cruel onslaught.

The obsession, the untreatable frustration and desolation it induced, as well as the deep pain of disillusionment and betrayal, made me petulant and edgy. I sought my creature comforts with frenzy, in quest of some solace. I judged others only on their worth to me.

None of my reactions were deliberate. Obsessive love, and what it makes us do, rarely is. It is only hindsight, sharpened by these past quiet months, which has cast light for me on what was going on beneath the surface of my life. As Tom himself might have said, we had ignored what was written in the stars.

And God made it clear to us He would not tolerate such a disruption of His celestial order.

III

AFTER OUR WEDDING, a new vigour, health and good cheer possessed the King—whom henceforth I shall refer to as Henry. He took to rising at dawn, when he would hear Mass, and then he would proceed on the hunt until dinner. He infected all at Hampton Court that summer with his merriment, and I am sure the many foreign ambassadors who enjoyed our hospitality sent back to their masters fulsome reports of their sojourn at the King of England's court.

I received my fill of his great generosity. It seemed every day he indulged me in some fresh caprice; soon, my coffers were bursting with rich jewels, my armouries bulging with exquisite gowns. When confronted with Henry's adoration and generosity, it was not possible for my heart to remain untouched by him. My past fears seemed absurd, as the year 1540 drew to a close.

At Christmas and New Year, Henry surpassed his earlier generosity. He presented me with a square containing table diamonds and clusters of pearls, as well as a brooch constructed of diamonds and rubies with an edge of pearl. The black velvet muffler he also gave me with was turned with sables and contained 38 rubies and—he proudly informed me as if he had counted every one—572 pearls.

Anne of Cleves rode over from Richmond with a gift for Henry of two horses with violet velvet trappings. She addressed me on her knees, and gave over to me a ring and two lap dogs. Her deference shocked and humbled me, and her gifts touched me. Despite the fact that I had usurped her and that Henry had openly humiliated her by showing his fancy for me whilst they were still married, she had never shown me anything but kindness. I welcomed Anne's friendship—and her person—literally, with open arms. On Christmas Eve, Henry, Anne and I shared an intimate supper, which included three pies made from the largest wild boar ever killed in France—a gift from King Francis. After Henry had retired, Anne and I danced and laughed long into the night.

The dour and plain Princess Mary—three years my senior—was not fond of me, try as I might to earn her trust and liking. She regarded me as a foreign, gaily coloured butterfly—with incomprehension, then indifference. Annoyance soon replaced my hurt when she failed to treat me with respect, and her ladies did likewise. In spiteful revenge, I endeavoured to have two of her maids removed from court, and it was only her complaint to Henry that prevented the full enactment of the vengeance. I was placated when, on hearing my own complaint, Henry reprimanded Mary for her behaviour. However, my relationship with the Princess of England was beyond repair.

By comparison, I enjoyed the company of the children—the Princess Elizabeth and the Prince Edward. Burdened with the unpleasant memory of the Cotton children, I had at first approached the royal children with wariness. However, I found pretty Elizabeth to be a friendly, merry child, who clearly relished that a first cousin of her mother was now her stepmother. The dear child was also intensely desirous of maternal affection. Fortunately, I found in myself motherly instincts I had not known I possessed, and Elizabeth basked in my attention. As for Edward—I doubt that the heir to the throne ever missed the presence of a mother, for he was spoiled and pampered by all; yet I found his childish ways and plump features to be adorable. Thus, much affection and laughter characterised the festive season with the children, while Henry looked on indulgently and no doubt envisioned another child being present the following year. And for the first time since my dealings with the Cotton tribe, having a child of my own was an enticing prospect.

Unfortunately, almost as soon as Twelfth Night of 1541 had passed, my life began to turn sour in the worst possible way.

IV

PREPARATIONS WERE UNDER WAY to move the court from its usual winter home at Greenwich to Hampton Court Palace. Henry and I frequently escaped from this bustle and tension into his music chamber, where he would play one of his many instruments and I would sew beside the window or sit by his side. We would dismiss all but one or two attendants, who remained at a discreet distance, and Henry would frequently interrupt his playing to kiss or caress me.

In those times, I fancied I saw in Henry the man he would have been if he had not become King—even-tempered, refined, and without the megalomania that had insinuated itself into his nature since his brother Prince Arthur died. It was always a disappointment to me when those times were interrupted by some call of duty.

Which is why, on one blustery January day, I groaned with annoyance when I saw, from the window of the music chamber, two figures disembarking from a barge and walking purposefully towards the Palace. I recognised one as my former guardian, the Dowager Duchess of Norfolk; the other was a cloaked man, his head covered and face hidden, but whose walk rang a vague bell of recollection in my mind. Very likely here was another family friend or relation who sought some preferment from me. Although I required my lord chamberlain or chancellor to deal with the many petitions that came my way, I had made a point of receiving my family myself; it appeared this duty would now call me away from this treasured time with my husband.

"What is it, sweetheart?" asked Henry, observing my scowl.

"My step-grandmother has arrived with a petitioner it seems," I said, walking over to where he sat with his pipes and bending down to slip my arms around his neck. "I shall have to leave you for a moment." I kissed his cheek.

He inclined into me and patted my arm. "We both have duties to our subjects," he said with a touch of sternness. He knew I preferred not to be bothered with the more tiresome obligations of my position. In months gone, he laughed and shrugged off this evidence of my flightiness, finding it a further illustration of my youth that he found so very attractive; but this last week or two, he had been less indulgent. This flightiness he now saw as just another example of my failure to fulfil my responsibilities to my realm.

The spectre of my possible infertility haunting me, I departed the chamber and hastened towards my own receiving-chamber. As I expected, on the way I encountered one of my ushers who had been sent to fetch me.

"The Dowager Duchess of Norfolk and a gentleman wish an audience with you, Your Grace," he said with abject servility, bowing low.

"I know," I snapped. I swept passed him, my nose in the air.

When I entered the receiving chamber, I saw at once the tense and pale form of the Dowager, sitting upright on a stool. The man stood by the window, his back to me, gazing out into the sleet. He still wore his cloak, so I could see nothing of his features. My guards watched him with suspicion—they were always wary of the possibility of assassination, and this man could be hiding any weapon.

"I told your guards they need not fear this man," complained the Dowager, noticing my assessment of the situation. "I can vouch for him. And in fact, please—rather—*may I* ask that you dismiss your attendants? You will want to speak to this man without an audience."

The Dowager often tried hard to speak to me with respect but failed. However, I had long since overlooked this force of habit, and would in any event have been uncomfortable if any of my close family had shown me deference, so I paid her tone no heed.

Her words stirred my curiosity. "Leave us," I said to my many attendants who gathered in the chamber. "I am in no danger," I said to the captain of my guard when he opened his mouth to protest. "This is a private family matter." He bowed low and followed the straggle of servants out through the door. It whispered closed behind him.

I did not sit down, my curious gaze still pinned on the man. He stood as still as a statue, but his tall form seemed to bristle with some acute awareness.

With shock, I realised he studied my reflection in the windowpane.

Annoyed at being at a disadvantage, for I could see only a dim reflection of his own hooded face, I strode over to him.

"So you want an audience with me?" I cried. "Speak then, what is your petition?" I laid a hand on his shoulder, bidding him to face me.

His broad shoulders lifted as he drew breath. Slowly, he turned around, removing the hood of his cloak . . . and I saw his face.

It was Francis Dereham.

V

I MUST HAVE FAINTED, or shock had rendered me temporarily senseless. When I was next sentient, I was sitting on the seat at the window embrasure, Francis kneeling at my feet, grasping my hands, the Dowager hovering behind him in agitation.

I stared into Francis' dear face. Thinner than of yore, it bore a thick silver scar stretching from the corner of his right eye, across his brown cheek, to his mouth. Deep grooves stretched from nose to mouth, and lines of tension radiated out from the corner of his eyes.

I had not thought it possible, but he was more handsome than ever.

I took his face in my hands.

"Francis!" I choked. "By all the saints—Francis!"

He closed his eyes and for a second seemed to press into my left hand, the one nearest his scar. Then he gently grasped my hands and pulled them down.

"You must not touch me like that," he whispered.

I paid him no heed. I lifted a finger and stroked his hair while with my other hand I grasped his shoulder, still hard and brawny. I saw a pulse thudding in the brown column of his neck and touched it. My gaze went to his alluring mouth and found it evoked sweetest memories. Unable to think, I leaned down and put my lips to it.

He shuddered at my kiss while he returned it with familiar ardour. It was a horrified gasp from the Dowager that had us springing apart and staring at each other with wide eyes and heaving chests.

"I thought you were dead," I whispered at last. "The Dowager told me your ship was attacked and that you—."

"It was attacked," Francis said. "As was I. But clearly I didn't die. Despite the best efforts of your uncle Norfolk!"

I flinched as if scalded. "What do you say?" I gasped.

The Dowager answered my question.

"Master Dereham believes the Duke of Norfolk devised the attack, to remove him from your life," she said with fury. "Quite a preposterous notion of course!"

Astonished that my suspicions should be thus confirmed, I looked from her red face back to Francis. He appeared to be studying his fingernails.

The Dowager surged on, spittle flying from her mouth.

"He also believes he is still married to you—what absurdity! However," her tone became ingratiating, "I believe that if you will give him a place in your household, he will not speak of such scandalous notions."

My stomach began to churn. If I was still legally married to Francis, then I was not Queen of England!

"Oh, Francis!" I whispered. "That would be blackmail."

He looked up at once, a flush creeping into his cheeks.

"This is your step-grandmother's idea," he mumbled. "However, I shall fall in with the plan for I believe your family owes me this much."

"How ridiculous!" raged the Dowager. "Madness—"

"Silence, madam!" Francis turned on the old woman, and she seemed to quail in the face of his anger. "Pray—go stand by the door and leave Catherine and me to discuss this matter alone."

The Dowager seemed to think better of protesting, for she snorted, swept her skirts aside and lumbered away from us. When she stood by the door, she shielded us from the view of anyone who might burst in unannounced.

Francis looked back at me, apology mingling with pride in his expression. I reached out and touched the scar on his cheek.

"I do not know what to think of this," I murmured.

This time Francis did not remove my hand.

"I want only to be close to you," he said. He turned his head and pressed a kiss into my palm. "If I must bribe you for it, then so be it."

I touched his lips. "You would have no need to resort to bribery," I said rashly. "A place in my household? 'Tis yours for the asking."

Francis' next move shocked me to the core. Moaning, he swung forward to wrap his arms around me and bury his face in my lap. Despite my numerous skirts, it was as if I could feel the heat of his mouth burning right through to my thighs as he held me tight. My fingers raked through his thick hair, and I closed my eyes with longing.

Uncaring of the Dowager's observance, Francis moved up my body until his mouth was against my bosom. Then his mouth found mine and I was lost.

A loud cough from the Dowager had us springing apart. Francis lurched to his feet.

"This is a mistake," he gasped. "I cannot be here with you, it places you in too much danger! We shall forget all about this."

"No!" I leapt up. Francis staggered backwards so I could not touch him. "No," I whispered, struggling for calm. "I want you here, Francis! I *need* you here!"

"If you are afraid that I will utter my suspicions, or reveal our previous closeness, I will not," said he in desperation. "I shall not accept a place if you offer me one! I have kept away from you for this long, that I can do so for however long it takes, now that I know you still love me—."

"You have kept away from me?" My head began to throb with confusion as I absorbed his words. I rubbed my perspiring temples in agitation.

He nodded. When he spoke, his tone was calmer.

"Aye, I have been in London since last spring. The Dowager knows it."

Since spring! And, was this another reason why my family had not mentioned to the King my friendship with Francis Dereham? Because if my marriage to Francis was valid, and he still lived, I was not free to marry and be Queen? I shot an accusing look at the Dowager.

"I heard rumours the King was interested in you," Francis continued, "so I stayed away . . . was *persuaded* to stay away," he said bitterly as the Dowager shifted in discomfort, "but in the end I could stay away no longer. And I was determined to right some wrongs in the process." He cast a stern look back at the Dowager. He sighed. "Now I see that it was a mistake. I'll leave you in peace, Catherine, and wait out the time until we can be together again." He bowed and backed away.

"No!" I expostulated again. "I will not have this! You must stay with me, I demand it! Francis—," I stretched out my hands pleadingly as my anguish took over. "I beg of you—I have need of people I can trust."

Francis was plainly torn. His disturbed gaze roamed over my face. He raked his fingers through his hair, shaking his head. He looked at me again with the pain of indecision contorting his features. Finally, he sighed.

"Yes," he muttered. "I will stay, for I can do no other."

VI

FRANCIS DEREHAM became my private secretary.

His close proximity to me each day and night became the most exquisite torment. Not only did I have to be in daily contact with him as we conducted my royal business, but his apartments were just across the hall from my own. In my need for relief and satisfaction from my inner tumult, some of my obsession with the elusive Tom was transferred to the more accessible Francis; my nights became restless as I imagined him naked in bed across the hall. I dreamed of joining him there, or having him come to me. I know I also subjected his splendid form to too much open and admiring scrutiny.

Francis at all times conducted himself in a decorous manner and never by word or deed did he betray that he suffered similar torment. In the silent watches of the night, I would unravel his every chivalrous remark, trying to discover some hint of his continuing desire and love for me, and then I would either dissolve into tears or fall into joyous dreams.

Francis may have been successful in hiding his passion, but I know I was not so skilful, and I had reason to wonder if Henry noticed my interest in my private secretary. In the weeks following Francis' return, Henry's temper became increasingly irascible, and often I found him staring at me with contempt. Terrified, as my dreams became filled with horrifying images of the block and the executioner's axe, I then attempted to restrain my desires, and focused all my efforts on charming my husband both in bed and out of it. To my relief, my efforts were fruitful and Henry became once more doting and indulgent.

However, disaster was only temporarily averted. In March, when we had been at Hampton Court for just over a month, I began to suspect I was with child. When I whispered my hope to Henry, in a fervour of renewed vitality he rode to the hunt one morning in inclement conditions. The next day, he was stricken with a mild infirmity and, with his defences weakened, the unpredictable ulcer on his leg became inflamed and closed up. Dangerous fever claimed him, and for a week he lay dying.

It seemed, for Tom and me, our dreams were being realised sooner than we had dared hope.

Chapter 23

"Be not rash with thy mouth, and let not thine heart be heavy to utter any thing before God: for God is in heaven, and you upon earth: therefore let thy words be few."

The Bible, Book of Ecclesiastes, 5:2

I

KING HENRY'S ULCERATED LEG TURNED BLACK, so that he writhed in constant agony, and I was barred from his chamber. I found solace in the Chapel, and there, under guise of devout prayer, I dared to dream of what this happening did portend—the rest of my life as Dowager Queen, the most powerful woman in England, with Tom at my side! I saw now that I should have trusted my uncle, so long ago, when he set me on this path; and I should have put aside my resentment of Tom, who also had foreseen my royal destiny!

When a note came from the King's Privy Chamber late one night while I lay awake, the ladies who rose to attend to me assumed it pertained to my lord's condition, especially when I dressed and left my bedchamber without ado, pausing only to burn the note.

Written in Tom's hand, the note summoned me to the Chapel Royal where prayers were being offered for the King.

In sedate and sombre fashion I made my way there and dismissed my attendants at the door, bidding them return for me in an hour. I waited for them to depart and entered the chapel, barring the doors behind me.

Two candles at the prie-dieu in the transept barely relieved the thick darkness, but the chapel appeared deserted. Nevertheless, I waited with pounding heart and breathless lungs for sign of movement, for I sensed I was being watched. After several minutes, when nothing happened, I moved down the aisle towards the altar, my skirts swishing loudly on the floor. I knelt before the altar and waited.

He slipped down beside me, the touch of his arm against mine sending a shock through my fragile being.

"We are alone," said Tom, "I am sure of it."

His eyes glowed in the dimness. He lowered his head and his lips scorched mine.

"It has been so long," he whispered a long moment later when we drew apart and I sagged against him. "Sweet Jesus, how I survived I do not know."

"It has to be this way, Tom," I whispered back. "You know that!"

"Aye, but perhaps for not much longer!"

As I stared at him, we heard a soft thud. We sprang apart and my heart began to beat with sickening rapidity. His fists clenched, Tom rose and strode through the archway to search for the source of the noise.

"It was only wax was from a candle falling!" he called with relief from the dimness. "Kate, come here—."

Trembling, I joined him. He grabbed a candle and gestured towards the choir stall. "Let us go in there, there is less chance of our being seen."

I allowed him to take me by the hand and we entered the stall. He laid the candle on a seat and hunkered down on his knees. He pulled me down into his arms.

After another long kiss, he drew away and took my face in his hands. "The King is dying!" he whispered with such intensity it made me flinch. "Perhaps soon our dreams will be realised!"

"Shush," I said placing my fingers on his mouth. "You must not talk like that, Tom. And we must not embrace like this, it is much too dangerous." I placed my hands on his chest and tried to push myself away.

"Kate, can we not talk? There is no one here and we have always been frank with each other! As for the other—ah, I do not care!" He pulled me closer and buried his face in my neck, where I felt his hot mouth and tongue against my bare skin. One of his hands groped at my bosom and the other stroked my buttocks and thighs through my skirts.

How to tell him that here, in the Chapel Royal, I felt as if God Himself saw and disapproved? That if God knew, Henry also knew? Yet, desire battled childish faith and for a time it conquered, as my hands passed under Tom's doublet, over the silken skin of his lean back, and roamed his masculine form.

But disquiet reasserted itself. I pushed Tom away, extricating myself from his eager touch.

"Kate, sweet Jesus, do not do this," he mumbled.

"Tom, we cannot! No, it would be adultery of the worst kind, God knows it and sees! If our time is at hand, then we can wait. Let us do what is right!"

With a groan, he fell back full-length on the ground. "Sweet Jesus! But you're right, I acknowledge it. We must wait."

But as he lay thus before me, it was as if he made me an offering of his body. I groaned, wanting only to partake of it. I reached forward to tug desperately at his clothing.

"What—?!"

"Shush!" I ordered. "Keep still." I pulled off his hose and shoes and scrabbled with the rest of his clothing. Tom did not assist me, nor did he resist, but only stared at me in astonishment.

"I thought you—," he mumbled as I stroked his naked chest and leaned forward to kiss him on the mouth.

"Shush," I whispered again, forcing him to lie flat. "Just let me—." My hand trailed downwards over his belly and slipped around him. It was like coming home. My eyelids closed fast, I kissed his mouth, and rejoiced in his response.

When I paused for air, he tried again. "Kate, you have to be sure. I do not want you hating me afterwards or regretting this."

"I shall not hate you, and I shall not regret this. For we will not be committing adultery!"

"What—?!"

"It is not adultery if we only do this, is it?" I said, sliding down his body and raining a soft kissing trail down his chest and belly to my final destination without waiting for his response.

II

I SUSPECT WE WERE FOOLISH and rash. Regardless, I can say with perfect truth that we never had any intention of making a cuckold of the King and we firmly believed we had not. However, it did set us on a feverish, dangerous path from which there was no return.

The adventure drove all thoughts of Francis, nay, any other man from my mind, and opened the floodgate of pent-up desire, and whatever armour I might have possessed against it was useless beneath its engulfing wave.

Perhaps it would have mattered little if the King had died, as everyone expected. However, he rallied the next day. And he lived.

And a week later, my bleeding arrived and I had to inform Henry that I was not, after all, with child.

Henry was not the same after that. He became fickle in his humours and violent in his passions. He made me his nursemaid and companion, and when I tried to be what he wanted, he complained constantly about his ailments and his age. Only when I summoned all my charm, and he succumbed, did my despair and fear abate. Then he saw in me once more the representation of his own youth, his vanity was flattered by my adulation, and he would lavish on me all the extravagance at his command.

One morning while he wallowed in one of his bitter moods, I persuaded him to accompany me to the tennis court to watch a match between Sir Edmund Knyvet and Thomas Clere, a gentleman retainer of the Duke of Norfolk. The match promised to be a good one, and I hoped it would restore the King to some good humour. He sat glowering beside me on the cushioned bench, and the Duke of Norfolk himself sat on my other side. Francis hovered near by and Tom umpired the game. My attention jumped between Tom, Francis, Henry and my uncle, which is why I missed the call that caused the rumpus. I only became aware of it when Tom stepped onto the court to separate the players as they stood face-to-face, exchanging angry words.

"Marry, take your positions again, gentlemen!" cried Tom in annoyance. "This lack of chivalry is an affront to our King and Queen!"

The King grunted his approval, but the rest of us watched with suppressed merriment. But amusement turned to shock when Sir Edmund drew back his arm and punched Master Clere squarely on the nose. A collective gasp rippled around the court.

Henry struggled to his feet.

"You know the penalty for such a crime," he bellowed, before thumping back down. "Take him away."

In an effort to quell fights amongst his courtiers, Henry had decreed by statute that such a punch be punishable by the loss of the offender's right hand. As Sir Edmund was dragged from the court by the King's guards, I turned in desperation to my uncle.

"Speak to your man," I whispered. "Demand that he not pursue the penalty on his honour!"

"It's a crime against the Kingdom, not the victim, Catherine," said my uncle. "Such a plea would be worthless." The crowd waited for Henry to indicate whether another game should proceed. He sat slumped in his chair, simmering with ill-humour, scarlet with anger. Tentatively, I laid a hand on his arm. The gesture seemed to irritate him more, for he shook my hand off and pushed himself again to his feet. Several attendants rushed to his aid and, without another word, he lumbered from the court. My Uncle Norfolk followed as the crowd began to disperse. I sat alone on the bench, sick with embarrassment, and anguished over the fate that lay in store for Sir Edmund.

Tom gave me a fleeting glance before sauntering away, but I knew from his paleness that his swagger was a ruse. I caught Francis' eye. He nodded at me, his gaze soft with understanding, as he moved towards me.

"Perhaps if you plead with the King, Sir Edmund will be pardoned," he suggested in a low voice as he came to my side.

"I am not in favour at present," I said. Francis looked sympathetic, and hesitated, as if in two minds whether he should linger with me. Then he bowed and backed away.

Following custom, Sir Edmund was tried; however, as with most trials, it was a mere formality—criminals who came before a jury were already deemed guilty and the jury bore the simple task of confirming fault. Sir Edmund was sentenced to have his right hand cut off. He pleaded that he should lose his left hand so he would better be able to serve his King, but the plea was ignored.

On the night before the enactment of the penalty I retired early to my bedchamber. I expected Henry to make his conjugal visit, as he had not been hunting that day and would have sufficient energy to perform his duty. I wondered about his mood, for he had been closeted with the Council for most of the day and had dined privately. At the usual time, I heard a flurry of activity in the outer chamber and, to my shock, Tom entered my bedchamber with several other gentlemen including my brother George, to conduct the customary inspection of the mattress. It was the first time since the night in the chapel that Tom had attended the King on his visits to my room, and I gasped aloud to see him. Tom flinched at the sound but did not look at me; George, however, glanced at me in surprise and turned a narrow-eyed stare on Tom's back. Flustered, I was more than usually openly affectionate towards Henry when he entered the chamber a second later.

"My dearest love, my lord!" I exclaimed, rushing to him and prostrating myself at his feet, grasping his hands and pressing kisses on them. "How I have missed you today!"

Henry was either already in an excellent mood, or my attitude placed him in one. He pulled me up and folded me into his arms.

"Sweetheart! And I have missed you!" He waved impatiently at his men. "Hurry and leave us, I wish to be alone with my Queen."

I stepped back while Tom and the others helped Henry disrobe from his elegant purple dressing gown. When he was stripped to his nightshirt, they backed out of the room. Tom did not look at me, but I detected a grim slant to his mouth.

While Henry partook of his usual mug of wine, I adjourned to the bed and waited for him. My thoughts swooped to Sir Edmund and the proceedings the next day, which—as I had attended the crime and given that I would have been offended by it—I had to attend. The thought made me ill and I barely registered Henry clambering into bed or his hot hands on my body through my shift.

I had long since learnt that overt enjoyment in the marriage bed shocked Henry, so there was no need for me to perform in that regard. I adjusted myself into a comfortable position as Henry kissed me and hauled himself on top of me to perform his obligation; a forced sigh of contentment from me, a few eager, perspiring thrusts from Henry, and the royal responsibility was fulfilled. Thankfully he rolled off me soon after so I could catch my breath.

Remembering Sir Edmund, I felt for Henry's hand, drew it to my lips and pressed it to my bosom with a blissful sigh. Henry propped himself onto his side, looked down at me with an affectionate smile.

"You have made me very happy," he said. Despite myself, his genuinely spoken words touched my heart. I smiled and reached up to kiss his mouth fondly. "You are indeed my sweet rose—my rose without a thorn!"

Again I kissed his hand and pressed it tighter to my bosom. "I am humbled by your kind words," I said. "It's unfortunate perhaps that tonight this rose is afflicted with the thorns of fear and unhappiness!"

"Ah, sweetheart, if you're unhappy that you have not fallen with child—fear not! I myself am confident it will happen in due course. I have been thinking—why should we not go on progress, and make a honeymoon of it? Perhaps an extended absence from the cares of ruling and petitions is just the key to ensure fertility!"

"A progress?"

"Aye! There has been more turmoil in the north—a small revolt that we suppressed. But I suspect the time has come for to make my royal presence known to the wicked and seditious citizens of the north. I have been thinking that a show of my military strength is appropriate!"

I murmured my approval and Henry looked pleased. I seized upon his continuing good humour at once.

"Dearest, I must tell you—it is the event tomorrow which is causing my fear and unhappiness," I said, my lips trembling. Henry at once looked concerned.

"Which event, sweetheart?"

"Sir Edmund's penalty," I cried. "It's such a horrible thing to cut off his hand!"

I covered my face with my hands. Henry was silent. When I chanced a peek through my fingers I knew at once that I had made a grave mistake.

Cold suspicion had replaced his goodwill.

"Why do you plead for this man?" he rumbled. "Do you find him handsome?"

"No!" Sincere denial fortified my exclamation. "It is the bloodshed, the ugliness, the pain . . ." I shuddered.

The King's faded eyes remained narrowed. "It is the law," he said. "I have decreed the penalty for his crime, for the good of my realm."

Rashly, I surged on. "If you made this law, you can unmake it . . . or pardon this man," I cried. I composed myself with an effort as deep colour swept into Henry's cheeks. "You are so great and merciful," I said with complete meekness in an attempt to explain my claim.

Henry pressed his lips together as he studied me.

"You are not in a position to plead for pardon," he said. He turned over and laboured to sit, dragging his legs over the side of the bed. "If you would fulfil your most important duty, then it would be a different matter." He cast me a bleak look over his shoulder. "I would then give you the moon if you asked for it."

His bitterness over my childless state having reasserted itself, he yelled "Enter!" at the closed door to the bedchamber. At once it opened and Tom, George and the others filed in. I pulled the bedcovers to my chin and waited miserably for Henry to be dressed; preoccupied, I was only dimly aware of Tom, going about his task of clothing the King's person with less reverence than usual.

At the door to the chamber, Henry stopped and looked around at me.

"It is required that the Queen attend the carrying out of the penalty on the morrow," he snapped. "Make sure of it."

III

"MY GREATEST WISH IS THAT HE SHOULD DIE," Tom whispered fiercely to me several hours later. "When I think of him sharing your bed—!"

Risking much to be with me, he had picked two locks, and had entered my chamber by way of the back stairs that led from the outer wall of the Palace to my privy. Regardless of the sleeping ladies in the alcove, he had then crawled to my bedside to awaken me. Without hesitation, I accepted his invitation to steal outside with him by the way he had come. Not content with that danger, Tom had risked our being seen by the night watch as he grabbed me by the hand and led me at a breathless pace across the King's Garden to the orchard. Once sheltered by the trees and high ivy-clad walls our pace slowed—clouds covered the moon and stars, making the way treacherous—until we reached a summer house alongside the wall. Tom pulled me inside, hauling me into his arms and uttering his treasonous words.

"You must not speak in this way," I whispered to him. "If someone should hear you—!"

"I do not care," said he with an imprudence that disturbed me. "I want only to take you away from here, to take you to *my* bed."

I groaned with despair as he kissed me. The warm and close atmosphere in the summer house pressed on us. Perspiration prickled my skin. It was a relief when he removed my heavy cloak. He slid down my body until he knelt before me, and pressed his face to the juncture of my thighs.

Perhaps he remembered, as I did, that the King had been there before him, for he made no further move. I bade him to stand up and we embraced tightly.

"This desperate situation is all my fault," he said. "I should have spoken up to our families at Oxenheath when we were there. They would have approved of our marriage, yea, I suspect my own family have been angling for it since you were born! Failing that, I should have done so immediately upon your coming to court. Yet I was too afraid that you did not love me, and I could not imagine marrying you without your love . . . it would have been the worst torture. As for how I persuaded you to this marriage . . . !"

"You must not blame yourself," I mumbled. "I should have realised I loved you in Oxenheath, but I was too wrapped up in childish notions about Henry Mannox to know what was really happening in my heart. As for your taking action when I came to court—it would have served you naught, since my family had already set me on this path. You would likely have got yourself killed!" I thought of Francis's claims about the attack on his ship and shuddered.

"There are different sides to every story," Tom said. "You and your family are no more culpable than I—and probably less!"

"Why do you dwell on blame?" I cried. "It serves no purpose now. We must remember what we all have striven for—the Howards, the most powerful family in the realm! Me, Dowager Queen! You, my husband! Think of that, Tom—it is you who first made me think of it, after all! You have said it is written in the stars that we shall be together, and I have no doubt it is—but perhaps it is also written that first we must survive this ordeal!"

He gave me a troubled look. "Must it be such a struggle, to do what fate intends? And so filled with pain and hardship, so reliant on the death of a man?" He sighed. "Sometimes as I lie alone in my bed and think of you with the King, unable to rescue you as I used to, I think we have defied God's plan. However, we are set on this course, we have no choice but to survive it and deal as best we can with the consequences—and hope for a swift resolution."

When he kissed me, I kissed him back in desperation, anxious to escape from the turmoil of my life. When I fell to my knees before him and pulled him towards me, I experienced the much-needed respite. But it was short-lived.

IV

I ENDURED A SLEEPLESS NIGHT. The next morning before dinner I chose my most sombre gown—brown velvet with cream satin underskirts—and made my way to the Clock Court where Sir Edmund's hand would be cut off. I wondered if anyone would stomach a meal afterwards. I knew I would not, even if I survived the ordeal without fainting.

I took my place beside Henry. The Duke of Norfolk sat on the other side, and aligned beside him on the cushioned bench were members of the Privy Council and various foreign dignitaries. Low murmurs rose from the gathering crowd. My uncle looked at me with concern. Henry glowered and hunched like a toad on the bench. I did not see Tom, but Francis, watchful and protective, had accompanied my train.

The royal surgeon appeared with his sergeant and equipment. The sergeant of the wood yard had set up the block and now stood beside it with his mallet. The master cook wielded the knife with red-faced importance and the sergeant farrier arrived with the searing iron. Even the sergeant of the poultry was present, holding under his arm the cock, which would be ceremonially beheaded on the same block at which Sir Edmund's hand would be removed. It seemed the only people missing were the yeoman of the scullery with the coal to heat the searing iron, and the sergeant of the cellar with the wine, ale and beer. And Sir Edmund himself.

There was a flurry of movement and Sir Edmund, ashen-faced, was dragged to the block. He fell to his knees before it and his hands were untied. The yeoman of the scullery finally appeared, accompanied by the sergeant of the cellar with his fare, who appeared to be arguing in an undertone with one of his minions about the beer borne on one of the trays.

Henry stirred in impatience. At last becoming aware of my presence, he looked down at me. I felt him studying me intently and, because it pained me, I slowly turned my head to look into his face.

A myriad of expressions passed across his face: concern, compassion and—at the last—love. I held my breath, daring to hope, afraid to hope.

The fuss with the beer was resolved and Sir Edmund's right hand was laid on the block, Sir Edmund giving a last cry and struggle.

Then the King straightened in his chair. He bellowed: "Halt!"

As his captors relaxed their hold, Sir Edmund snatched his hand away and looked in our direction in anguished pleading. The crowd murmured. Henry looked at me again and lowered his head towards me.

"I remember you have pleaded for many criminals," he murmured. "Sir Thomas Wyatt, Mistress Helen Page, John Legh. You are too soft-hearted and gentle, sweetheart."

I could not respond, for tears congested my throat. As Henry continued to study me with sympathy and understanding, the tears rose to my eyes and began to trickle down my face. My head began to drop, but Henry placed his fingers beneath my chin and kept my gaze locked with his. He smiled.

"Those are qualities which make me love you," he said. His fingers left my chin and he pushed himself to his feet. Some of his attendants rushed to his side but he waved them away.

"Sir Edmund," he roared. "You have committed a crime against me, my Queen and my realm and you ought to pay the just penalty!" Sir Edmund began to weep and my heart ached for him. "However—," the King held up his hands and an expectant hush settled on the watching audience. "Because my Queen wishes it, I shall pardon you!"

I gasped. Sir Edmund wept louder, crying "I thank you, I thank you, my lord and majesty! My Queen, I thank you!" The stirring and exclamations of the crowd became louder. Henry lifted his hand and there was immediate silence.

"Go about your business, all!" he bellowed. "And mind my laws always!"

He slumped heavily back into this chair. The crowd began to disperse. The foreign dignitaries and the members of the Council filed away, the Duke casting me a swift look of approval before he departed. Francis was flushed with delight and pleasure, and nodded to me in appreciation.

Henry grasped my hand and pressed it to his mouth. On impulse, I leaned forward and threw my arms around him. He embraced me fiercely, and my soul soared with the exhilaration of power: the greatest and most powerful man in all the land, who had ever lived and would ever live, loved me above all others.

Chapter 24

"The family is the association established by nature for the supply of man's everyday wants."

Aristotle
Greek Philosopher, Scientist and Physician
(384-322 BC)

I

POWER LENT ME SELF-CONFIDENCE, which in turn made me arrogant. In my arrogance, I began to take risks.

I openly favoured Francis by lavishing attention and praise on him. I elevated him by seeking his participation in meetings with my lord chamberlain and chancellor, and I urged him to sit at their table at meals. I sensed many in my household began to despise him for being so preferred, and regarded my favouring him as suspicious, but this did not deter me.

I meandered on the Mount one afternoon with my ladies when I heard from over a hedge the voices of Francis and his friend Roger Davenport in idle conversation while they too strolled the pathways. I heard an eager exclamation: "Master Dereham!" followed by the sound of approaching footsteps on pebbled pathway.

I paused to listen in.

"Aye, good man?" asked Francis

"I have a message from Master John." I cocked my head. Master John, one of my gentlemen ushers, had recently shown himself to be resentful of Francis, and as a consequence relations between them were strained.

"What's your message?" said Francis.

"Nay, a question—he wishes to know whether you are of the Queen's council."

Francis detected the sarcasm.

"Go and tell Master John," he said, "that I was of the Queen's council before he knew her and shall be there long after she has forgotten him!"

I imagined the messenger bowing before more crunches over pebbles announced his departure. I heard an inaudible comment from Roger Davenport, and a grunt of consent from Francis before they too moved off.

When we encountered Francis and Roger on the path a minute later, I drew Francis aside and walked ahead with him.

"Take heed of what you speak, Francis," I urged. He bowed his head.

"Aye," he murmured. "I know I spoke boldly to Master John's messenger just now. Your attentions to me of late have renewed hope that some day I shall be known again as your husband, it is my only excuse."

"Then I have been wrong to encourage you," I whispered, horrified. I swivelled on my heel and walked back to my ladies. Francis looked shocked but composed himself with admirable swiftness, before rejoining Roger Davenport at their stroll.

The incident should have jolted me from my complacency; however, I had other preoccupations that diverted me.

Still consumed with the intense fever of lust, I had begun to think of ways to see Tom in private, and decided almost at once that I would need an accomplice. Of course, the first I thought of for the role was Father Vyncent, but I dismissed the idea as soon as it formed—my old friend would never countenance such dangerous meetings, particularly as he seemed to have appointed himself my guardian angel ever since the night Tom had persuaded me to marry the King. Francis was also out of the question, and my brothers, as fond as they were of me, held the interests of the family uppermost. Potentially adulterous meetings were most definitely not in the family's interests. For that reason I also dismissed Isabel, Lady Baynton, my half sister, and Anne, the wife of my brother Henry. Next, I assessed my other ladies. Ever since her blackmail letter, I had not trusted Joan and I would not consider asking her assistance when she might have an inkling of my past with Tom and therefore reason to be suspicious of my wanting to meet with him. The other ladies from Horsham and Lambeth days were better prospects, particularly romantic, giddy Katherine Tylney, yet I knew good reason existed to be wary of them also, for they knew so much of my past and my nature.

My attention turned to Jane, Lady Rochford, the widow of my cousin George Boleyn. As one of the chief instigators behind my cousin Anne Boleyn's death and that of her own husband, I knew I ought not trust her; certainly she seemed a strange, high-strung and restless woman, and ever watchful of me. However, she seemed to see in me a friend, and her attitude towards me was always ingratiating and subservient. I did not know if I could trust her, but I suspected I could tempt her with adventure. It was the most I could hope for.

One night, a week after the pardoning of Sir Edmund, I dismissed all my ladies except Jane. I then asked that she summon a messenger and beg his discretion for a reward. I had earlier crafted a note to Tom, bidding that he proceed to the outer door of the back stairs, where he would be met and brought to me. This note Jane ordered the messenger to deliver. I then sent her down the back stairs to wait for Tom.

She returned a short time later, bristling with excitement. Tom, white-faced, followed her, pausing to hover just outside the door to the privy, watching Jane warily.

"Jane, please sit outside my bedchamber and see that no one enters, on the excuse that I have a headache and require some quiet and darkness," I said. "Should someone wish an audience with me, call for me at once. And please, no word of this to anyone. I will summon you shortly."

Jane nodded and curtseyed, smiling broadly. When the door closed firmly behind her, I turned to face Tom, barely able to contain my exhilaration at being alone with him.

He looked aghast. "Kate, what are you doing?" he whispered.

By way of answer, I unwrapped my dressing gown and let it fall. Naked, I walked towards him and sank against him, winding my arms around his neck.

He grasped me and returned my kiss, yet there was an unnatural tension to his body.

"Jane will call for me if someone wishes to enter," I said, trying to reassure him as my eager palms found their usual route over his body.

"What of rumour? It is so easily incited!"

"The King so loves me he will regard any rumour as scurrilous," I said airily. "Come, my love—."

I fell with him onto the bed where we were able to attain some minor satisfaction. Unfortunately, denied the deepest intimacy, it was nowhere near as fulfilling as our encounters before my marriage. In an effort to hide our mutual disappointment, our verbal expressions of love and pleasure were more effusive than usual, and Tom scrambled into his clothes and departed the bedchamber by way of the back stairs, as if pursued by the Devil himself.

Soon after, I sent him a gift of a velvet cap garnished with a jewelled brooch, bidding him by note in a moment of sense to hide it beneath his cloak "that nobody see it." An absurd gift perhaps, as Tom rarely wore a cap, and an equally odd request. However, I longed to make overt demonstrations of my love, now that I felt I had more freedom to do so, and given the failure of our sexual unions, which I feared would ultimately drive Tom from me.

The following day, Lady Rochford told me in an undertone that Tom had been taken ill with a mild fever. At once, I ran to my writing desk and wrote a hurried, passionate and somewhat garbled note:

> It was showed me that you was sick, the thing which troubled me very much till such time that I hear from you praying you to send me word how that you do, for I never longed so much for a thing as I do to see you and to speak with you, which I trust shall be shortly now. The which doth comfort me very much when I think of it, and when I think again that you shall depart from me again it makes my heart to die to think what fortune I have that I cannot always be in your company. It is my trust always that you will be as you have promised me, and in that hope I trust upon still, praying you then that you will come when my Lady Rochford is here for then I shall best be at leisure to be at your commandment.

After more lines in the same rambling, incoherent vein I signed the note "yours as long as life endures" and sealed it with a kiss. With perspiration prickling my face and dampening my palms, and with agitated voice and gestures, I bade a messenger deliver the note while Jane looked on with intense interest.

When Tom was well, he met me at a time of Jane's devising and this time made no protest. We fell on each other with desperate and frantic—but ultimately futile— fervour.

II

MY UNCLE NORFOLK was sent ahead to make preparation for the northern progress. On the last day of June we departed, leaving behind Archbishop Cranmer, Chancellor Audley and the Earl of Hertford to rule in the King's absence.

Five thousand horses carried the King's army and all required supplies, except for the artillery pieces, which went by sea to York. Our supplies included two hundred tents, the King's richest tapestries and our finest plate, as well as his and my richest apparel.

Our first major stop after Greenwich was Lincoln on the ninth day of August. When we entered eighty archers with drawn bows preceded us. Surrounded by the noblest dignitaries in the realm, the King and I entered in our open chariot, and the King's horse of state followed us. The royal princesses proceeded after, dressed in crimson velvet and cloth of gold. The ladies and gentlemen of the court, ranked according to precedence, brought up the rear. The Prince Edward had not accompanied us, for fear of his health and safety in the restless north.

At the gates of Lincoln, the citizenry met our procession, and we advanced through the city, admiring its gay decorations—pennants, badges and various escutcheons commemorating the greatest of Tudor triumphs. Church bells pealed, and at the town hall the mayor presented Henry with the sword and mace of the city, as symbols of submission to the King. It the midst of such splendour I forgot my cares, and Henry, sensing my happiness, showed his own pleasure by being openly affectionate and indulgent of me, which the gathering crowds cheered to witness. A rumour rapidly swept through our company that I would soon have my long overdue coronation, most likely at York.

At all ceremonial occasions, my dress was of silver tissue or brocade. At other times I wore crimson velvet. Many times I had it said ingratiatingly to me that I was the most beautiful woman in the realm. Privately, I would dismiss such compliments as gallantry—except when I saw Henry struck mute by my appearance, or the Duke of Norfolk staring in wonder, or Francis flushing, or Tom unable to look away. I then did wonder if there was some truth in the notion, at least to those men who loved me.

After Lincoln, we stopped at Pontefract Castle and finally reached York on the sixteenth day of September. The King had ordered a vast lodging constructed for our use on the site where stood the King's Manor, formerly the abbot's house of Saint Mary's Abbey. By the time we arrived, tents and pavilions, all grandly appointed, had been added, and a large and glorious rose garden had been set out in the grounds. At York, much was made of the Pilgrimage of Grace suppressed many years before—those who had remained loyal to the crown were received, decently welcomed and given favours; those who had been less than loyal were required to prostrate themselves at the King's feet and give sizeable monetary donations.

I received a surprise visitor—Sir William Norris, husband of my friend and cousin Mary Norris. A short man whose good looks were marred by a wide gap between his front teeth, he bestowed on me a soft woollen muff as a gift, although he offered no message from Mary. I bade him sit beside me, eager for news of my friend. Always I was aware that somewhere in my world was the faithful and devoted Mary Norris.

"Tell me, Sir William, how goes my cousin Mary? And the babe? I have heard nothing since Mary departed Greenwich—is the child a girl or boy?"

Sir William looked pained. "The child *was* a girl," he said. I did not miss his emphasis. Childbirth was treacherous, and I ought not to have been overly surprised or upset; however, the news struck me with deep sorrow for my friend's loss.

"Sir William, I am sorry to hear such distressing news. You and Mary have my deepest sympathy."

He dropped his gaze to his hands, which twisted in agitation in his lap. "Your Grace, I wanted to request an audience of you as Mary spoke often of your closeness while she was at Greenwich. I wish to express my thanks—."

"Spoke?" I stiffened at his use of the past tense. Sir William's countenance became more pained.

"Aye, Your Grace—I am sorry to tell you, but—my wife and the child both died in childbirth."

I stared at him, as if his words had cut me adrift on a raging river in a fragile boat. I lowered my head to my hands, and Sir William departed in haste and discomfort.

Learning of Mary's death had me searching for a replacement confidante. I imagined I found the required traits in Lady Rochford and Katherine Tylney, and I trusted them perhaps more than I should have, in making my assignations with Tom.

During our stay at York, Jane revealed cunning skills in arranging the trysts. If it was not possible for Tom to visit my bedchamber, she arranged meetings in the rose garden, on the back stairs, or in the cellar, no matter what the weather or time.

On our second to last afternoon at the King's Manor, while Henry was out hunting, I was in my apartments with Francis and some of my ladies. Francis stood beside the window, reading over a page of accounts, the ladies talked amongst themselves while sewing, and I jotted another note to Tom. Of late, I often amused myself in that way, and had even attempted poetry, but more often than not, anything I wrote was tossed in the fire. This one was no exception, and after I had watched it turn to ashes, I wandered over to the window where Francis stood, to gaze out at the soft skies and dull green rolling landscape in the distance.

Francis shifted so that his back was to the room. His arm brushed mine, but he moved away at once. I glanced at him in idle curiosity. His attention was still on the page of accounts in his hand, his lashes casting crescent shadows on his cheeks. He looked paler than usual.

"You are ill, Francis?" I asked, concerned.

He looked up at me and I reeled at the pain in expression. He struggled for composure. When he spoke, his tone was bland.

"I am ill in my heart," he said with astonishing frankness. He cleared his throat. "May I give you some advice, Catherine?" he asked in a voice so low I had to strain to hear it.

"Aye, of course," I murmured. "You know I value your opinions, Francis."

He bowed his head.

"Then I must say—you should stop what is placing you in mortal danger! Do you know of what I speak?" He looked at me intently.

The notes . . . the meetings with Tom. I flushed, shocked and embarrassed that Francis knew of my actions.

"We are doing nothing," I whispered. "There is no adultery."

Relief passed across Francis' face, rapidly placed by renewed concern.

"All the same, you should stop . . . that there be no adultery is hard to prove, as your late cousin Queen Anne would attest!"

I fought rising giddiness. "I cannot stop," I whispered in despair. "I think of him always . . . I have a fever for him . . . I need him as those roses need sunshine." Anguished, gestured at the vast gardens below. Francis shifted in discomfort.

"You *can* stop, Catherine!" he said, his voice rumbling with such dread that I dredged up a measure of control. "You must! I beg of you."

I nodded my consent, wondering in sudden fear how he had come to know of that which he warned against. Evidently, Tom and I had not been careful enough. Francis looked relieved. He inclined his head, and moved away.

However, I did not keep to my resolve. That very night, Jane arranged for a meeting with Tom. In the early hours of the next morning, while the manor slept, she smuggled Tom once more to my bedchamber and I welcomed him with open arms.

III

TOM ROLLED OFF ME AND SAT UP with his back to me, shoulders drooping. I noticed his hair had lost its sheen. I wrapped my arms around his waist and pressed a kiss against his bare shoulder.

"You have been ailing of late, my love?" I asked.

"I am not ailing," he said with a trace of curtness. "It simply grieves me when I cannot love you as God intended!"

Pained by his tone and his words, I moved to his side and directed his face to mine with trembling fingers. Now for the first time I noticed with dread how pale his face was. A nervous pulse flickered wildly at the corner of his eye.

"Our meeting like this is making you ill," I whispered in horror. "*I* am making you ill!" New resolve gripped me. "Tom, we shall stop this," I said. "This is the last time until I am free. It must stop, I see that now."

"No," he growled. "I need to be with you." He pulled me onto his lap and began to kiss and grope me in desperation.

"Then not like this," I cried, shifting and straddling him. "If you must have me, then let it be in the way that is written in the stars!"

He swung away from me.

"Kate! No!"

"Yes," I said. Indeed, I was aching so deeply I could not deny myself.

Tom stopped the intercourse. As I lowered myself, he hauled himself up the bed, and rolled away to lie face down on the pillows. With a cry of anguish and frustration, I tumbled down beside him. As I railed at our misfortune into my pillow, I felt Tom take my fist and entwine his fingers with mine. We lay thus, until dawn began to streak the sky above the barren moors.

IV

THE DUKE OF NORFOLK'S base-born mistress, Bess Holland, had accompanied the royal court on its progress. She was rarely seen. The Duke's wife, the Duchess of Norfolk was still alive and well at Hertfordshire, but Mistress Holland's absence from social circles was more because she was heavy with child. The court understood, even though it was not confirmed, that the babe she carried was my uncle's. It was unusual for a pregnant woman to travel, and even more unusual for an unmarried pregnant woman to flaunt her state—but then, my uncle and his mistress had never made a habit of heeding custom.

At York, the child was born—a girl, Jane. Of late, my enjoyment in the company of the Princess Elizabeth and the Prince Edward had grown into a deep fascination with babies. My imagination would take wing, and often I would imagine having my own child. It was something of a struggle for I had beheld no good example of motherhood. Solicitous to learn more of this mysterious state of being, when I heard that Bess Holland and her child were well enough, I decided to pay them a visit. My first encounter with Bess Holland at the Horsham joust long ago had been inauspicious; however, the promise of holding a tiny, warm and innocent infant, who was also of my blood, was too intoxicating a prospect to ignore, and it would be a welcome diversion from my other preoccupations.

Bess Holland sat alone with her child in a comfortably furnished bedchamber set aside for her use. It was the first time I had seen her in close proximity, and her beauty made me stare—she wore a green velvet dressing-gown, the colour matching her cat-like eyes and complementing her creamy complexion. She possessed full pink lips of astonishing sensuality, and her thick flaxen hair flowed loose past her waist. Her gown gaped open, for she nursed her child.

Unflustered when I was admitted, she stood and bobbed a curtsey, the babe remaining firmly attached to her white, full breast. She bore no trace of the antagonism she showed me at the Horsham joust long ago. I could see that having a family of her own had granted her an enviable serenity.

"Pray sit," I said at last.

She inclined her head and sank back down. I took a seat opposite her, unable to take my gaze from the nursing child.

"You feed the babe yourself?" I asked.

"Of course, Your Grace," she murmured. She added with some spirit, "Jane is my child, she should have my milk."

She had a soft voice, and accents that betrayed her common breeding. I found myself studying her—her beauty was such as would have caught the Duke's eye, but to keep him as she had, Bess Holland had to have some substance that was not so visible. I remembered the shocking passion of the embrace I had witnessed one night at Norfolk House—and in it an inkling of the hold she had on the Duke.

At that moment, the door opened and we both jumped. The Duke of Norfolk himself walked in. During a second of awkwardness, he glance at Mistress Holland, who smiled at him with great tranquillity. He moved to her side and together they faced me, a united front . . . a family . . .

Bess Holland spoke first.

"Her Grace has been gracious enough to pay us a visit," she said. "I am very honoured and I am sure Jane would be pleased to know her cousin has paid her this great honour."

The Duke grunted his agreement. For a second he seemed as captivated as I was by the child at the breast, and stroked a finger across the tiny, fragile head. The child stirred and turned away from her sustenance. Mistress Holland at once scrabbled for her gown and pulled it across her breast.

"Here, let me," muttered my uncle, reaching down and taking the child from her mother. I gaped as he laid the baby across his shoulder and began to pat her back. He *tch*-ed when the child bubbled milk over his doublet. Mistress Holland uttered an exclamation and began to dab at the stain with a cloth, while the Duke expertly switched the child to his other shoulder. Mistress Holland's touch I found to be subtly intimate. Suddenly distressed by the domestic scene, and feeling like an intruder, I rose to my feet.

"My cousin is beautiful," I said in a strained voice, rushing to the door. "And I am pleased mother and babe are both well . . . good morrow to you!"

I heard a startled, "Catherine!" from the Duke as I left the room, but he did not follow me. I swept ahead of my attendants at a brisk pace, seeking the sanctuary of my own apartments. In my bedchamber, I dismissed all my ladies except Jane and Katherine and fell face down on my bed. Those two kept a discreet distance from me, although I heard them whispering in agitation.

Jane moved to my side.

"My lady, would you like me to fetch Master Culpeper?" she asked.

I shook my head furiously. The last thing I wanted was to see Tom—he represented all that fate had denied me: love, passion, family, *babies!*

But, no—not denied me, I reminded myself. I only had to wait for the King to die and all that—and the contentment that came with it—would be mine.

I trembled with need. And, like a child, I was not prepared to wait for something I wanted. I wanted it—nay, *needed* it—now! I realised I might have to forsake love and passion for the time being, but I could have the other! I could start my family—with my husband, the King of England.

Yet, the way I led my life would not bring me to possess the tranquil, domestic happiness embodied by my uncle, his mistress and their child. I had to start behaving as a Queen should, with maturity, dignity and soberness. No wonder, I thought—in the anguish of realising a stark truth—that God had thus far denied me a child—I did not deserve one! If I now resumed my duties, receiving all my petitioners and taking dutiful care of my estates, if I became interested in political and religious affairs, and if I ceased my irresponsible liaison with Tom, God would surely grant me and Henry a child!

And so I made another vow. But, as I resolved on a life without Tom, the memory of him and of his intimate touches flashed through my mind, and I writhed in desire for him. I gripped my head with vice-like fingers in a fruitless effort to force out the memories . . . then wondered in despair—bearing in mind my many broken vows—how long my resolutions would last.

V

THE COURT WAS SOON ON THE MOVE AGAIN, and opportunities for meeting Tom grew limited, even if I had desired one. However, I discovered I was right to doubt my ability to stay away from him; my old obsession, somewhat appeased of late by his attentions, surged again to the fore. Thus, when I saw him from the window at Hatfield early one morning, I stopped what I was doing to stare at him with open-mouthed yearning. With a group of boisterous, laughing men, he emerged from the direction of the river and traipsed across the fields closest to the castle. From their appearance, the men had been swimming—a brave feat, for the weather was turning cold—and Tom, like the others, wore only his hose, slops and shoes while he swung his other clothing from his grasp. As they drew closer to the castle, Tom lagged behind the rest to watch another courtier at sport with his hawk. I gazed at the sheen of moisture on his pale skin and absorbed into my being the vision of every muscle and sinew of his body.

I think I may have made some foolish sound for Margaret Morton moved to my side and her curious gaze followed my own. Her head swung back to me, her interest heightening. With heat in my cheeks, fire in my belly and my heart thudding in nervous agitation, I managed to turn from the window.

Just then, I heard activity outside the bedchamber, and Henry and his train entered with their usual glamour and ceremony. Garbed in his dressing-gown, he was buoyant and exuberant. His expression became ardent when he beheld me, and he waited with obvious impatience as his gentlemen conducted their search of the mattress and chamber. Stunned, I realised he was making a conjugal visit, something he never did outside the nighttime hours. He dismissed his men with alacrity just as the purpose of his visit occurred to my ladies and they sprang to disrobe me.

When the door had closed behind the last of our attendants, I stood only in my shift, shocked into immobility. Henry strode towards me and wrapped his arms around me.

"I had a dream last night," he said into my ear. "In my dream my good friend and servant Hans Holbein painted our portrait, and in the portrait were you and I—and three of our children, sons amongst them! Is that not a wondrous dream, sweetheart?" He hugged me tight. "Tis a sign, surely. I determined at once to share your bed."

My cheek remained pressed against his gown and my gaze was drawn inexorably to the scene outside the window. Tom still watched the hawking . . . lusty Tom, with his swinging black hair and striking body. I shuddered and closed my eyes, but his vision remained imprinted behind my eyelids.

The King led me to the bed. With my eyes still closed fast, holding onto my vision, I surrendered to my husband as he filled for a short time the aching void in my loins. For the first time with him, I attained satisfaction. Afterwards, he said to me: "I am sure of it now! God's power surged through you, I felt it! We will be blessed soon with a son."

However, when we returned to Hampton Court on November the first, I still bore no child in my womb.

Chapter 25

"Pain will force even the truthful to speak falsely."

Publius Syrus
Roman author
(85-43 BC)

I

Hampton Court Palace
November, 1541

THE FLOWERS OF HAMPTON COURT were fading and the trees growing bare, their russet and orange leaves turning black on the ground. The atmosphere pressed grey, close and misty, but the Palace's dusky red walls glowed with a warm welcome through the gloom.

I awoke the next day resolved henceforth to be responsible. I dressed with unusual sombreness in a dark gown of midnight blue velvet with silver tissue underskirts and proceeded to my privy chamber to commence the day's business. Henry was at Mass and afterwards we would dine; I believed he then intended to meet with Chancellor Audley, Archbishop Cranmer and the Earl of Hertford to review happenings in London whilst we were away.

I was in consultation with my chancellor and chamberlain and other of my men, including Francis, over our plans for the coming week when Father Vyncent was announced. Gratified, and not a little curious as to the purpose of this visit, I rose to welcome him.

However, as soon as he entered the chamber, a chill of apprehension snaked down my spine—his face was ashen. I took an anxious step towards him, opening my mouth to exclaim my shock—but he shook his head. I stopped short. A dart of his fretful eyes advised me of my next action.

I cleared my throat.

"Gentlemen," I said with calm. "I wish to be alone with my chaplain. Pray leave us."

I waited while all present filed out. Father Vyncent stared anguished at Francis as he went by, which did little for my composure.

"Father Vyncent, what ails you?" I cried when we were alone, rushing to him. "What is wrong?"

"Everything," said Father Vyncent in a tone guttural with anxiety. "If it please you, let us sit."

Trembling and confused, I sank down into a chair and Father Vyncent pulled up a stool to sit before me. He grasped my hands. His own felt cold and clammy.

He swallowed and drew a deep breath. "I was at Mass just now," he said. "The King was there. I saw Archbishop Cranmer hand him a note. I recognised the Archbishop's own seal."

I shrugged. "We no doubt will have much urgent business to attend to for a few days—."

"No!" Never before had he shown such agitation. He struggled for some self-possession. "The King read it while still in chapel," he said tremulously. "I had remained behind with my prayers for I was curious. I heard him exclaim: 'Why, this is abominable lies! Who has started these scurrilous rumours of my Queen?'"

A wave of fear swept over me. "What did the note say?" I whispered through cold lips.

Father Vyncent shook his head. "I do not know. For some minutes afterwards, Archbishop Cranmer talked in a low tone with the King and then they left. I returned to my chambers, hoping it was nothing to be concerned about—forsooth, the King seemed disbelieving of the note's contents. I thought some idle mischief perhaps."

"Of course, that is all it was!" I exclaimed with relief. "You are worrying for naught, my good friend."

But Father Vyncent shook his head. "The note came from Archbishop Cranmer. If it pertained to something that occurred while you were on progress, he would have consulted with Chancellor Audley and the Earl of Hertford, and therefore the writing of the note would have had their endorsement. And why a note? Why not raise the subject with the King in person? Perhaps the answer to that question is that the contents of the note are so shocking that they feared the King's wrath. Dear God," he whispered, "If it is rumour of your association with Master Dereham, or Master Culpeper . . . !" He closed his eyes and squeezed my hands in his torment.

Now I laughed with genuine amusement. "Father Vyncent, I believe that in your care for me you have made some wild suppositions. I am sure it is nothing like what you have described, except idle mischief signifying nothing!"

"Perhaps," whispered Father Vyncent, his shoulders slumping. "I will pray that it is so."

Just then we heard a commotion in the outer chamber—loud words, scuffles. Father Vyncent sat straighter and we looked at each other in puzzlement before we rose simultaneously and moved to the door.

With Father Vyncent at my shoulder, I stepped into the outer chamber and stopped short. On either side of Francis, gripping his arms, were two guards. Standing to the side was Sir Thomas Wriothesley, the King's secretary of state, looking stern and self-important. Francis was white to the lips.

"What is the meaning of this?" I burst out, my astonishment and horror lending outrage to my voice.

Wriothesley bowed his head, yet somehow the gesture was devoid of respect. I bristled at his insolence.

"Master Francis Dereham is under arrest, Your Grace," he said.

"On what charge?" I cried.

A pause thrummed in the chamber. Wriothesley appeared to suppress a smirk.

"Piracy off the coast of Ireland almost two years ago, Your Grace."

I do not know which emotion was the stronger—relief or confusion. As one battled the other within me, rendering me mute, Wriothesley inclined his head once more and, at a signal from him, the guards led Francis from the chamber.

When the door slammed shut behind them, I turned to face Father Vyncent and felt as if I drowned in own apparent terror. Discreetly, he grasped my hand and pulled me back into the inner chamber.

He helped me to my seat and pressed a mug of wine into my shaking hand. I took a gulp and turned in anguish to my old friend.

"What does this mean, coming directly after that note?" I whispered.

Father Vyncent looked as if he had aged twenty years and his expression was bleak.

"I fear," he said, "that which we have dreaded has begun."

II

HOWEVER, FOR THREE DAYS life at Hampton Court proceeded in the normal fashion, although Francis did not return and my enquiries after his welfare met with ignorance. Henry showed no sign of anger or distress, and exhibited the same deep affection he had showed me in the final days of our progress. I began to believe that Francis' arrest and the note were unrelated, and that the note itself had indeed been idle mischief. Although we worried about the outcome of the piracy charge against Francis, both Father Vyncent and I relaxed. The reprieve was fleeting.

On the fifth of November I returned to my apartments after dining to find the number of my ladies reduced. Joan Bulmer, Katherine Tylney, Margaret Morton and Alice Restwold were absent. No one knew of their whereabouts. I did not need a horrified Father Vyncent to point out to me what all these ladies had in common—knowledge of my days at Horsham and Lambeth, including my relationship with Francis Dereham. Father Vyncent assumed they had been held for questioning.

Sick with dread, hoping fresh air would relieve the aching of my head, I wandered through the cold and dank gardens with Lady Rochford. We were descending the Mount when crunching footsteps from below announced the approach of several people. I stopped with a gasp when Sir Thomas Wriothesley and several of his minions rounded the corner of the pebbled path.

Once again his bow was devoid of respect; again he wore an insolent smirk and a self-important air. My hand itched to slap him. My jaw snapped into an arrogant tilt and I glared at him.

"Your Grace, I am here to escort you to your chambers where you will remain confined until further notice. Under orders of his most high majesty, the King!"

It was only my overwhelming and sudden hatred of this towering, thin man with his curly tawny hair and jutting, axe-like chin that kept me from bursting into storms of protesting tears. Nose still in the air, I brushed past him and strode on ahead. Lady Rochford, after a second's hesitation, scuttled after me.

However, in the confines of my chambers, with all but four of my ladies dismissed and guards stationed outside my closed door, I gave way to the deepest fear imaginable, and collapsed on my bed. Lady Isabel Baynton, my half-sister, made weak attempts to console me but soon gave up. She must have wondered, as everyone did, why I was confined, and decided to reserve her loyalties in the interests of self-preservation.

"The Duke of Norfolk has returned," I heard my brother Henry's wife, Anne, say to Isabel in an undertone later that night. They thought I was sleeping but in truth I had lain awake, my agony turned to numbness, a headache robbing me of sleep. "What do you think that portends? He was supposed to be away in Kenninghall until January."

"Only a meeting of the Council would bring him back," replied Isabel. They fell silent. I turned my face into the pillow, praying for oblivion.

The next afternoon, Father Vyncent was admitted. I had been incapable of any activity since rising from my bed, and had spent the long, quiet hours sitting beside my window. I was not surprised that Father Vyncent again looked aged and distraught. Again on the pretext of wanting to pray with my chaplain, I dismissed my ladies.

"What more have you heard?" I whispered in a voice husky with tears. "I need to know what ensues, Father!"

Father Vyncent bowed his head in acknowledgement. A deep wheeze rattled in his chest, signifying that care had taken a toll on his own health. "I know only what rumour has reached my ears and what careful questioning has taught me," he said.

"Then tell me, please. I cannot stand not knowing!"

"Sir Thomas Wriothesley returned yesterday—from Sussex. It is believed that while he was away he called on the Dowager Duchess of Norfolk, at Horsham. What he learnt there, I do not know. But as a result of it, and of some questioning of your ladies, a meeting of the Privy Council was called. This morning, the King met with Wriothesley, your Uncle Norfolk and Chancellor Audley in the field. He then boarded a small barge and headed to the Bishop of Winchester's residence at Southwark. I believe that is where the meeting will take place." Father Vyncent sighed. "Beyond that, I can only speculate. Nothing has been said publicly."

"Then, please—speculate, Father! Tell me your thoughts!"

He sighed. "I believe it is possible that information has come to light regarding your relationship with Master Dereham, confirmed perhaps by the Dowager and your ladies."

"Not the Dowager," I protested. "She would only be incriminating herself, for she vouched to the King for my pure state before we were married!"

"Then perhaps the servants." Some realisation dawned on his face. "I heard one piece of information, which I dismissed as unimportant, but perhaps it may shed some small light on this. Apparently, the Archbishop received a certain Protestant fanatic in October and was closeted with him for an extended period—one John Laschelles." Father Vyncent paused meaningfully.

For a second the name rang only a distant bell, then I knew. Laschelles . . . Mary Laschelles, now Mary Hall . . . the chambermaid who for years had displayed a deep animosity towards me. Was there a connection? Had she wreaked the ultimate revenge by informing a relative—a father or brother perhaps?—of my past? A relative with his own religious agenda?

Father Vyncent sighed and shrugged. Indeed, it mattered not now the origin of the rumours. What mattered was survival.

"What do I say if I am questioned, Father?" I whispered. "I need your guidance."

Father Vyncent bit his bottom lip in deep thought. "It depends," he said at last, "on what you are asked—for the questions will reveal what has been said—by your accusers, by your friends—and by Master Dereham himself."

"Francis is being questioned, do you think?" I asked, horrified.

"Oh, without a doubt. The matter of piracy was a ruse, I see that now. And Catherine, you must know—." He paused, unsure whether to continue. I urged him along with a whispered "What?"

"Also without doubt," Father Vyncent said slowly, not meeting my eyes, "Master

Dereham is being subjected to—the rack."

The final word seemed to echo and re-echo through the chamber . . . or was the echo in my mind?

My beautiful Francis, strung on the rack, or compressed in the scavenger's daughter! Starved or denied water!

I moaned, pressing my hands against my head in a futile effort to drive out the images and the guilt from my mind. I began to rock back and forth, the motions becoming progressively wilder. In my tumult I heard Father Vyncent praying in a low, beseeching voice.

Then it occurred to me—*both Katherine Tylney and Francis knew of Tom!*

Katherine was beyond the reach of torture and was a mere corroborator of information pertaining to Francis. She was foolish enough to see no connection between questions about my past and my present relationship with Tom. If not asked about him, she would say nothing. But *Francis!* To divert his tormenters, Francis might utter Tom's name!

Frantically, I interrupted Father Vyncent's desperate prayers.

"Tom! What of Tom, Father Vyncent?" I begged, clutching him. "Francis knew there was something between us. Oh, if Tom has been arrested—!" In my terror I could not finish the sentence.

I had not thought it possible, but Father Vyncent blanched whiter.

"He has not been arrested," he said through stiff, colourless lips. "Nay, he even appears ignorant of what has happened, as is most of the court, although I have not had a chance to speak with him in private. He is merry and bright, out hawking . . ."

"I hope he remains safe and ignorant," I whispered. "Although I am innocent of adultery, I shall not utter a word of him if I am questioned."

"Yes, tis better if you do not. Torture can wring all manner of confessions from people," Father Vyncent said bitterly.

He turned to me.

"And *you* shall be questioned, Catherine, I am sure of it—you must be prepared."

He was right. The next day Archbishop Cranmer entered my chambers unannounced. My uncle, the Duke of Norfolk, accompanied him.

III

"PLEASE, MY LADY, SIT," said the Archbishop with a smile that did not reach his eyes. He waved towards a vacant chair. The Duke pulled up two others to face it. We all sat down. My ladies had been dismissed, but in the corner sat a simply-garbed man I assumed was a secretary, ready to transcribe the proceedings.

The Archbishop wore a mitre, a russet brown cassock and cincture; the weak sunlight streaming through the nearby window fell on his pectoral cross and it flashed, causing me to blink and see its outline behind my lids when they closed. I took in only his austere face before I turned to my uncle.

At once I quailed and I felt my lips tremble in distress. He wore a cold and inscrutable expression, his mouth pressed into a cruel line. I dragged my gaze away. I preferred the blinding pectoral cross to the fearsome countenance of my uncle.

"Some information has come to light," said the Archbishop mildly "regarding your life before you married the King. We are here today to talk over the information with you."

I swallowed the lump in my throat and nodded. The Archbishop laced his fingers together, leaned back slightly in his seat and pressed his hands against his stomach. His expression was puzzled and dreamy.

"There are two men in the Tower," he said, "who—."

"Two?"

"Why, yes—."

"Oh, sweet Jesus! Oh, no!" I burst into a wild storm of tears, and began to rock back and forth, wailing my despair, clutching my head with biting fingers. *Tom! Tom! Tom!* "Oh, God," I cried, tumbling to my knees, throwing myself across the seat of my chair. "Dear God, no! *No! No!*" My wails grew higher with every uttered word.

"Catherine!" I dimly heard my uncle exclaim in deep shock. ". . . Henry Mannox . . . Francis Dereham."

Henry . . .

Not Tom. Tom was safe!

But, was *I* safe? And what of Francis? And Henry? What manner of torture were they subjected to?

I burst into a new paroxysm of weeping

My wild rocking impelled me backwards and I rolled over almost at once, as if in the throes of some physical agony that no position of my body could relieve. On my hands and knees, I lurched to my uncle.

"Oh, please, uncle, please!" I clutched his legs and hauled myself up. He swayed away from me, his face now distorted, and he tugged at my hands in an attempt to disengage them. I held fast. "I beg you, uncle, call a halt to this madness. I have done nothing wrong, you know it! I am innocent, *innocent!*" My hands flew up and grasped his doublet with all the ferocity my desperation could lend me! "You promised me you would take care of me, you promised me!" I threw back my head and wailed. "*You promised me!*"

Spent, I collapsed forward, sobbing, falling face down into his lap.

But for my racking sobs, there was silence. The Duke did not move, did not touch me. A creak of the Archbishop's chair, then I felt his touch beneath my arms.

"Come, child, this frenzy of lamentation and heaviness serves you ill."

He pulled me away. Once free of me, the Duke sprang to his feet, strode to the door and opened it. I heard him say something in an impatient tone, and then there came hurried, light footsteps approaching me. I was lifted and fell against Isabel. Assisted by Anne Howard, she led me into the bedchamber. My ordeal had concluded—for now.

The next day, Archbishop Cranmer arrived once more in my chambers to continue my interrogation. This time, but for the scribe, he was alone.

IV

HE FETCHED ME A MUG OF WINE and made sure I was seated comfortably. When I had thrown back the drink, he pulled up a chair close to mine and grasped my hands, *tut-tut*-ing in concern at their chill. His kindness touched my heart and I smiled tremulously at him. He returned my smile; I noticed his eyes were like ice-chips—pale blue, cold, hard.

"My dear," he said, abandoning the royal form of address in favour of parental concern, "have you eaten today? You look very pale and weak."

"I cannot eat," I said, "until this matter is resolved!"

"And it shall be resolved—and very soon I am sure of it!" said he with hearty reassurance and a stiff smile which revealed yellowed teeth. "All you need to do is help me, then your friends will be released from the Tower, and life will go on as normal! Would that not be wondrous? We simply need some clarification of information we have received, and you can supply that clarification. Why, I will help you! Let us be partners in solving this mystery, what say you, child?"

I sniffed and nodded, immeasurably comforted. "I have committed no wrong," I said, "that is the solving of the mystery at once!"

"I am sure you never consciously intended to do any wrong," said he ingratiatingly. "There may perhaps have been one or two—shall we say?—childish indiscretions? Why, we all commit those!" He laughed—a harsh, braying sound. "Knowing that, I am sure the King will pardon you—and all will be well! So let us examine the matters that have been raised." He nodded at the secretary who lifted his quill, ready to scribble. The prospect of the King's pardon filled me with wild hope.

"Now, let us begin with Master Mannox, shall we?" said the Archbishop, releasing my hands and leaning back in his chair in the same way as he had done the day before—interlaced fingers pressed against his stomach, dreamy and puzzled look. There seemed to be a trace of harshness in his tone and I stiffened. With an effort, he smiled. I willed my body to relax.

"Let me try to remember what he has told us," he mused, blinking in heightened puzzlement. "Ah, yes . . . he was your music teacher, I understand? However," he continued when I nodded, a frown beetling his bristly grey eyebrows, "it appears he was a young man intent on corrupting a very young girl by instructing her in more than music!"

I seized upon the excuse at once. "Aye!" I exclaimed, widening my eyes in a show of innocence. Then I remembered Henry's plight. "However," I rushed on, "there was no—no—"

"He did not know you carnally?" urged the Archbishop, suddenly inclining foward and staring at me.

"No, he did not!" I said with all the fervour and indignation I could muster.

The Archbishop thumped back in the chair and scratched his head. "Yet—if I can recall his statement—he said he did know intimate parts of thy body."

Heat scorched my cheeks. I began to bluster my denial when the Archbishop sprang to his feet and took one stride forward until he towered over me.

"You must speak the truth!" he shouted and threw up his arm. His voice rang through the chamber. With a whimper, I flinched expecting him to strike me. Instead he thrust a pointing finger at the ceiling. "God sees the truth! Do not mock him by falsehood!"

"It's true," I blubbered, shaking. "Master Mannox did touch intimate parts of my body . . . *I suffered him* so to touch!" I began to weep, dropping my face to my hands.

There was a creak of the chair as the Archbishop resumed his seat. When I looked up it was to see he had resumed his puzzled and dreamy pose.

"Master Mannox said nothing about *forcing*," he murmured.

Oh, dear God, I thought in agony. What had I done in my efforts to vindicate myself, but set Henry up for more torture?

However, the Archbishop shrugged and smiled. "He did though avow there was no carnal knowledge of you. It seems then that Master Mannox is guilty of nothing more than attempting to take advantage of a young woman of noble birth—a deplorable exploit indeed but not, unfortunately, a crime." He sighed. "It appears we no longer require him to assist us in our investigations."

I almost collapsed with relief, but the Archbishop's next words caused a sickening fear in my breast.

"It is a different matter, however, with Master Dereham, is it not? Master Dereham did know you carnally both before your marriage to the King—*and after?*"

"No!" I exclaimed at once in deep horror. "Not after!"

Too late, I realised my mistake. The Archbishop tilted his head as if listening to the echo of my words. I whispered "Oh, sweet Jesus," and crumpled into renewed storms of weeping.

"You were his lover before you became Queen?" pressed the Archbishop. I could only nod. "Ah! Well, certainly, Master Dereham has admitted to such, although he swears there has been no adultery. That of course would be unforgivable! However, carnal knowledge before your marriage?" I dashed tears from my eyes to see him shrug thoughtfully and bare his teeth in a smile again. "Perhaps pardonable, depending on the details. You can help me clarify those details, my dear—will you do that?"

I nodded. Again the prospect of pardon was enticing.

"Good, good!" said the Archbishop heartily. "Let me recall again." He pinched his nose and frowned. "Ah, yes." His hands clenched on his knees and his head thrust forward. Involuntarily, I swayed back from the fervour in his expression. "My Lady, were you ever naked with Master Dereham?"

I gasped at the apparent absurdity of the question. However, it was a simple enough query and I could not see how a truthful answer would incriminate me or Francis. If the rest of the questions were like this . . . ! I answered in a whisper forced between dry lips, "Aye."

"How many times?"

"I know not!"

"Was there times when he laid with you when he was not naked?"

"Sometimes at Horsham . . . he would be naked but for his hose, and sometimes he would be fully clothed . . . I do not understand such questions!" I wailed.

"I am merely corroborating information Master Dereham has given us," said the Archbishop. "And you have done well—why, perhaps we shall also see that Master Dereham no longer is required to help us with our enquiries! Would that not be wonderful, my dear?"

I knew there was a purpose behind the bizarre questions. In my tumult, I just could not discern what that purpose was. I could only nod, and hope that neither by word nor by action did I betray Francis or endanger myself.

"How many times did you lie with Master Dereham?" asked the Archbishop.

I rubbed my head in agitation. "I know not," I whispered. "Many times."

"How long did your carnal intercourse endure?"

"I—I am not certain." We had commenced our intimacy at the time of the Horsham joust, I remembered . . . that was in May . . . three years before? And we had ceased our familiarity just before I had gone to court, and Francis to Ireland . . . that was in the same year, or the following? "Perhaps a year . . . half a year, perhaps less," I mumbled. "I am not certain."

"I see, I see. Now, my dear, I confess I am confused. You expressed justifiable horror at the notion of adultery, yet you bring into your close household someone who at one time was your lover! Wherefore did you do such a thing if you held no desire to take this handsome young man to your bed again?"

It is marvellous how in retrospect one can easily arrive at the correct and proper answers to difficult questions; later that night I was to rail at myself for not pointing out to the Archbishop that one of my roles as Queen was to seek preferment and positions for my friends and family. I could also have emphasised with truth that it had been the Dowager Duchess who had petitioned for Francis at the outset. However, all I could do at my interrogation was to sniff and insist, "I never wished to commit adultery, there was no adultery."

"Hmm," said the Archbishop with interest. "No adultery—because *you were never legally married to the King ?*"

At last I realised the purpose of his questions! The Archbishop wished to establish a degree of intimacy and fidelity between Francis and me that indicated a marriage had existed!

He rose from his seat and approached me with menace in his stride and on his face, an avenging angel who made me quiver and recoil in dread. I dropped my head and held my hand out in a feeble attempt to protect myself from his onslaught.

"Never married to the King, because you were already promised to Francis Dereham?" the Archbishop roared.

"No, no," I whimpered. "I am rightfully Queen of England! I am!"

"It was a long and intimate association you had with Master Dereham—was there an *understanding ?* Did you both call each other *husband* and *wife ?*"

"Yes—no!—yes . . . I know not . . . there was no promise . . . no promise . . ."

"I cannot hear you! Do you say there was no promise to wed Francis Dereham?" The bellow grew louder with every uttered word, and I quailed further at the onslaught of his fury.

"No promise! I am rightfully Queen of England . . . I am . . . I am . . . I am." I sobbed in desperation, clutching hold of my only worthy achievement, the pride of my family.

"Does Master Dereham *lie* then?"

Slowly, I nodded.

"What do you say! Speak!"

I looked up into the Archbishop's thunderous countenance.

"Yes," I cried. "He lies. There was no promise to be wed. *I am rightfully Queen of England.*"

V

MY CONFINEMENT CONTINUED. I remember little about the following days, except being stricken with a headache, which rendered me insensible, blinkered my vision and cast all I saw into blurry shapes and colours of grey and white. I bore a constantly upset belly and a trembling of my hands that I could not control. Father Vyncent came often, but he had no further information except a rumour that Henry Mannox had been released from the Tower, although Francis remained there. The King had not returned from London and Tom remained at liberty—I realised then that Francis was withholding the information about Tom, most probably to his own detriment. He was far braver and more honourable than I. I despised myself for my weakness.

I had further reason to despise myself. Desperate for his pardon, I wrote the King a letter, in which I repeated the details I had given the Archbishop, although embellishing it with inaccuracies that I thought would save me from death and deliver me from my current terror. I must have no shame in revealing some of what I wrote, for it is my punishment, and by confessing to the lies I vindicate Francis, and poor Henry Mannox.

I wrote in regard to Henry Mannox that "I suffered him at sundry times to touch and handle the secret parts of my body." Francis Dereham had "by many persuasions procured me to his vicious purpose."

Of course there had been no suffering and no vicious purpose. I am indeed, as I truthfully said in the letter, the most vile wretch in the world.

On the thirteenth of November, Sir Thomas Wriothesley came to my chambers.

He ordered my household to gather around before he addressed me. With Isabel and Anne on either side of me, ready to catch me lest in my weak state I should fall, I faced him. His chin jutted more than ever and his hollow cheeks were flushed.

"My Lady Catherine Howard," he said, his address the first indication that he bore ill news. "You will be charged with treason." There was a collective gasp from my attendants. I swayed. Isabel and Anne gripped my arms, holding me upright. Wriothesley continued relentlessly. Even in my tumult, I hated him.

"It has come to light that you entered into marriage with His Royal Highness, King Henry VIII, having knowledge of a previous betrothal to Francis Dereham, whom you also employed in your household with the full intention of continuing your sordid association with him. You have brought shame upon your name and have grievously sought to destroy His Majesty the King. Do you wish to address these charges?"

"I am innocent of that which you speak," I whispered. "They are lies, treacherous lies."

Wriothesley sighed. "So be it! Tomorrow you will be taken to Syon Abbey. There you shall remain under house arrest to await the King's pleasure." Without inclining his head, he turned his back on me and clumped from the chamber.

I wanted to run from the chamber, screaming for Henry, and, on finding him, plead for his forgiveness; indeed, such was my insensible state that the vivid scene played itself out in my mind's eye as my last hope. However, I did not do as I imagined—my weak legs would not have supported such an effort, and I knew the King was not in residence at the Palace. Instead Isabel and Anne half-carried, half-led me to my bedchamber where for many hours I lay supine on my bed, praying for sleep to deliver me from this suffering. My prayer was not answered.

The next day armed guards arrived in my chambers to escort me and four ladies and a handful of servants to Syon Abbey, which had been dissolved and claimed by the Crown. Isabel was chosen to accompany me, but not Anne. Father Vyncent was selected as my accompanying chaplain.

As a few of my belongings were gathered, I became aware that one other of my ladies was missing. I turned to Isabel, made my strained enquiry and received her reply.

Just in time I reached the chamber pot, where I retched into it, over and over, until all that was expelled from my mouth was clear, burning liquid.

Lady Rochford had been seized for questioning.

SYON ABBEY—or what until two years ago had been called Syon Abbey—is situated on the north side of the river Thames, more than three leagues west of the city of London. It had once been a double monastery of monks and nuns. Until it was dissolved in 1539, it had also been a centre of preaching and learning and had boasted one of the largest libraries in England. The nuns had had their own convent on one side of the double-aisled church, while the brothers had occupied the other. Of cathedral-sized proportions, the Church preserved separate enclosure within. When I arrived there in 1541, part of its south wall had been desecrated, the grey stone removed and reused elsewhere. Vast sections of the interior of the church were now in effect a stone quarry, and home to hundreds of pigeons. On approach to the abbey by an overgrown pebbled pathway leading from the dock, the echoing coo of these birds was the only discernible sound. Wildlife and weeds had overtaken the vast parkland, the orchards were untamed, the vegetable and flower beds uncultivated.

We were to occupy what had been the convent—along with a legion of rats, and curtains of spider-webs. Fortunately, the dormitory, kitchens, a number of cells, what had been the library, and a chapel had been prepared for our use. It was with saddened spirit that we all set to, to restore the abbey to some life and order. For myself, at least in the daylight hours, the frenetic activity served to distract me from my present ordeal. At night, while submerged in thick, eerie silence, memories of Tom and Francis beset me, and terror for my own fate and theirs kept me wakeful.

Several days after our arrival, Father Vyncent brought the horrifying news that the questioning of Lady Rochford had borne fruit. Tom had been arrested.

Images of him being subjected to the rack, his fine body that I had loved and knew so well torn and broken, were an intolerable torment. Then Wriothesley and the Archbishop called on me at Syon to continue my inquisition. This time, their questions were only of Tom, their purpose to establish adultery. They expressed avid interest in our meetings, and I detected the hand of Jane Rochford behind their questions. At the last, they presented me with the note I had written to Tom when he had been taken ill. Had I written this note? they asked with ill-concealed glee. I could only nod, my attention fixed on my closing salute: "Yours as long as life endures." If that salute did not suggest adultery, it certainly could indicate that I wished for it . . .

I weakened under the blistering, relentless and hateful interrogation. I cannot recall my answers, although I know I admitted to meeting with Tom in private after our marriage; however, I am abjectly ashamed to confess that I blamed Tom and even Lady Rochford for these meetings. I have no excuse except that I wished for the assault of angry questions to cease and strove only for my own survival—perhaps I am more like my uncle Norfolk than I had realised! It was a deplorable personal weakness, when Lady Rochford was experiencing the same desperation . . . and Tom was . . . but best not to think on what Tom was enduring . . .

I did not confess to adultery nor any wish for it, certain that neither the act nor the inclination had existed. I know my denial of both held the ring of truth, for I detected in my inquisitors a shade of annoyance and uncertainty when I made my answers on that crucial question. However, on the twenty-second of November Wriothesley took great pleasure in telling me that a public announcement had been made, in which it was revealed I had forfeited my honour and would be prosecuted by law. From that day, I would also no longer be Queen but only Catherine Howard.

Two days later, I was formally accused of leading an "abominable, base, carnal, voluptuous and vicious life." I expected to be dispatched with due haste to the Tower and to death, following my indictment. However, my imprisonment endured. I dared to hope— as I know even Father Vyncent did—that the King intended to pardon me or divorce me. Sometimes, in desperate hope, I imagined Tom, Francis and me walking free from this horror. At other times, I searched frenziedly for distractions. If the hectic bustle of settling in to Syon happened to subside during the day—and as we grew more comfortable in our surrounds—I found the required diversion in music and dancing, in conversation, eating and drinking. I amused myself by imposing my rank and demanding respect and deference from my servants.

Such efforts to avoid reflection were wearying, not only for myself but also for my companions, who—except for Father Vyncent—began to avoid me. Often I did find myself alone and too tired to turn my mind from my predicament

On the evening of the tenth of December, Father Vyncent found me slumped in solitary dejection on a stone bench in the cloisters, huddled in my cloak, tears drying on my cheeks. He had been in London for the last few days. It pleased me to see him, though he was thin and haggard. Too depressed to summon even a modicum of politeness, I turned my regard away from him and closed my eyes.

When the silence had endured for several minutes, I murmured:

"I sometimes imagine my summons to the Tower . . .when it will happen . . . how it will happen. Who will come for me, do you think? Wriothesley? The Earl of Hertford? Will I be taken by surprise one night, or will a servant announce the arrival of my escort one sunny, bright morning? Will it be a dull or bright day? I think it would be best it were dull and ugly, to make my parting from this world easier . . ."

Father Vyncent gave a strangled sort of sound, interrupting my musings. I opened my eyes and looked at him properly.

I froze as I beheld his haunted countenance.

"You have news," I whispered. "Tell me."

To my further shock, my old friend began to weep and his large hands trembled violently as they covered his face. In between weeping and keening, he prayed: "*Sed et si ambulavero in valle umbrae mortis non timebo malum quoniam to mecum es; virga tua et baculus tuus ipsa consolabuntur me* . . . Yea, though I walk through the valley of the shadow of death, I will fear no evil, for thou art with me; thy rod and thy staff they comfort me . . ."

"Father Vyncent," I interrupted in desperation, "what has happened? Tell me!"

Never have I beheld such desolation as distorted the face that was lifted to mine. I reached for him at once. His hands were like ice. At last, in a voice so thick with feeling that it could barely escape his lips, he uttered the words.

"Master Dereham . . . and Master Culpeper . . . have been put to death."

The doors in my mind yawned. Evil swept out and engulfed every corner of my being. My bones so chilled that I shivered violently, and sickness invaded my belly so that I was ill with its vileness. The evil squeezed my heart with pain and my soul with guilt. I tumbled to the ground.

On and on Father Vyncent spoke. His words only caused me to wretch again, ". . . both drawn to Tyburn . . . Master Culpeper . . . beheaded . . . Master Dereham suffered the full force of the law . . . hung, dismembered while conscious, disembowelled . . . at last, beheaded . . his body quartered . . . Their heads now on London Bridge . . ."

I do not know how long I lay on the cold, stone ground, how long Father Vyncent swayed on the bench, praying and keening. All I know is that when he lifted me up, the violence of our grief had passed and God had rendered me mercifully numb.

He called my ladies who rushed at once to clean me up and assist me to my bed. There I remained for several days in a stupor of pain and grief.

Father Vyncent recovered sufficiently for my sake to keep his ear to the ground and he received secret dispatches from London on a regular basis. From him I learnt that all my relatives had been taken to the Tower—including the Dowager, my uncle Lord William, the Countess of Bridgewater, my brothers, even my sister-in-law Anne. All the Howards, except the Duke of Norfolk, bore the full impact of the King's jealousy and wrath. The constant warrior, fighting always for survival, my uncle Norfolk retreated to Kenninghall.

I heard his voice had been the loudest in condemning me, and that he had even offered to strike me down himself. He had been present at the arraignment of Francis and Tom, and had laughed at their plight. He had denied any knowledge of crimes, accusing his stepmother, his brother and his sister-in-law for their part in convincing the King that I had led a pure life before I married. His forceful protestations saved him.

I understand his actions. He fought for his survival, and I cannot expect less of him. His betrayal hurts, but I feel no bitterness towards him—unlike the others who had nothing to lose by supporting me. My half-sister, Isabel, for example, adopted a cool and haughty manner towards me, as did my other ladies. The conclusion that my former friends—Joan, Katherine, Margaret and Alice—had without compunction revealed sordid details of my earlier life was difficult to endure. Only Father Vyncent, who had mercifully escaped the attentions of the inquisitors, remained true and loyal.

I remained under house arrest all through the dismal Christmas season. Ever resilient, with every passing day that I remained alive I began to hope again. Why did the King take no action? Did he love me still? Was the evidence against me so weak?

Perhaps it was . . . or perhaps to condemn me the King required something more substantial, and beyond the world's refutation, than evidence extracted under torture. Something like an Act of Parliament . . .

On the twenty-second day of January 1542 a Bill of Attainder was passed. I do not understand its nature—and it matters little to me now. However, I do know that it sounded my death knell. Relinquishing all hope, I waited for my summons to the Tower.

On the 10 February it came, with that ominous pulsing sound rising from the direction of the river, the approach of my escort to the Tower.

VII

TWO DAYS AGO, while I remained incarcerated in the Queen's House at the Tower, the Bill of Attainder was made law. Last evening I was commanded to dispose my soul and prepare for death. Today I die. I am scared beyond endurance—of the pain, the violence, and the ugliness. That is what is in my future, and there is nothing earthly beyond it, nothing I can comprehend. With the present and future so agonizing, only the past has beckoned my tormented mind with its promise of refuge.

I have prepared for death as I was bidden. I have asked for the block to be brought to me, so I could practice laying my head on it. Over and over, while the guards looked on, I walked up to where it rested on the stone floor of my chamber. Countless times I knelt, placed my hands on the ground and lowered myself until I felt the wood against my neck. I thought I heard sniffs from my guards, but the realisation barely penetrated my tumult.

It was then time for the disposal of my soul. I made my final request of my guards.

"I wish to see a priest," I said. "I wish to see Father Vyncent."

Epilogue

"Endure and persist, this pain will turn good by and by."

Ovid
Ancient Roman classical poet and author of Metamorphoses
(43BC-17AD)

I

Tower of London
13 February 1542

MY LADY SUMMONED ME to her cell. I heard her confession and we prayed together for a time. As dread had weakened her, I then assisted her to the narrow bed. There she lay, eyes closed, death-like in her stillness, silence and pallor.

"How can a heart stand such terror?" she whispered at last. She lifted her hand and pressed it against her chest. "Such pain, yet still it beats on . . . *pom, pom, pom* . . . a persistent pulse, just like when they came for me . . . it began as just a pulse . . ."

And so I urged her to remember, to take refuge in her past. When she finished speaking, her voice was hoarse, dawn streaked the sky, and without the chamber could be heard sounds of the Tower of London stirring to a new day.

"My dear?" I asked tentatively when she had been silent for many minutes. She made no response. Observing her chest rising and falling in slow rhythm I realised she slept. I tapped quietly on the door of the chamber, and again louder. I heard a scuffle outside the door and the grating of bolts before it yawned open. A blinking, sleepy guard beheld me.

"You prayed long into the night, priest," he grumbled, in an attempt to excuse his laxness.

"When you are in the position of Her Grace, you may judge the propriety of praying all night before your execution, and not before!" I snapped, purposely using the royal form of address. "I will return anon should Her Grace call for me . . . now she sleeps in God's mercy."

I did not wait for a response but stalked away, trying not to wince at the pain in my legs and back.

I used the privy and begged a chunk of bread from the kitchens. As I made my way back to Catherine's chamber, I saw that a gathering had formed on Tower Green—I recognised at once members of the Privy Council and a handful of foreign dignitaries, but saw no sign of the Duke of Suffolk, he who had brought Catherine here to the Tower, and nor was the Duke of Norfolk present. I could not help but wonder at the significance of their absence. Did guilt or regret keep them away? I suspected both.

I returned to Catherine's chamber.

"A woman is helping her dress," the guard said gruffly. I nodded my curt acknowledgement and turned my back on the man to gaze out of a small window on to the Green. Someone had brought out the block and the crowd had moved to the perimeter.

The door opened behind me. At once I swung around and lumbered inside. Catherine stood in the centre of the room, a small, pale and pathetic creature in black. She tried to smile.

"I'm ready—to go to them," she said, startling me. *Them?* To her executioners? Or to those she had loved? "You'll accompany me part of the way, my friend?"

"Of course," I said in a voice thick with unshed tears. I moved to her side and she hooked her arm through mine. She leaned on me as we left the chamber, and made our way through cold hallways to the outside.

The sun shone without warmth. White puffs of moisture billowed from the mouths of all who gathered at the Green and a sharp breeze stirred cloaks and hair. Guards with glinting swords moved towards us and I had to stand back to allow them to take position on either side of Catherine.

I wanted to speak but the grief in my throat prevented words. I coughed to clear it. Catherine looked around at me as she stumbled away, smiled and nodded.

"God be with you," I cried hoarsely. My cry was taken up by a handful of Londoners who had also gathered: "God be with you, my lady, God be with you."

It was time for her to make her final address.

"I desire all Christian people to take regard of my worthy and just punishment for my offences," she said in a weak, high voice; a few of the women around me began to weep. "I have sinned against God heinously from my youth upward, in breaking all his commandments, and also against the King's Royal Majesty very dangerously . . . I have been justly condemned by the laws of the realm and parliament to die . . ."

It pained me to listen, even though I knew such death's door "confessions" were customary. I hated to think of my lady admitting such culpability. I clasped my hands together and began to pray, concentrating on my entreaties so I would not have to hear to her words.

By a stirring of the people around me, I sensed she had finished speaking. I looked up. Blindfolded, she stepped towards the block, but stumbled and had to be assisted. Her neck came to its final rest and a hushed, taut pause settled over the crowd. The masked executioner lifted his axe. It flashed in the sunshine . . . and swung downwards in a wide arc.

It landed with a loud *thwack*. Her body jerked, bright red blood gushed forth, her head tumbled into straw.

That is all it took. By God's mercy, the end was swift and clean. I lingered to make sure her body was treated with respect afterwards. Then, tears blurring my vision, I left.

I don't know how long I walked the streets of London. I know at one stage I contemplated the two heads on the Bridge. There would be three souls reunited in the hereafter now. I fancied they wandered a restless eternity, desirous of justice, yearning for vindication and understanding.

For most of my life I had wielded the written word, at many and varied tasks. I now had before me another task, more important than any other I had undertaken. I reiterated my vow to those three souls—through my writing, they would earn their eternal peace.

December, 1560
St Bartholomew's Priory, Kent.

WHAT YOU READ HERE is the enactment of my role—Catherine's story as she told it to me, and by extension the story of those who loved her. I have corroborated her account with my own recollections and writings over the years. I have honed it with my literacy and with my knowledge of her nature and of those other figures of her story. Some further elucidation is now required.

When no solid proof of wrong-doing could be established on the part of Masters Dereham and Culpeper, the inquisitors sought to find in them the intention or wish to harm the King, thereby establishing treason. Master Dereham did not break. His friend Roger Davenport did.

Under torture, Davenport provided condemning evidence against Master Dereham. He attested that Master Dereham had once declared of Catherine: "If the King were dead, I might marry her." In glee, the inquisitors pounced on that at once, finding in the innocent pronouncement the motive and intent to harm the King. Therein lay Master Dereham's high treason.

Master Culpeper had been more defiant and rash under torture. At the end, he declared he wished to possess Catherine carnally. This too was deemed to be a confession of treachery.

Doctors of theology were undecided on whether Catherine's pre-contract with Master Dereham constituted a legally binding marriage making Catherine guilty of bigamy. It was for this reason also that Master Dereham and the Dowager Duchess of Norfolk could not be condemned for deceiving the King on the matter of an existing pre-contract—if there was no marriage, there could be no deception of it. Catherine would be happy to know that she was, after all, rightly Queen of England.

It was the Act of Attainder, and not the evidence extracted in the main under torture or duress, which condemned Catherine Howard. Try as the Council might to see in her actions an intent to commit adultery or otherwise harm the King, it was insufficient to convict her, at least in the eyes of the ever-watchful world. The Act solved the problem of how to placate the King's jealousy and wounded pride, and convince the world of Catherine's guilt, by making it high treason for a woman who married the King not to reveal the details of her unchaste life. Such neglect could now be seen as intent to cause detriment to the throne. It signalled Catherine's demise.

On 22 December, those of the Howard clan arrested were tried and found guilty of misprision. Their worldly goods and possessions were forfeited to the Crown and their bodies condemned to perpetual imprisonment.

The Duke of Norfolk, having escaped his relatives' fate, eventually returned to London, with his authority and reputation only slightly tainted. Within two months— no doubt as a result of the Duke's indomitable sway—Lord William's wife, Margaret, and Anne Howard, wife of Catherine's brother Henry, were pardoned and released from the Tower. Soon after, all other Howards were set free with pardons. However, their influence and standing had been damaged beyond repair.

Only Lady Rochford went to the block, directly after Catherine. Some would say it was a just punishment for the disloyal hand this devious lady had in the deaths of her own husband and two Queens of England.

King Henry VIII endured three more years of ill health and his last wife, Queen Katherine Parr, outlived him. She bore him no children.

The Duke of Norfolk and his son, the Earl of Surrey, were arrested in the King's final months and convicted of treason. The Earl was beheaded. On the very night before the Duke's execution, the King died, and the Duke's sentence was suspended. That constant warrior had survived another assault on his family line. He died peacefully in his bed six years ago.

Queen Catherine Howard has been long dead now, and England has seen many years of strife and turmoil, with one new King and three new Queens. It swung to virulent Protestantism when Prince Edward became King under the guidance of the Seymours. In his will, King Edward left the throne to his Protestant cousin, Lady Jane Grey, who reigned for a pathetically brief and inconsequential period, until Princess Mary, with great popular support, seized the crown and had Queen Jane sent to the block. When Princess Mary became Queen no other religion but the Church of Rome was tolerated and a bloody rule ensued. Then, when she died without issue, Catherine's niece—Anne Boleyn's daughter—Elizabeth, ascended the throne, installing an easier and more peaceful mode of Protestant worship. The Howards had their triumph! England seems to have embarked now on a period of stability and harmony, although it seems I have observed it all from a detached distance, intent only on completing this mission.

III

A KNOCK COMES AT THE DOOR OF MY CELL. It creaks open and the merry, piquant face of Marius, my companion, appears in the gap. When he sees me at my writing table, he frowns in exasperation.

"You still write! Always you write! When will you finish this task?" he exclaims, entering the room and throwing up his hands in agitation.

Soon after Catherine's death, I embarked on a pilgrimage to the Holy Land. Marius was a young lad I rescued from a certain life of vagrancy on the streets of Lyon—he was at that time a wayward, impetuous vagrant, in need of guidance, and I a weary and lonesome traveller requiring a needy friend to distract me from my own misery. Each serving a purpose to the other, Marius accompanied me while I journeyed on to Rome, thence to the Holy Land, and finally back to England. Now a tall young man, recently married to a local lass from the village, he has remained with me as my carer and companion, and staunch assistant in my efforts to write Catherine's story—that is, until very recently when great age and illness have left me almost a cripple, and his concern for me has made him less indulgent of my task.

"It is you who has urged me on all these years to write this tale," I say to him now with a touch of asperity that carries no great force, for I am fond of the boy. "Now you complain?"

Marius has the grace to look shamefaced.

"*Oui, c'est vrai,*" he admits. "But all this time you have been writing! And now you are so old and frail, and in need of rest! I am anxious—."

"Aye, Marius," I interrupt his ravings, finding it difficult to be annoyed, for his protests clearly arise from his high regard for me. "You will be pleased to know then that Catherine," I hastily scribble on to my conclusion, emitting a long sigh, "is quiet now."

Marius comes closer and lays a hand on my shoulder.

"You mean she no longer speaks to you?" he whispered in some awe. He knows, does Marius, that every time I have dipped my quill to write Catherine's story, her voice has been in my ears—just as it was that long, last night in the Tower—and that my hand has moved only to her intonations.

"Aye," I say, "she is silent. My job is done, and I will now go to my Maker happily."

Marius scoffs at my prediction of imminent demise, yet I know his exclamation of denial comes from sadness rather than a refusal to accept the truth. I reach up to pat his hand.

"Now, you must remember your mission, Marius," I say. "I am relying on you to place this," reverently I rest my palm on my work, "in the right hands. Catherine needs this story told, for the good Lord knows her family will not do it." Bitterly, I recall that in an effort to eradicate all memory of Catherine, the Howards destroyed every portrait and record ever pertaining to her life before she became Queen of England. She now lives on only in the ignominy of her short reign—*but not for much longer.*

Marius sniffs. "Aye, I remember what I must do with your work," he mumbles, although he is clearly distracted, causing me a dart of anxiety. As I reassure myself that he can be trusted with Catherine's story, Marius grips my shoulder, urging me to stand. "Come, to bed! No more of such talk. You will feel much better in the morning."

I expel a long sigh, cock my head for a second, listening, to be sure there are no more echoes of the past resounding in my head. With relief and gladness, I realise all is silent . . . and restful.

I recall my Lord's last word, the word that turned His apparent tragedy into a victory that changed history; the word that implies that something has come to an end; something has been completed, perfected, accomplished in the full! And that something has enduring consequences. I humbly recognise its appropriateness here.

"*Tetelestai,*" I murmur.

The End

Recommended Reading

I consulted many works of reference in the preparation of writing of this book - including large and small articles, encyclopaedia references as well as texts. Not many references were in agreement with each other as to the events and people that featured in Catherine's life. Although I found the inconsistency in materials to be frustrating at times, I do believe it accorded me some considerable freedom in writing this fictional memoir. Thus, in An Unchaste Life I describe some events that did not occur and feature some people who did not exist, all in the interests of augmenting a story that I believe should be told with a degree of compassion, understanding and sympathy. Nevertheless, I have taken pains to depict all events noteworthy in Catherine's life and to portray as accurately as I believe possible those people who played a major role in her fate. Any inaccuracy in the telling or description, which cannot be excused by the apparent wielding of literary license throughout, is my fault alone and not that of the writers and historians who produced my list of recommended reading, below:

Tudors and Elizabethans - Costume Reference 2; Marion Sichel (Anchor Press Limited for BT Batsford Limited, 1977)

Tudor Women, Alison Plowden (Atheneum, 1979)

England in Tudor Times, L.F. Salzman (B.T. Batsford Limited, 1926)

Life in Tudor England, Penry Williams (B.T. Batsford Limited, 1964)

Hampton Court The Palace and the People, Roy Nash (MacDonald & Co (Publishers) Limited, 1983)

A Tudor Tragedy: The Life and Times of Catherine Howard, Lacey Baldwin Smith, (Jonathan Cape, 1961)

Henry VIII and his Court, Neville Williams (Weidenfeld and Nicholson, 1971)

The Life and Times of Henry VIII, Robert Lacey (Weidenfeld and Nicholson, 1972)

Tudor Costume and Fashion, Herbert Norris (Dover Publications, Inc, 1997)

The Ebbs and Flows of Fortune: The Life of Thomas Howard, Third Duke of Norfolk, David M. Head (The University of Georgia Press, 1995)

Anne Cato

Printed in the United States
96566LV00003B/96/A